SURVEYING CRIME

PANEL FOR THE EVALUATION OF CRIME SURVEYS
Committee on National Statistics
Assembly of Mathematical and Physical Sciences
National Research Council

BETTYE K. EIDSON PENICK, *Editor*
MAURICE E. B. OWENS III, *Associate Editor*

NATIONAL ACADEMY OF SCIENCES
WASHINGTON, D.C. 1976

This study was sponsored by the Committee on National Statistics, Assembly of Mathematical and Physical Sciences, and is submitted to the Law Enforcement Assistance Administration, Department of Justice, under provisions of Contract No. 74-SS-99-6002 from the Department of Justice to the National Academy of Sciences.

Library of Congress Cataloging in Publication Data

National Research Council. Panel for the Evaluation of Crime Surveys.
  Surveying crime.

  Includes bibliographical references and index.
  1. Criminal statistics—United States. I. Penick, Bettye K. Eidson. II. Owens, Maurice E. B. III. Title.
HV6787.N37 1976   364'.973   76-50120
ISBN 0-309-02524-9

Available from
Printing and Publishing Office, National Academy of Sciences
2101 Constitution Avenue, N.W., Washington, D.C. 20418

Printed in the United States of America

Preface

The Panel for the Evaluation of Crime Surveys was established in early 1974 by the National Academy of Sciences, at the request of the U.S. Department of Justice. Within the department, the request originated at the Statistics Division of the National Criminal Justice Information and Statistics Service (NCJISS), a unit within the Law Enforcement Assistance Administration (LEAA).

The panel was asked to evaluate a new statistical series, the National Crime Surveys (NCS). This series was and is located administratively within the Statistics Division of LEAA's NCJISS. Thus, the primary audience for this report is the small set of individuals within LEAA who directly are responsible for the planning and management of the NCS.

We hope the report is of interest to a variety of audiences. Survey methodologists should be interested in issues flowing from the sheer size of the NCS enterprise. In terms of the number of cases interviewed, the NCS is second only to the decennial census and comparable with respect to field costs to the Current Population Survey of the U.S. Bureau of the Census, the vehicle that yields our national estimates of employment and unemployment.

Statisticians might be intrigued by problems of inference posed by multistage sample designs and by uniform sampling criteria, especially where the sampled events are rare among the surveyed population, as in the case of rape or robbery incidence.

Social scientists might view this report as illustrative of the difficulties in institutionalizing an innovation, for the NCS is almost as new as the art of victim surveying and still in a preliminary stage of development. The NCS is also extremely complex and expensive. It costs the public in excess of $10 million per year to operate, and its innovators and managers are pressured to demonstrate that the knowledge it ultimately might yield can help to reduce the nation's crime rate within the next fiscal year. All statistical series are subject to pressures with which budget and personnel ceilings collide, but the NCS especially is vulnerable, for it is located in an operating agency, LEAA, whose own charter is not permanent. For a large-scale series in which designated households remain in the sample for 3 years, the operational need for long-term planning and budgeting is manifest. Equally manifest is the political need to justify data collection in terms of its short-term utility.

Our evaluation falls naturally into two parts. In the first part, the NCS is evaluated as an ongoing statistical survey in terms of its completeness, accuracy, reliability, analysis, and dissemination. The second part treats perhaps more fundamental issues: It assesses the substantive utility of the NCS results and offers suggestions on future directions the program should take to improve the usefulness of the results.

While we hope that many aspects of this report will be applicable to the range of decisions that the sponsoring unit of LEAA will face in the next few years, our evaluation has focused far more on areas requiring long-term planning and assessment than on day-to-day issues that arise in the management of any large-scale survey. Our evaluation has not been structured by the sponsoring agency in terms of the areas we have chosen to emphasize. Neither have we adjusted our recommendations in recognition of agency constraints of personnel, budget, and other plateaus. In short, we were invited to evaluate the NCS, independently and as objectively as possible. We were not asked to provide consultation on issues as defined by the sponsor nor on how best to accommodate a given set of bureaucratic constraints. And we have not.

The one respect in which this report is influenced heavily by the sponsoring agency is the directness of the criticism of its version of a victim survey. Because the report is addressed primarily to individuals who are responsible for the continued development of the NCS, we have not conducted a broad review of the criminological literature, held symposia on crime control, invited experts to draft working papers on issues of measurement, and so forth. We have not because at this stage the experts on victim surveys in this country and internationally are the individuals to whom this report is addressed. The intellectual terrain is uncharted. Our role has been to track these individuals across it, to reconstruct their decisions, to consider their options, to identify issues that crosscut the many components of this complex survey operation, and to make specific recommendations, if warranted.

Hence, the criticisms raised in this report are addressed to a highly professional audience and one not bound in any way to accept our assessments or recommendations, as is appropriate when one set of professionals invites another to render an independent judgment.

Some of our recommendations can be implemented with present resources; others would require additional funds or additional personnel. Whether such resources can be allocated to the NCS can only be decided by LEAA administrators, by Congress, and by the Administration, when they have weighed the claims of the NCS against other claims for public support. We have tried to indicate what could be accomplished if additional resources were available or if current resources were reallocated.

Another panel, with different members, might have different views about goals and priorities for the NCS. We have tried to learn from the staff of the Statistics Division of NCJISS, from the Bureau of the Census, from the Federal Bureau of Investigation, from the Office of Management and Budget, from each other, and from colleagues outside the panel as we went along, but our final product must be taken for what it is: the considered collective judgments of a particular group of scientists and administrators, drawn mostly from the social science disciplines and not presuming to represent our colleagues who are statisticians, sociologists, political scientists, economists, lawyers, and law enforcement administrators.

We are grateful for the cooperation we have received in the course of our evaluation. We owe special thanks to Charles R. Kindermann, Dawn D. Nelson, Carol B. Kalish, and Benjamin H. Renshaw, all of the Statistics Division of NCJISS, and to Linda R. Murphy, Daniel B. Levine, George H. Gray, Earle J. Gerson, Robert P. Parkinson, Marvin M. Thompson, Richard W. Dodge, Adolfo L. Paez, David V. Bateman, Henry Woltman, Chester E. Bowie, Caesar G. Hill, and Tyler R. Sturdevant, all of the Bureau of the Census. Robert D. Conger and later Paul A. Zolbe of the Uniform Crime Reporting Unit of the Federal Bureau of Investigation also contributed to our discussions.

Joseph H. Lewis, of the Police Foundation; Albert J. Reiss and William Elliot, of Yale University; Wesley G. Skogan, of Northwestern University; and Hans Zeisel, of the University of Chicago, provided us with thoughtful comments on our interim reports, as well as new prospects from their own work on crime statistics.

Within the Academy, Margaret E. Martin, Executive Director of our parent Committee on National Statistics, has shared with us since we began her wisdom about the federal statistical system and the impact of its strengths and weaknesses on policy formulation. The panel is also appreciative of the contribution made by our two consultants, Walt R.

Simmons and Richard F. Sparks. Throughout its 2-year life, the group was fortunate to have had excellent administrative and secretarial support from Gloria A. Wise. In the final stages, Wilma Hill's careful assistance with bibliographic, editorial, and clerical work was much appreciated.

The Chairman of the Committee on National Statistics, William H. Kruskal, also has shown a keen interest in the substance and quality of our work. Many flaws no doubt remain in what we are pleased to call the final product, but they are far fewer than would have been made public without his careful and consistent scrutiny. Earlier versions of this report also benefited from comments by Frederick Mosteller, Nathan Keyfitz, and Morris H. Hansen, who are members of the Committee on National Statistics, and from James A. Davis, on behalf of the Executive Committee of the Assembly of Behavioral and Social Sciences.

George E. Hall and Anthony G. Turner, now of the Office of Management and Budget and the Bureau of the Census, respectively, were responsible primarily for the initiation and early development of the NCS. They also were responsible for the decision to invite an evaluation of the NCS by the National Academy of Sciences. In doing so, they presented a unique opportunity for an independent review of a major federal statistical series before design, concepts, and methods become hardened through repetition.

Above all, the panel would like to express special appreciation to Bettye K. Eidson Penick and to Maurice E. B. Owens III, staff for the panel during the life of the evaluation. They were indispensable in enabling the group to perform its tasks, in compiling the material on which this report is based, and in drafting and editing this document. Their ability, dedication, and unflagging interest contributed immeasurably to the panel's work. Our admiration is enormous and our gratitude profound.

CONRAD F. TAEUBER, _Chairman_
Panel for the Evaluation of Crime Surveys

PANEL FOR THE EVALUATION OF CRIME SURVEYS

*Dean Goldstein and Dr. Patterson were unable to serve full terms.

Contents

ix

LIST OF TABLES AND ILLUSTRATIONS

1 The National Crime Surveys

INTRODUCTION

A major statistical series, The National Crime Surveys (NCS), was instituted by the Law Enforcement Assistance Administration (LEAA) in July 1972 to develop new information on the incidence of crime and its impact on society. The new series was to provide information on the victims of crime, and on crimes not reported to the police and to give uniform measures for the types of crime selected.

A national sample survey included personal interviews at 6-month intervals in approximately 60,000 households and 39,000 business establishments. Initial plans also called for sample surveys designed to provide data for individual cities. Such surveys have been conducted in 26 cities; in 13 of them a second survey has been taken to provide a measure of changes over time. The Bureau of the Census, on behalf of LEAA, is responsible for the collection and tabulation of the survey data.

The surveys provide measurement of the extent to which persons 12 years old and over, households, and places of business have been victimized by the following crimes, including attempts: rape, robbery, assault, personal and household larceny, burglary, and auto theft. In the case of commercial establishments, measurement is taken only of attempted or completed robberies and burglaries. In general, information is collected on the circumstances under which the event occurred, the effects on the victim, and whether the incident was reported to the police.

1

Although the NCS was launched only after some detailed field testing and after some small-scale surveys by nongovernmental agencies had been analyzed, many questions remained and new questions arose once data became available.

It was known that many criminal incidents are not reported to the police, but for the nation as a whole there was little knowledge about the characteristics of the crimes not reported to the police and the reasons for nonreporting. Would victims be willing to report events in the course of a survey interview even though they had not reported them to the police? Would victims likely be willing to report one type of crime but not another to the interviewer?

People's memories are notably faulty in placing events in the correct time frame. Could survey techniques be developed that would over-come this difficulty and thus provide the basis for a measure of change over time? Could victims give reliable information about the characteristics of the other party in those cases in which there was a confrontation between victim and assailant? In many instances victims, after calling the police, fail to proceed with prosecution. Could some light be thrown on such situations? Rates of robbery of business establishments are affected by the fact that some business establishments are frequent victims of robbery. Are there also areas and groups of people that are particularly prone to victimization, and do repeated victimizations account for a significant part of all crimes against persons? Becoming a victim of the types of crimes surveyed is a relatively rare event, despite general public impressions to the contrary. Can the risk of victimization be estimated for groups in the population such as the young and the old, men and women, black and white? Are certain areas or types of business more likely to become victims than others, and what are the factors that lead to the greater risk? What factors correlate with lower levels of victimization? Does risk appear to be modifiable by individual or by collective action? Is the list of crimes that are included in the survey too narrow, and could other crimes of significant proportions be included, thus making the results even more informative?

From the standpoint of survey methods, a particularly difficult problem is the proper manner of accounting for those events that happen so frequently that the victim is unable to assign any one of them to a specific time period. This might be the case with frequent assaults. The manner of dealing with such events affects not only the number of victimizations that are counted, but also the efforts to provide information about the relations between the person committing the crime and the victim.

Other questions related to the degree to which the NCS was meeting the objectives set out for it and the extent to which it was providing essential information on the basis of which improved systems of crime prevention and criminal justice can be designed, operated, and evaluated. A question raised early was the degree to which the data supplied could be related to other data already available, especially to the Uniform Crime Reports, which provide data on crimes known to the police.

Shortly after the surveys were underway, LEAA asked the Committee on National Statistics of the National Academy of Sciences–National Research Council to evaluate the surveys. The Committee selected a panel representing a variety of disciplines and recruited a staff to carry out the investigations necessary to perform the work envisaged. The study covered the period January 1974 to June 1976. Throughout the time of the study, the staff and the panel had the full cooperation of the staffs of the Bureau of the Census and LEAA.

PRINCIPAL FINDINGS AND MAJOR RECOMMENDATIONS

The main body of this report examines the methodology and utility of the National Crime Surveys (NCS). This section provides a guide for that examination by setting forth very briefly the most important findings and recommendations. Fuller explanation of the items in this summary and the evidence upon which they are based are provided later in the report.

The principal findings were as follows:

1. The design of the NCS generally is consistent with the objective of producing data on trends and patterns of victimization for certain categories of crime. Some reservations about specific design components of the surveys are detailed later in this report, including the scope of crimes surveyed.

2. Conceptual, procedural, and managerial problems limit the potential of the NCS, but the panel considers that, given sufficient support, the problems ought to be amenable to substantial resolution in the long run.

3. A major shift of resources to analytic and methodological research is essential in order for the NCS to yield data useful for policy formulation. This shift should be accompanied by the development of

administrative mechanisms to enhance this large and complex series' capacity for self-correction.

4. The primary uses envisioned originally for the NCS were of a social and policy indicator nature. The panel agrees that a subsequent objective of producing operating intelligence for jurisdictions is inconsistent with the original purposes of the NCS and with the design informed by those purposes, except insofar as operating intelligence is a by-product of understanding broad trends and patterns of victimization.

The major recommendations were as follows:

1. A substantially greater proportion of LEAA resources should be allocated to delineation of product objectives, to managerial coordination, to data analysis and dissemination, and to a continuing program of methodological research and evaluation. We are concerned about the current balance between resources allocated to data collection and resources allocated to all other aspects of the victimization survey effort.

2. The staff providing managerial and analytic support for the NCS should be expanded to include the full-time efforts of at least 30 to 40 professional employees. Without this expansion, the NCS cannot be developed to achieve its potential for practical utility.

3. A coordinator at the Bureau of the Census should be appointed whose responsibilities would crosscut the various Census operations that support the NCS.

4. The staff that performs NCS analysis and report-writing functions, whether LEAA employees or otherwise, should have an active role in the management of the NCS. Specifically, the analytic staff should participate in the development of objectives for substantive reports and publication schedules. Once analytic plans are formulated, the analytic staff should have autonomy in specifying tabulations to be used in support of the analysis, and it should have direct access to complete NCS data files and to data processing resources. It should be the analytic staff's responsibility to formulate statistical or other criteria used in hypothesis testing. Finally, a feedback mechanism should be instituted through which the staff can influence decisions on the content of survey instruments, on field and code procedures, and on analytic and methodological research to be undertaken.

5. Resources now used for the nationwide household survey and for the independent city-level household surveys should be consolidated and used for carrying out an integrated national program. The inte-

grated effort could produce not only nationwide and regional data, but, on the same timetable, estimates for separately identifiable Standard Metropolitan Statistical Areas (SMSA's) and for at least the five largest central cities within them. For some purposes, it would be practicable and perhaps useful to combine data for 2 or more years and to show separate tabulations for a large number of cities and metropolitan areas.

6. A review and restatement of the objectives of the commercial surveys should be conducted and data collection should be suspended, except in support of experimental and exploratory review of these objectives.

7. Five percent of the NCS sample in the future should be available to interview in order to explore different forms and ordering of questions, and for pretesting possible new questions. Chapter 6 is devoted to discussion of alternate measures of victim events, to the scope of victim events surveyed, and to the need for independent variables. Measures of the concepts of vulnerability and opportunity for victimization are recommended additions to the interview schedule.

8. Routine NCS tabulations should include results on the risk of victimization, where the unit of analysis is the surveyed individual, and that analysis of risk should be a significant part of NCS publications on a recurring basis. If the NCS data are coded and tabulated so as to yield a cumulative count of personal and household victim experiences of *all* surveyed respondents, analyses of multiple victimization, including events now excluded as "series" incidents, could and should be routine components of official publications.

9. A major methodological effort on optimum field and survey design for the NCS should be undertaken. Toward this goal, high priority should be given to research on the best combination of reference period, frequency of interview at an address, length of retention in the sample, and bounding rules. Part of the recommended research in this area should be a new reverse record check study in order to assess: (a) differential *degrees* of reporting for different types of victimizations and different classes of respondents, (b) problems of telescoping and decay; and (c) biases in the *misreporting* of facts.

10. Local interest in victimization patterns should be addressed through LEAA–Census joint development of a manual of procedures for conducting local area victimization surveys. The federal government should produce reports on the NCS that contain detailed analyses of patterns and trends of victimization so as to allow law enforcement personnel, the public, and policymakers to draw inferences that might be applicable to the issues with which they are concerned. Informing

the public and their policymakers of the distribution and modifiability of risk should be the primary objective of the NCS.

ORGANIZATION OF THE REPORT

Chapter 2 describes the NCS in terms of its field designs and sampling and estimating schemes. Chapter 3 reviews and discusses the victim survey pretest and pilot studies sponsored by LEAA and conducted by the Bureau of the Census and appraises the impact of these test results on the current design of the NCS.

Chapter 4 recommends survey design changes and resource shifts in order to enhance the managerial and technical coordination of the NCS operation.

Current LEAA–Census research and development activities associated with the NCS are examined and recommendations for a continuing and expanded program of research, development, and evaluation of victimization survey methodology are offered in Chapter 5. In addition, Chapter 5 recommends specific analytic research that could be performed on the NCS data now available.

Chapter 6 assesses the NCS collection instruments and procedures, including their effect upon the analytic potential of the series. Recommendations are offered for expansion or substitution of independent variables and for changes in the baseline counts of incidents surveyed. Chapter 7 outlines the principal features of the NCS analysis, publication, and dissemination program to date and contains specific recommendations on the organization of the analytic function and on the choice of a primary descriptive statistic.

Chapters 8 and 9 consider the once, present, and future objectives for the NCS. Chapter 8, especially, considers whether the early and current objectives are realizable in view of what is known or is likely to be discoverable about NCS capabilities in particular and victim survey methodology in general.

Chapter 9, the final chapter, presents a statement on the potential utility of the NCS.

This report represents a summary of the consensus views reached in many discussions of the panel, the review of interim reports, and the review of early drafts of the final report. It was not intended to secure agreement of all members of the panel to every word in this text. That would have been an unwieldy procedure. However, it is believed that this text reflects the major concerns that were expressed by the panel members and correctly presents the recommendations that the panel wishes to have brought to the attention of LEAA. It is our hope that by this presentation we will have made a contribution to the full development of what can become a major element in the statistics relating to crime in the United States.

2 Description and Comment on Survey Design

INTRODUCTION

The NCS was conceived as a set of probability samples of both victims and potential victims of selected crimes. The survey design and the sampling and estimating schemes are among the most complex and elaborate in the social science field. Much of the technical design was produced by the U.S. Bureau of the Census, building on and adapting from long experience with large-scale probability social surveys. The formal structure of the NCS exhibits high technical standards.

To describe the NCS comprehensively and in full detail is quite beyond the scope of this report. The NCS comprises four different surveys: (1) a continuing monthly interview survey of a rotating national probability sample of households and their members, (2) a continuing national interview probability sample of business establishments—called the commercial survey, (3) a set of one-time or intermittent household probability samples of each of selected cities, and (4) a concomitant set of commercial surveys of each of the same cities. Accounts of these surveys, in varying detail and specificity, have been published.[1]

[1] Especially notable are these six documents: Marie G. Argana, Marvin M. Thompson, and Earle J. Gerson, "The Measurement of Crime through Victimization Surveys" (Paper presented at the Annual Meeting of the American Statistical Association, New York, December 27, 1973); U.S. Department of Commerce, Bureau of the Census, *National Crime Survey, Central Cities Sample Survey Documentation* (Washington,

8

The present chapter does three things: (1) provides a summary brief description of the surveys, (2) identifies several prominent special and distinguishing features of the NCS, and (3) comments on some strengths of the NCS and also its weaknesses as an instrument for accomplishing certain objectives for which it is not well suited.

Main emphasis will be on the national household sample, because it is the largest component of the program and because it appears to have the most promising future.

SURVEY OBJECTIVES

The NCS was planned as a multipurpose undertaking. The objectives are treated elsewhere in this report. At this point it is sufficient to recall that the objectives are of two broad types. The first is to produce general-purpose time series on criminal victimization, with wide ranges of descriptive characteristics. These series should display levels of events, trends, and relationships among relevant variables. In time, they may become the central source of background, reference, and baseline intelligence on criminal victimization for policymakers, administrators, students, and the general public. The second objective is to supply specific evidence that will facilitate resolution of particular problem-oriented issues and circumstances. For example, what kinds of crimes in what volume are not reported to the police? Or, what is the relationship between crime incidence and various protective actions that the populace can take?

Generally speaking, the NCS seeks to measure events and experiences that are comparatively rare phenomena. Fortunately, criminal victimization is not a frequent experience for most members of our society. Unfortunately, for purposes of this survey, this means that a large number of persons must be questioned in order to secure enough victimization cases to permit useful analysis. When a survey is aimed at more frequent phenomena, a smaller sample usually suffices.

A survey—or any measurement process—should be designed to meet stated objectives in so far as feasible. Evaluation of the survey or the measuring instrument should in large part be an assessment of the

D.C.: U.S. Government Printing Office, May 1974); *idem, National Crime Survey, Interviewer's Manual 1971* (and current revision); *idem, National Crime Survey Documentation* (no date; released 1976); U.S. Department of Justice, Law Enforcement Assistance Administration, *Criminal Victimization Surveys in 13 American Cities* (Washington: U.S. Government Printing Office, June 1975); *idem, Criminal Victimization in the United States, 1973 Advance Report,* Vol. 1 (May 1975).

degree to which it meets or can meet objectives. As will be apparent later, the panel feels the NCS thus far is doing a better job of meeting its general objectives—producing general-purpose time series and other social indicators—than of meeting some of the more local or more specific problem-oriented objectives that certain students of crime had envisaged earlier.

PRETESTS AND PILOT STUDIES

NCS planners recognized a considerable number of both major and lesser problems that would be encountered in the prospective victimization surveys. Accordingly, over a 2-year period, they conducted a series of six pretests and pilot studies before moving into full-scale operation. This commendable course is discussed in Chapter 3. Among the matters investigated were the range of topics (crimes) to be covered; questionnaire construction; choice of respondent; recall failure; telescoping, or displacement of events in time; underreporting, as judged by reverse record checks; and operational feasibility. This exploration and research undoubtedly made the NCS a better instrument than it otherwise might have been. Such exploratory research unfortunately was all but discontinued after the main survey began, and only recently have there been signs that it is being reinstituted.

THE NATIONAL HOUSEHOLD SURVEY

The national survey is based on a sample of about 60,000 households, each interviewed at 6-month intervals. This sample is divided into subsamples of 10,000 households interviewed each month. A housing unit—as distinct from a household or the persons residing in the housing unit—remains in the sample for 3 years. The subsamples are organized in such a fashion that one group of 10,000 is rotated out of the sample each 6-month period and is replaced with a new group.

At each interview, household members are queried about victimization experiences in each of the 6 months preceding the month of interview. Under present practice, events are tabulated according to reported month of occurrence. Thus, events reported in July interviews as ones that occurred in June are combined with reports of events that also occurred in June from interviews conducted in August, September, October, November, and December, in order to secure the final estimate for June.

Events reported in one interview of a household are checked to see if they were reported by that same household in the interview conducted there 6 months earlier. If they were previously reported, they cannot have occurred in the 6-month reference period of the later interview and, accordingly, are deleted from the second report. This editing technique is a one-directional use of methodology that is known as conducting "bounded" interviews. Note that data for a person or household that appears in the sample for the first time are not bounded for that first appearance. The first time a panel-rotation is in the sample, the data are not used. In continuing panel-rotations, new construction is introduced, over time, so that some new addresses are interviewed for the first time in continuing panel-rotations, and these are used in the official estimates.

Sampling is carried out in stages. The nation is first divided exhaustively into approximately 2,000 Primary Sampling Units (PSU's). A PSU is a Standard Metropolitan Statistical Area (SMSA), a county, or a small group of contiguous counties. The PSU's are then stratified on the basis of size, density and mobility of population, and other socioeconomic criteria into 376 strata. In the first stage of sampling, one PSU is selected from each stratum with probability proportionate to the size of its population. In subsequent steps, within the sample PSU's, clusters of approximately four neighboring housing units are selected systematically in such a manner that each housing unit in the nation has a known, nonzero, roughly equal probability of inclusion in the final sample.

Interviewing is carried out by a crew of approximately 500 enumerators, supervised and controlled from the Census Bureau's 12 regional offices. At each contact with a housing unit while it is in the sample, attempts are made initially to obtain face-to-face interviews. Questions on household characteristics and victimizations are handled by a household informant—any competent adult 18 years or older—and those on personal victimizations are answered by each eligible household member.[2] For these latter questions, about 75 percent of interviews are face to face, and the remainder are conducted by telephone. Proxy respondents are specified for the personal questions when the person affected is age 12 or 13, hospitalized, incompetent, or temporarily absent for the duration of the interview period.

---

[2]Since August 1975, the household informant has been specifically required to be at least 18 years old, unless the head or wife is under 18. Prior to that date, any competent adult, 14 years old or older, could serve as the informant on household characteristics and household victimizations.

THE NATIONAL COMMERCIAL SURVEY

The commercial survey consists of a two-stage probability sample of business establishments in the United States. For this survey, the universe of business establishments is grouped into PSU's, which are classified on the basis of geography and other socioeconomic factors into 58 strata. The first stage of sampling consists of 10 large, self-representing PSU's selected with certainty, because there is only one PSU in each of 10 strata, and 48 non-self-representing PSU's, one from each of the other 48 strata. The second stage is systematic sampling of clusters of neighboring establishments. There are 889 sample clusters in the self-representing PSU's and 1,580 in the PSU's that are non-self-representing. The overall sample contains approximately 39,000 establishments.

The commercial sample also is divided into monthly subsamples of approximately 6,500 establishments, each interviewed at 6-month intervals with reference periods for the preceding 6 months. Unlike the household sample, the commercial clusters remain in the sample indefinitely.

Another important difference between the household and commercial samples is the scope of crimes covered. The household survey is concerned with rape, robbery, assault, burglary, household larceny, personal larceny, and automobile theft. The commercial survey coverage is restricted to robbery and burglary.

THE CITY HOUSEHOLD SURVEYS

The city household surveys follow the pattern of the national survey, with the following differences:

1. Some cities are surveyed once only. In all cities, the sample for each survey is selected at the time of the survey. There are no subsamples or rotation groups, and the interviews cannot be related to earlier interviews at the same housing unit—consequently, the bounding procedure cannot be used.

2. The reference period is 12 months rather than 6 months.

3. Each city survey is restricted to households within the corporate limits of a single city.

4. Each city sample consists of approximately 10,000 interviewed households in 5,000 clusters.

5. Enumerator cadres must be newly formed for each city survey,

since interviewing is concentrated in a 6-week period and is not a continuing activity in any given community.

6. Estimation is different than in the national survey because independent controls of city populations are not available by age, sex, or race. (See pp. 18–20 for a discussion of the significance of this circumstance.)

7. Between 1972 and 1975, the 5 largest cities and 8 others have been surveyed twice each and 13 have been surveyed once.

THE CITY COMMERCIAL SURVEYS

The city commercial surveys take place in the same cities as the city household surveys. They bear the same kind of relationship to the national commercial survey as do the city household surveys to the national household survey.

The city commercial samples vary in size among cities, the range being from 1,000 to 5,000 establishments.

The above brief descriptions of each of the four types of surveys that make up the overall LEAA–Census victimization survey may offer sufficient background for some readers of this report, who wish to focus on the panel's findings, evaluations, and conclusions presented in later chapters. Others may feel the need for additional information on certain features of the sampling design and estimating technique— some of which are unique to the NCS. Knowledge of these features should contribute to better understanding of precisely what is sampled and what is or is not measured and, consequently, of both current and potential output of the survey. The following section, somewhat technical in character, provides modest additional detail on design and estimation for the national household sample.

SELECTED SIGNIFICANT FEATURES OF THE NATIONAL HOUSEHOLD SURVEY

THE BASIC DESIGN

The NCS is fundamentally a sample of clusters of addresses (housing units). The interviewing process records measures of what has happened during the previous 6 months to the households and persons currently living at those addresses, as reported by the residents. Primary emphasis is placed on victimization events and certain descriptors, including demographic and socioeconomic characteristics of the residents.

Continuity of the sample over a 3-year period is that of the clusters of addresses, or more precisely, of the physical area defined by those addresses. There is no assured continuity of households and persons: If the composition of a household at an address in the sample changes entirely, the experiences of the new occupants are reported for the address on subsequent interviews, rather than the experiences of those who previously lived in the unit. Thus, NCS data do not disclose the experiences of a fixed cohort of households or persons, but instead tally victimization events as reported by the residents at the sample addresses at times of interview.

The *person* coverage is restricted to the civilian noninstitutional population. Census procedures require that every person discovered at a sample address be associated at any given time with some one address—even those with "no fixed address." It is in this sense that the NCS is a sample of persons at fixed points in time and space. In other words, the NCS over time is a sample of addresses—if people move, they are not followed up—and, accordingly, it is not a cohort sample of persons or families. This important fact needs be kept in mind in assessing the NCS capabilities.

Out-migrant losses restrict longitudinal analysis of fixed panels of persons and invite questions on whether the experiences of out-migrants are different from those of persons who do not move. With respect to the latter point, relevant evidence could be obtained at low cost. The sample contains in its entirety a national sample of in-migrants who were out-migrants from other areas. Additional questions to these in-migrants, and careful tabulation of responses, could provide much of the desired information. It should help in making a decision as to whether information that might be gained by follow-up of the out-migrants would justify its high cost. To be sure, analysis of longitudinal experience *at a location* has obvious advantages when geographical interests are central.

The 60,000 households in the total sample are located in 15,000 address-clusters that contain an average of four households each. Setting aside the first month of interviewing, used only for bounding, the parent sample of 15,000 address-clusters, after the rotational pattern is in full operation, comprises many subsamples, each of which is itself a probability sample of all addresses in the United States. In fact, the estimate for each *reference* month is constructed from 72 distinct such subsamples. The rotation groups and six subsample panels within each rotation group are interlocked in such a fashion that, for any reference month, there are two subsample estimates for each cell of the following 6 × 6 dummy table. There are two subsamples in each cell rather than one, because the overall sample consists of two sets of corresponding, or replicate, address-clusters.

Number of Times Address-Cluster Has Been Interviewed	Distance in Months Between Interview Month and Reference Month for Measures					
	1	2	3	4	5	6
1						
2						
3						
4			X			
5						
6						

The cell containing an X identifies a pair of samples for which a particular reference month is 3 months prior to the interview month for addresses that are being measured for the fourth time—i.e., for clusters that have been in the parent sample for 1½ years. Each of the 72 subsamples consists of approximately 208 clusters and 832 households, yielding an average of 1,910 sample persons.

Viewed in a still broader context, a block of information from one of the sets of subsamples can be described by a five-part label that identifies its key characteristics (g, p, i, m, r): g = serial number of the rotation group; p = serial number of the panel within that rotation group; i = chronological number of first month in which the gth rotation group enters the sample; m = chronological number of months of data collection; and r = chronological month of reference (i.e., the month to which the data relate). Suppose we use "1" for January 1973, "13" for January 1974, and so on. Thus, for example, the descriptor (4, 3, 19, 33, 32) identifies the collection month 33 (September 1975); reference month 32 (August 1975); obtained from the third panel of the fourth rotation group, which first entered the sample in month 19 (July 1974).

It turns out that in this set there are 36 blocks of data or subsamples that contribute to the estimate for month 32 (August 1975): six panels from each of five rotation groups, four from one rotation group, and two from a seventh rotation group. The *collection* months include September 1975 through February 1976. Since there are two sets of subsamples, the full design yields the 72 subsamples that contribute to the August estimate.

From the perspective of collection month rather than reference month, we find one panel in the sample from each of 12 rotation groups, while collectively the panels provide data for approximately 2,500 address-clusters and 10,000 households. Each of these 12 panels produces six estimates, one for each of the preceding 6 months.

Focus next on a *reference* year—say calendar 1975. We find that 72 subsamples contribute to the estimate for January. All but two of these also produce data for February, while two new subsamples apply also to February. For each of the subsequent 10 reference months of 1975, two new subsamples are added, so that finally 94 subsamples have contributed to the 1975 estimate. Table 1 displays the patterns, and Table 2 summarizes the contributions.

The sample structure when matured—i.e., when the rotation pattern is fully operative—is well designed to balance time-in-sample in order to secure equal representation from first, second, third . . . sixth time interviewed and to balance elapsed time between interview and reported event (ranging from 1 to 6 months), as well as the interaction of the two influences. The structure also offers opportunities for an analysis of these factors. However, it is not immediately evident what impact the highly complex structure has in the period prior to full maturity—which occurs first with respect to data for January 1977—or with respect to some particular interim statistic, such as the difference between estimates of burglaries for 1974 and 1973.

By most standards in social statistics, this is not only a carefully constructed sample, but also a large sample. Monthly interviews include 10,000 households and more than 22,000 persons. Data for a reference month rest on samples of 60,000 households and more than 138,000 persons. Data for a reference year are based on samples of approximately 78,000 households and 180,000 persons, although not all households contribute reported experience for each month of the year. Estimates for a reference year are derived from more than 1 million reported person-months of experience.

Yet even for this relatively large sample, there are serious limitations on utility if one wants to study specific geographic areas, particularly the smaller domains within specific geographic areas. For example, for one reference year, the 180,000 sample persons include about 9,500 black males. These 9,500 males collectively will have reported fewer than 800 robberies in a year, and less than 10 of this number are likely to have occurred in any particular fairly large metropolitan area. The rarity of events in the population also imposes limitations on many

TABLE 1 Illustration of Relationship between Collection Month and Reference Month in the NCS

Collection Month	Panel	Rotation Groups	Jan.	Feb.	Mar.	Apr.	May	June	July	Aug.	Sept.	Oct.	Nov.	Dec.
1975														
Feb.	2	1–12	X											
Mar.	3	"	X	X										
Apr.	4	"	X	X	X									
May	5	"	X	X	X	X								
June	6	"	X	X	X	X	X							
July	1	3–14	X	X	X	X	X	X						
Aug.	2	"		X	X	X	X	X	X					
Sept.	3	"			X	X	X	X	X	X				
Oct.	4	"				X	X	X	X	X	X			
Nov.	5	"					X	X	X	X	X	X		
Dec.	6	"						X	X	X	X	X	X	
1976														
Jan.	1	5–16							X	X	X	X	X	X
Feb.	2	"								X	X	X	X	X
Mar.	3	"									X	X	X	X
Apr.	4	"										X	X	X
May	5	"											X	X
June	6	"												X

Reference Month in 1975

17

TABLE 2   Numbers of Subsamples Contributing Specified Numbers of Reference-Month Estimates for a Given Reference Year

Number of Subsamples	Number of Reference-Month Estimates per Subsample	Total Number of Contributed Monthly Estimates for the Reference Year
All 94	—	864
4	1	4
4	2	8
4	3	12
4	4	16
4	5	20
4	6	24
4	7	28
4	8	32
4	9	36
4	10	40
4	11	44
50	12	600

cross-classifications, on estimates for a calendar quarter, and on estimates for parts of a metropolitan area.

The lesson is obvious. Caution is in order when analyzing data for smaller cells. For in such cells, not only is sampling error very large, but so too is the risk from occasional gross mistakes in execution of the survey. Such gross mistakes in coding, programming, tabulation, and other processing are inevitable in any large survey.

ESTIMATION

In probability sampling, initially reported data are converted to estimates of population parameters through selection of appropriate computational rules. In many, if not most, sampling operations, this operation is accomplished simply by multiplying sample observations by the reciprocals of their probabilities of inclusion in the sample. In more complex surveys, theory and practice have evolved to produce more elaborate estimators in order to reduce the mean square error of the resulting statistics. Since the mean square error encompasses both bias and variance of sample estimates, some of the more elaborate estimating techniques seek a reduction in bias, while others are chosen to minimize variance and thus increase the precision of estimates. The NCS employs a number of such techniques, in addition to the built-in features of the sampling design itself. The necessary computations are accomplished by applying a series of multiplier weights to each reported observation. These weights are identified and described briefly in the following list:

1. *The Basic Weight*   This is the traditional reciprocal of the initially designed probability of selection. It has varied somewhat in different time periods, but, calculated on a month-of-collection basis, it typically is around 1,000.

2. *Duplication Weight*   In a few situations, the field operation finds that an initially designated address-cluster contains substantially more households than had been expected. When this occurs, the address-cluster may be subsampled to obtain a tolerable workload. The reciprocal of the subsampling fraction becomes a duplication weight.

3. *Within-Household Noninterview Weight*   This weight is applied to convert data for responding persons to reflect all persons in the sample household. Its determination is in itself a rather complex calculation, described here in modest detail because it reflects a *pattern* of imputation used also in other steps of the estimating process.

(a) The weights are calculated separately for each of four geographic regions of the United States.
(b) Within region, separate multipliers are obtained for each of 24 cells: two races by four age groups by three relationships to head of household.
(c) No multiplier in a cell is allowed to be greater than 2,000; that is, no responding person is allowed by himself to represent more than one nonrespondent. This particular purpose is accomplished by collapsing cells in the 24-cell table if the standard is not met for an individual cell. The collapsing is done by combining neighboring cells of the table through use of a scaling of cells so that one cell or even a combination of cells is merged with its nearest demographic neighbor.
(d) The arithmetic for the noninterview factor (NIF) for a single cell is

$$\text{NIF} = \frac{I_c + NI_c}{I_c} ,$$

where I_c is the number of responding persons for the cell and NI_c is the number of nonrespondents within interviewed households.

4. *Household Noninterview Weight*   This weight is designed to

adjust for entire households that are in the sample but do not respond. It is calculated with the same strategy that is used for within-household nonresponse. Separate sets of weights are computed for each of 22 clusters of housing units, with cluster being defined by type of housing, population density factors, and predominant racial composition.

5. *First-Stage Ratio Factor*   As noted earlier, the NCS is a multi-stage sample. The first stage is the selection of 376 PSU's from among approximately 2,000 PSU's. The first-stage ratio factor is a set of multipliers that relate the 1970 population of the 376 sample PSU's to the 2,000-PSU universe. When the multipliers are introduced, they cause the aggregate counts for sample PSU's to match the 1970 official census population figures exactly in each of 48 cells, defined by region, population density, and race.

6. *Poststratification*   After the above weights have been applied, an estimate x' for any specified measurement for a category of persons is secured and also an estimate y' of the number of persons in the universe population for the same demographic category. The estimate x' is then refined by a poststratifying operation to

$$x'' = x' \left(\frac{y}{y'}\right),$$

where y is the official independent estimate of current population in the target category, as determined by the Census Bureau using counts of births and deaths from the National Center for Health Statistics, migration figures from other sources, and aging of the 1970 cohorts to the current date. The quantity (y/y') is the poststratification factor. It is calculated and applied separately for each of 72 age–sex–color classes. Once again, a scaling technique is used to collapse cells if the multiplier would otherwise be greater than 2.000.

The weights 1 through 6 apply to statistics for personal victimizations and to their characteristics. Since tabulations produced are based on incidents, an incident adjustment is included to account for crimes committed against more than one person and (possibly) reported by more than one person. For household crimes, the *principal person weight* is used. The principal person is defined as the wife in husband–wife households and as the head-of-house in other cases, both excluding the within-household noninterview weight.

This estimating and imputation procedure is intended to minimize mean square error within the assigned budget and prevailing environment.

THE COMPLEX OF RECALL DECAY, TELESCOPING, AND LENGTH OF REFERENCE PERIOD

For many reasons, an event or circumstance reported by a respondent and recorded in the survey may not be accurate. In a continuing survey with a retrospective reference period, prominent among these reasons are recall decay, telescoping (or, the displacement of events in time), and the number of times a respondent has been interviewed on the topic. Both reasonable hypotheses and empirical evidence in the NCS and in other surveys demonstrate that each of these factors and their interactions affect results. From the start of NCS planning to the present, Census and LEAA staff have recognized these problems and tried to cope with them both in terms of design and data analysis.

Recall decay refers to the phenomenon that the greater the distance between the date of an event and the date of interview, the less likely is the event to be reported, other things being equal. A burglary that occurred about a year ago is less likely to be reported than one occurring a week ago. Telescoping indicates a reported displacement of the event in time. If an event is reported as occurring earlier than it actually occurred, the displacement is called backward telescoping. If the event is reported to have occurred later than it did, the displacement is called forward telescoping. There is widespread opinion and limited evidence that forward telescoping exceeds backward telescoping, especially as the length of reference period increases, although there is certainly some telescoping in both directions.

A Washington, D.C., pretest selected a small sample of crimes reported to the police and subsequently included among interviewed households persons who were the recorded victims of those crimes.[3] This type of reverse record check can provide evidence on underreporting in the household interview, but not overreporting. The record check may reveal displacement by households of events in time when the events are reported both to the police and by the household respondents. The Washington data on this point are shown in Table 3. A similar study was a part of the San Jose pretest.[4] The San Jose data appear in Table 4.

The nature of this tabulation is such that cases in the police record 1–3 months ago could not be shown as telescoped forward, and cases in the police record 10–12 months ago could not be shown as telescoped

---

[3]U.S. Department of Commerce, Bureau of the Census, "Victim Recall Pretest (Washington, D.C.)" (Internal Memorandum dated June 10, 1970).

[4]U.S. Department of Justice, Law Enforcement Assistance Administration, *San Jose Methods Test of Known Crime Victims*, Statistics Technical Report No. 1 (Washington, D.C.: U.S. Government Printing Office, June 1972).

TABLE 3 Extent of Forward and Backward Telescoping of Events as Reported in Interviews, Washington Pretest, March 1970

No. of Cases in Police Record	Police Record Shows Event Occurred	Percent of Events as Reported in Interview				
		All Cases	Not Reported	Telescoped Forward	Reported in Correct Month	Telescoped Backward
86	3 Months ago	100	14	5	73	8
77	6 Months ago	100	22	9	60	9
63	11 Months ago	100[a]	22	14	49	6

[a]Five victimizations were reported in interviews but are not included in the percentage distribution because the respondent could not recall the month of occurrence. Thus, the row totals for events occurring 11 months before the interview do not add up to 100 percent.

22

TABLE 4 Extent of Forward and Backward Telescoping of Events as Reported in Interview, San Jose Pretest, January 1971

No. of Cases in Police Record	Police Record Shows Event Occurred	Percent of Events as Reported in Interview				
		All Cases	Not Reported or Month Not Known	Telescoped Forward	Reported in Correct Quarter	Telescoped Backward
101	1–3 Months ago	100	22	—	70	8
100	4–6 Months ago	100	36	8	50	6
103	7–9 Months ago	100	32	14	46	8
90	10–12 Months ago	100	41	13	46	—

backward. (A somewhat different partitioning of the original San Jose data and a more detailed account of that pretest is presented in Chapter 3.)

Recall decay and telescoping occur together in raw reported data, and this complicates analysis of their effects. Both do have bearing on the choice of optimum length of reference period.

If reporting were equally reliable for each month of a retrospective reference period, it would be better to use a 12-month rather than a 6-month reference period. The longer period has several advantages. It permits discovery in one interview of what may be total experience for an individual over a full year and thus provides, for example, a classification of persons by *number* of victimizations in a year. It provides more information per dollar cost, since it yields 12 person–months in a single interview rather than in two interviews with 6-month recall. It avoids seasonal distortions that may otherwise be present within an immature panel.

Census–LEAA have chosen a 6-month reference period for the national surveys (although a 12-month period is used for the city surveys). Their studies led them to believe that the quality of reporting for the shorter period justifies the greater cost and the loss of other capabilities. This choice also may have been influenced by the decision to adjust reported data for forward telescoping into the reference period by a bounding procedure, but not to adjust for telescoping backward out of the reference period, nor for either backward or forward telescoping that might occur within the reference period itself. In the present procedure, bounding entails deleting events reported for a given 6-month period if apparently the same events were also reported in the previous 6-month period. It should be emphasized that the bounding procedure is geared to address-clusters and thus has no effect on interviews where the respondent is an in-migrant to the cluster since the previous interview of that cluster or previously was not interviewed or not in the sample. The intention of this form of bounding is to remove forward telescoping from the most recent 6-month-period's interview. None of the editing procedures adjust for recall decay.

Whatever the contribution of the above effects, it has been observed that the volume of victimization per month reported in the NCS interviews decreases rather sharply as the distance between the reported event and the date of interview increases. Evidence of this phenomenon is clear in Table 5. Data in the body of the table are partitioned average monthly victimization rates *within the reference period* for all NCS personal crimes per 1,000 persons interviewed, as reported in the national survey from June 1973 through September 1974.

TABLE 5 Reported Average Monthly Victimization Rate for Total Personal Crimes Using Data for Differing Intervals within Reference Period

Length of Interval within the Reference Period	Average Monthly Victimization Rate for the Interval
1 Month	262
2 Months	228
3 Months	203
4 Months	187
5 Months	174
6 Months	162

The NAS–NRC panel is ambivalent on the choice for length of reference period and is both hesitant to endorse the 6-month reference period or to suggest adoption of a reference period of a different length. There are conflicting interpretations of the limited evidence available. This is a very important matter that affects both the quality and cost of the NCS. Many combinations of reference period, frequency of interview, and tabulating tactics are possible. A configuration that might be studied is one that uses a 12-month reference period for different purposes. Estimates of total incidence might be based on data reported for the most recent 6 months of the reference periods, while the percentage distribution of persons by number of victimizations in a year, for example, could utilize the full 12-month data.

The configuration should be compared with estimates based on shorter reference periods in order to take into account, among other factors, the effect on respondent productivity of the longer attention span required in interviews employing longer reference periods. The effects on different classes of respondents of different reference periods also should be assessed. Chapter 5 of this report discusses this proposed research in more detail and recommends assignment of high priority to it.

CURRENT ESTIMATES AND TABULATING PATTERNS

The NCS places major emphasis in its tabulations and publications on the volume of victimizations in reference periods of occurrence. The sample design is particularly appropriate for this objective, especially if a prime consideration is the study of annual totals. A necessary consequence of the tabulating scheme is a considerable delay between reference period and the earliest possible publication of estimates for that year based on all subsamples that will contribute data for that year. For example, data for calendar year 1975 will not all have been collected until July 1976 and probably cannot be published before the latter part of 1976 or perhaps in 1977. Even data for the month of December 1975 have the same timetable. After the NCS was in the field, there began to be a demand for current publication of estimates for calendar quarters. Most such estimates would have high sampling variance in any event, as well as seasonal and irregular characteristics. But currency is not feasible with the present tabulating scheme. For again, full data for, say, January, February, and March of 1976 are not collected until September 1976 and probably could not be analyzed and published before 1977, if anything like present operating timetables obtain.

If currency is an objective, either a different field design or a different tabulation pattern is required. For the latter option, probably the essential step would be tabulation and publication on the basis of collection month rather than, or in addition to, reference month. But at present, a collection month's data come from a sample of 10,000 households, whereas a reference month's data are based on a 60,000-household sample. This suggests that, if frequently published current estimates are deemed desirable, a possible pattern is a rolling 12-month reference, based on 12 successive collection months, published perhaps at quarterly intervals.

VICTIMIZATIONS, VICTIMS, RATES, RELATIONSHIPS, AND ALLIED STATISTICS

Given that NCS is a continuing survey and at any given time provides a probability sample of housing units and the entire population of persons, victims, victimizations, and associated descriptors, there is a wide range of items that might be tabulated and presented, in various formats. Decisions about priorities are or should be set by LEAA, taking into account the collective demands of consumers. LEAA has up to the present put the main emphasis on presenting estimates of *numbers* of victimizations by types occurring in specified time intervals and on "victimization rates." A victimization rate is defined as the ratio of victimizations to the number of persons (or households or businesses) classified at the time of interview into categories corresponding to the victims of the crimes. The NCS design is well suited to this output, although both levels and rates are subject to most of the measurement errors inherent in the victimization counts. But the raw data have a much wider potential.

The victimization rates say nothing about how many of the persons in the denominator contribute to the victimization counts in the numerator. It is surprising that no attempt has been made to tabulate persons—both victims and nonvictims—by number of victimizations in a time interval. With the present design of the national component of the NCS, this is possible for a reference period of 6 months. The victimization rate alone is a poor indicator of the likelihood of a person in the category being victimized. For example, suppose that among 1,000 persons in a given category there are 800 who are not victimized at all, another 150 persons are victimized one time in a period of a year, while the remaining 50 persons are victimized an average of five times each. The victimization rate for this category of 1,000 persons, as currently calculated in the NCS, is (400/1,000). Too often such a rate may be interpreted incorrectly as implying that any person in this category has a 40 percent chance of being victimized within a year. The rate does little to help in describing the characteristics of persons who are victimized or in comparing them with persons who are not victimized, since tabulations of nonvictims are not published at all.

Trends, or comparisons over time, may as the NCS matures become one of the most significant outputs. Fortunately, many of the measurement biases that affect levels may have less impact on trend statistics because the measurement biases tend to remain constant. Thus LEAA may wish to consider computation and release of certain indexes of trend.

Another fundamental objective is the discovery of relationships among the measured variables. The crude victimization rate is an unsatisfactory statistic for this purpose. Rather, what is required is finer cross-classification of data, along with the use of multivariate techniques.

NONRESPONSE AND UNDERCOVERAGE

Response rates in the NCS are far above those in most surveys and, indeed, are among the highest in major social surveys. Overall nonresponse for households is only about 3.5 percent, with 1 percent of this figure indicating refusals and the other 2.5 percent representing failure to find a suitable respondent after repeated attempts. There is an additional 1.1 percent of person nonresponse within responding households. The effect of such nonresponse as exists is considerably lessened by the imputation procedures and post-stratification described earlier in this chapter.

Yet nonresponse and undercoverage cannot be ignored. Both vary by demographic categories, and it is a fair presumption that under-coverage is greatest for persons with no usual place of residence and for some classes of persons who have higher-than-average exposure to victimization. These differential undercoverages pose a hazard in comparing rates for different groups and in establishing relationships among variables.

Some insight into the degree of differential nonresponse and under-coverage can be gained from comparing data for two groups of persons: white males, ages 40–44, and nonwhite males, ages 30–34— deliberately chosen for the example in Table 6 because they represent extremes. Entries for Row 1 in Table 6 show the ratios by which responding sample persons must be multiplied to convert them to the independent population controls; Row 2 figures reflect the officially estimated undercounts of the 1970 population Census controls them-selves. It is reasonable to assume, on the basis of the evidence in Table 6, that the sample white males, ages 40–44, are randomly representa-tive of the corresponding universe. There is less confidence in making the similar assumption about nonwhite males, ages 30–34. For the latter group, the realized sample is only some 68 percent of the expected proportion of the universe.

Although it is distinctly possible that those not interviewed had different victimization experience than those who were, there are two features of the NCS estimation method that would tend to mitigate the effects of nonresponse and undercoverage. First, miscounting in both denominators and numerators should be in the same direction if persons missed are not radically different in victim experience from those enumerated. If they are not, rates should be less affected than aggregates of victimization numerators, and the imputation procedures should dampen errors that reside in the raw data.

OPERATIONAL CONTROL

Quite aside from the readily determined nonresponse volumes, there are numerous other respects in which execution of a survey may not correspond precisely with designed intent. Steps taken to keep execu-tion faithful to design can be termed operational control. We have not had the resources to evaluate operational control of NCS in any depth. But the Census Bureau's reputation in this regard, as well as surface indications, suggest that NCS performance is good.

Control is exercised largely through four mechanisms. The first is the initial training of staff and the retraining when weaknesses are dis-covered. Second is detection of interviewer oversights and mistakes

TABLE 6 Measures of Differential Nonresponse and Undercoverage

	Category of Persons	
Source of Potential Bias	White Males, Ages 40–44	Nonwhite Males, Ages 30–34
Necessary sample person adjustment (average values, 1974)	1.012	1.201
Estimated net undercount of the population estimates (Census, 1970)	3.2%	17.9%

through continuing monitoring of questionnaires by field supervisors and through central office editing. Third is a reinterview program of approximately 5 percent of all households by supervisors or senior interviewers. This reinterview procedure identifies both the questions and the interviewers that appear to have least stability and provides rough indicators of measurement variance. Early tabulations suggest that measurement variance for the great majority of items is of the order of 5–20 percent of total variance. The reinterview method of calculation probably results in some understatement of these percentages, since it does not adjust for any conditioning effect of the first response on the reinterview response. Further, it may be that some reinterviewers, contrary to instructions, allow their recording of the second response to be influenced by the response given in the first interview. The net difference—reinterview aggregates after reconciliation minus original interviews—is one approximation of the bias of the original and published data. The small reinterview samples restrict interpretation of early data. The limited scale of the reinterview program, and some delay in analyzing results, mean that there is sometimes a passage of many months before the benefits of reinterview can be fully introduced to operational collection and analysis.

A fourth control procedure is the feedback from analysis, highlighting anomalies, surprises, and suspected peculiarities that are discovered in preparation of reports. We would like to see this process strengthened by giving it more formal attention and by more often introducing change when weaknesses are discovered. Change can be better tolerated in the earlier stages of an ongoing program than in later years, when continuity has heavier weight.

SAMPLING ERROR

The calculation and presentation of measures of precision for a multi-topic survey that seeks to present data on both levels and trends are

formidable tasks. Calculation in the NCS is difficult because the alge-
braic models are extremely involved, because the estimates of variance
themselves have substantial variance, because the estimates of sampling variance are incomplete measures of mean square error, and
because there is such a large number of specific primary statistics for
which knowledge of precision is needed. Presentation, too, is difficult
for these reasons. It is nearly impossible to display the mass of results
in a format that is convenient for ready use.

LEAA and the Census Bureau use several devices to cope with these
issues. (As our evaluation study ended, estimates of standard errors
and components of variance, calculated from NCS data, became available through 1974.) Estimates of variance have been calculated for a
number of statistics, although they are based on data from pilot studies
and other Census surveys, rather than on the full NCS itself. Selections
from these estimates are published in tables in the substantive reports.
Also published are approximate formulas for securing estimates of
variance for other statistics, starting with the published tables. The
published standard errors are estimates that include pure sampling
error and a part of measurement variance, but do not include any
elements of bias.

Another device used is analytic in character. An editing procedure
insures that all statements of comparison appearing in the published
reports are significant at a 1.6 standard error level or more. This
certainly is not a completely satisfactory screening device. It overlooks
patterns in the data and neglects multiple comparisons. It is an arbitrary level. And, it is of little help to the consumer who wishes to use
tabular data to make comparisons that the LEAA has not attempted.
Still, overall, it is helpful in avoiding conclusions that rest on sampling
artifacts.

The panel recommends that LEAA and the Census Bureau continue to search for methods of presentation that simplify the user's
task of determining the precision of a published statistic. Improved
estimates of the components of variance would be useful in assessing
the value of any proposed design modifications and might be informative in analyzing the sources of variation among elements of the
population.

In one area there is a more pressing need: LEAA expects the consum-
ing public to depend heavily on public-use tapes for analytic research.
These are computer tapes of microdata from the survey, with geographic and other descriptors that might identify individuals sup-
pressed in order to protect confidentiality. They offer material for a
variety of estimates and data manipulations. At present there is no

advice to consumers on how to estimate precision of these estimates. This problem is common to many, if not all, public-use tapes that are available and not unique to NCS. Some approximating device for estimation of public-use tapes variances should be included in tape documentation.

Pending discovery of a better technique, the following course might be taken. Define the "design effect" as the ratio of estimated variances for a designated statistic from the NCS to what the variance would be in a simple random sample of the same size for that same designated statistic. Calculate the design effect for a number of statistics. It may well be that many of the survey statistics can then be grouped into classes for each of which an average design effect is close to the true relationships between the NCS and a simple random sample. Publication of these results would permit users of tapes to calculate sampling errors with sufficient accuracy for most purposes, employing the elementary rules of simple random sampling.

3 Review of LEAA-Sponsored Pretest and Pilot Studies

INTRODUCTION

The first victim surveys, carried out for the President's Commission on Law Enforcement and Administration of Justice, a decade ago, raised a number of methodological problems concerning this new research technique.[1] These problems included the fundamental questions of the extent to which survey respondents would accurately remember, and accurately report to interviewers, incidents that had happened to them. But there were many other problems that were explored, to some extent, by those surveys. For example: Which person or persons in a household would be most likely to know about offenses such as burglary? Which could be regarded as having been committed against the whole household? What effects do class-linked factors

---

[1]See the following reports of the President's Commission on Law Enforcement and Administration of Justice (Washington, D.C.: U.S. Government Printing Office, 1967): Albert D. Biderman *et al., Report on a Pilot Study in the District of Columbia on Victimization and Attitudes Toward Law Enforcement,* Field Surveys I, 1967; Philip H. Ennis, *Criminal Victimization in the United States: A Report of a National Survey,* Field Surveys II; Albert J. Reiss, Jr., *Studies in Crime and Law Enforcement in Major Metropolitan Areas,* Vol. 1, Field Surveys III. For a general discussion of many of these methodological problems, see Albert D. Biderman, "Surveys of Population Samples for Estimating Crime Incidence," *The Annals of the American Academy of Political and Social Science* 374 (November 1967): 16–33; Albert D. Biderman and Albert J. Reiss, Jr., "On Exploring the 'Dark Figure' of Crime," *The Annals of the American Academy of Political and Social Science* 374 (1967): 1–15.

such as level of education—which have been identified as sources of bias in many surveys based on interviews—have on the reporting of crime incidents? What would be the effects of different interviewing strategies and conditions (variation in length of interviews or in content of screening questions, for instance) on respondents' "productivity"? What is the best way of coping with series victimization, that is, cases in which the respondent says that he was a victim on numerous occasions but cannot recount dates of specific incidents, much less other details? What are the best ways in which to analyze incident reports and to carry out procedures analogous to "unfounding" by police of false or baseless reports?

There was thus a substantial agenda of methodological issues to be investigated at the time when the NCS first was being planned. It appears, however, that only a few of these issues have so far been studied by the Census Bureau or by LEAA. The panel recommends, therefore, that the methodological research program of the NCS be greatly expanded to provide for a thorough examination of those problems that have already been identified, as well as those that may emerge in the future.

Before the current NCS surveys were implemented in the field in 1972, LEAA and the Bureau of the Census did conduct a number of pretests and pilot studies, a review of which is presented in this chapter. These pretests included:

1. a reverse record check in Washington, D.C.[2] (March 1970, 326 persons interviewed);

2. a reverse record check in Baltimore[3] (July 1970, 362 persons interviewed);

3. a reverse record check in San Jose, California[4] (January 1971, 394 persons interviewed);

4. pilot surveys of households and businesses in Santa Clara County (San Jose), California, and Montgomery County (Dayton), Ohio[5] (Jan-

[2]"Victim Recall Pretest, Washington, D.C.: Household Survey of Victims of Crime" (Unpublished memorandum, Bureau of the Census, June 10, 1970, no author).

[3]Linda R. Yost and Richard W. Dodge, "Household Survey of Victims of Crime, Second Pretest: Baltimore, Maryland" (Unpublished memorandum, Bureau of the Census, November 30, 1970).

[4]U.S. Department of Justice, Law Enforcement Assistance Administration, *San Jose Methods Test of Known Crime Victims*, Statistics Technical Report No. 1 (Washington, D.C.: U.S. Government Printing Office, June 1972).

[5]Carol B. Kalish, *Crimes and Victims: A Report on the Dayton–San Jose Pilot Survey of Victimization* (Washington, D.C.: U.S. Department of Justice, Law Enforcement Assistance Administration, June 1974).

uary 1971, approximately 5,500 households and 1,000 businesses interviewed in each county);

5. feasibility tests of businesses in Cleveland and Akron, Ohio[6] (May 1970, approximately 300 businesses in Cleveland and 200 in Akron); and,

6. four victimization supplements to the Quarterly Household Survey[7] (January 1971, 18,000 households; July 1971, 18,000 households; January 1972, 18,000 households; and, July 1972, 18,000 households).

In these projects a number of important methodological problems inherent in victim surveys were addressed. The main ones were (a) the extent of memory failure (or, more strictly, the nonreporting of incidents to survey interviewers) and the selection of reference period length; (b) the effects of telescoping and respondents' ability to recall the precise month in which an incident occurred; (c) questionnaire development; (d) the choice of self-respondent versus household or proxy respondent; and, (e) the possibility of using mail questionnaires.

THE EXTENT OF MEMORY FAILURE AND THE CHOICE OF AN OPTIMUM REFERENCE PERIOD

Retrospective surveys, in which respondents are asked about things that may have happened to them in the past, may be inaccurate, because respondents fail to remember the events in question or because (through deceit or misunderstanding) they simply fail to tell interviewers about them. In reverse record check studies—like those carried out in Washington, Baltimore, and San Jose—a sample is selected of persons who are known, from other data, to have had the experiences in question (in this case persons who have been recorded by the police as having reported a crime to them). Those persons are interviewed, and their responses are compared with what is known about them from other sources (in this case, police records).

The reverse-record-check technique has been used to investigate recall, telescoping, and related phenomena in social surveys on many

[6]Karen Joerg, "The Cleveland–Akron Commerical Victimization Feasibility Test" (Draft of Statistics Division Technical Series Report No. 2, U.S. Department of Justice, Law Enforcement Assistance Administration, no date). Unpublished.
[7]Anthony G. Turner, "Methodological Issues in the Development of the National Crime Survey Panel: Partial Findings" (Unpublished memorandum, U.S. Department of Justice, Law Enforcement Assistance Administration, December 1972).

TABLE 7   Reporting of Victimizations

Recorded by Police	Reported to Interviewers		
	Yes	No	Row Sums
Yes	N_{11}	N_{12}	N_{1+}
No	N_{21}	N_{22}	N_{2+}
Column Sums	N_{+1}	N_{+2}	N (Total)

other subjects (for example, medical treatment and household expenditures).[8] Potentially, the technique is capable of validating survey responses, since it uses a sample drawn from those for whom there is an independent measure (in this case, police records) of what those responses refer to.

Yet for several reasons one should exercise caution in applying inferences based on reverse record checks to victimization survey results. For instance, experience has shown that there is a serious problem in locating for interview persons who are identified in police records as victims.[9]

Moreover, while an important objective of the NCS is to obtain estimates of the incidence of crime that are not affected by the nonreporting by victims of offenses to the police (and the nonrecording by police of offenses that are reported or otherwise known to them), reverse record checks usually are based on incidents that have been reported to the police. The presumption would be that these may be more likely to be reported to survey interviewers than incidents where the police were not notified. Theoretically, victimizations can be classified depending on whether they were recorded by police and reported to interviewers, as illustrated in Table 7.

What is desired is that most victimizations will be reported to survey interviewers, whether or not they were reported to the police: that is, that the ratio N_{+2}/N will be very small. But since it is in practice impossible to observe N_{22}—those crimes not recorded by the police nor reported to survey interviewers—the reverse record check uses a sample of the N_{1+} victimizations that have been recorded by police to

[8]See, for example, Percy G. Gray, "The Memory Factor in Social Surveys," *Journal of the American Statistical Association* 50 (1955): 344–63; W. P. D. Logan and E. M. Brooke, *The Survey of Sickness, 1943 to 1952,* General Register Office, Studies on Medical and Population Subjects (London: Her Majesty's Stationery Office, 1957). For a general discussion, see Seymour Sudman and Norman M. Bradburn, *Response Effects in Surveys* (Chicago: Aldine Publishing Co., 1974), Chapter 3.

[9]For example, the noncontact rates in the Washington, Baltimore, and San Jose pretests ranged from 31.3 percent to 36.5 percent of the sampled cases.

determine if the proportion of this sample not reported to interviewers, N_{12}/N_{1+}, is indeed small. Clearly, however, the ratio N_{+2}/N is a weighted average of N_{12}/N_{1+} and N_{22}/N_{2+} and thus depends in part on the relative magnitudes of N_{1+} and N_{2+}—those victimizations that are, and are not, recorded by police. There is abundant evidence, from the NCS and other victimization surveys, that the great majority of crimes are not recorded by police, so that N_{2+} is greater than N_{1+}. If—as also seems likely—crimes that have not been recorded by the police are less likely to be reported to interviewers than those that have, then the reverse record check may give misleading results. For example, suppose that 90 percent of crimes recorded by police were mentioned to interviewers in a reverse-record-check study, but that only 10 percent of all events that police might have judged to be crimes actually were recorded by police. If a victim survey like the NCS captured half of those crimes that had not been recorded by the police, the actual "success" rate of the survey method would be 54 percent and not 90 percent, as the reverse record check would suggest.[10] The point is that a reverse record check cannot be used to validate victim surveys any more than victim surveys can be used to validate police records. On the other hand, if all of the incidents included in a reverse record check were mentioned to interviewers (so that $N_{12}/N_{1+} = 0$), the survey method clearly could be regarded as a comparably reliable indicator, at least of those types of events that both victims and police judge to be crimes.

With respect to the reliability of victimizations reported to interviewers, the results of the three reverse record checks carried out by the Census Bureau raise a number of provocative questions. For several reasons, it is not easy to compare the results of the three pretests in any straightforward way. For example, in Washington, D.C., cases used to investigate recall involved incidents occurring 3, 6, and 11 months before the interviews; in Baltimore, the incidents had occurred 3 and 6 months before interview; and in San Jose, they went back as far as a year before interview. The questionnaires used in the three studies also differed, as did certain of the interviewing and

[10]Other strategies, such as the "multiple recapture" technique, which requires two or more interviews of the same sample, might be employed to explore this problem. For a discussion of multiple recapture methods, used in estimating the size of a closed population where complete enumeration is impossible, see R. M. Cormack, "The Statistics of Capture–Recapture Methods," *Oceanographic Marine Biology Annual Review* 6 (1968): 455–501; S. E. Feinberg, "The Multiple Recapture Census for Closed Populations and Incomplete 2^k Contingency Tables," *Biometrika* 59 (1972): 591–603; Yvonne M. M. Bishop, S. E. Feinberg, and P. W. Holland, *Discrete Multivariate Analysis, Theory and Practice* (Cambridge, Mass.: MIT Press, 1975), Chapter 6.

fieldwork methods. Furthermore, a substantial proportion of victims initially selected from police files for the studies were not interviewed; completion rates ranged from 63.5 percent to 68.7 percent across the three cities. Ignoring these problems, however, the overall "success" rates—defined as the percent of interviewed persons who acknowledged the target event—in the three surveys, for all types of incidents and for all reference periods considered, were 81 percent in Washington, D.C., 67 percent in Baltimore, and 74 percent in San Jose.

There was wide variation in the reporting to the interviewers of incidents, according to type of crime: The reporting of some kinds of victimizations was much lower than average. Since the percentage distributions of types of offenses in the three pretests differed from what might be expected in a true probability sample of victims—crimes of violence were overrepresented—these overall "success" rates accordingly differ from those which would be obtained in such a sample. Reweighting the pretest results to take account of this fact, it could be estimated that for the offenses of burglary, robbery, assault, and larceny (both personal and household), the overall "success" rate of a national victim survey would be between 70 and 80 percent, so far as crimes recorded by the police are concerned. That is, a victim survey that achieved a true overall "success" rate (in terms of recall and reporting to interviewers) like that suggested by the three Census pretests would understate the level of personal and household victimization by at least 20 to 30 percent.[11]

It should be emphasized that the accuracy of this estimate is problematic, for at least two reasons. First, it seems likely that the incidents used in the reverse record checks, which had been reported to the police, would be more likely to be recalled and mentioned to survey interviewers than incidents not reported to police, partly because they are likely to be (both objectively and subjectively) more serious and partly because the fact of having called the police, given details of the incident, possibly having appeared in court, etc., might make the event more salient to the survey respondent. Secondly, in the cases of Washington, D.C., and Baltimore, the conditions under which respondents were interviewed may have increased the chances of recall: It appears that in both cases interviewers knew that the respondents had been victims of crime and in both cases respondents were contacted by telephone in advance of the actual interview. Thus, if we were to consider all incidents of victimization occurring during 6 months or a year prior

---

[11]If the proportion of underreported cases remained constant over time, a series of surveys might still give a reasonably accurate measure of trends in victimization. But it is not known whether nonreporting to interviewers does in fact remain constant.

to interview, and if the interviews had been conducted in exactly the same way as those now being done for the NCS and city surveys, the surveys might understate the level of personal and household victimization to an even greater degree than the pretests suggest.

It is possible that this underestimate to some extent is offset by the effects of forward telescoping (discussed further below), as well as by the false or mistaken reporting of incidents that were not in fact crimes. Also operating in the opposite direction is the fact that the average criterion incident in the reverse-record-check studies was much less recent than the average incident in the NCS 6-month reference period. Too, questions used to elicit victim experiences were altered after the Washington, D.C., and Baltimore pretest studies. The point is that on the issue of recall and reporting considered by itself, the results of the three Census pretests leave much to be desired, and further research on this problem is well worth doing.

The foregoing analysis, in terms of overall percentages of known incidents reported, ignores differences that were found in all three pretests in the "success" of the survey method, according to the reference period used and to the type of offense. In the Washington, D.C., pretest, whether a recalled incident was placed in the correct month varied according to the number of months between the incident and the interview: 73 percent of the incidents occurring 3 months before interview were reported to have occurred in the correct month, compared with 60 percent of those taking place 6 months before the interview and 49 percent of those occurring 11 months earlier (see Table 3, Chapter 2).

In the San Jose reverse record check, the only reference period used in the interview was 12 months (calendar year 1970). The San Jose data showed, however, that there was little difference in the proportions of incidents placed correctly within the time period in which they were known to have occurred: Of cases occurring up to 3 months previously, 69.3 percent were reported as having taken place within the past 3 months, whereas for cases occurring up to 12 months previously, 67.3 percent were reported as having occurred within the past 12 months. (These percentages were affected only slightly by weighting for sample size differentials and by noninterview adjustments.) Even when allowance was made for incidents mentioned by respondents who could not give the month in which the incident occurred, the "success" rates for 3-, 6-, and 12-month data intervals were similar. However, since all respondents were asked to report events for a 12-month reference period, the effect on recall decay or on productivity of a 6- versus 12-month reference period, or of a 3- versus 6-month reference period, was not tested. The authors of the San Jose study concluded "that a reference period of 12 months is basically as reliable as the other reference periods shown (3, 6, 9, . . .), as long as the precise month of the occurrence is not a criterion for consideration."[12]

A 6-month reference period was selected for the National Crime Panel. This decision apparently was affected by several factors (including telescoping, which is discussed in the next section). One argument offered in support of the 6-month reference period, in the *San Jose Methods Test* report, is as follows:

. . . when considered in connection with a continuing survey, a 6-month reference period is better than a 12-month period for producing calendar year data and for obtaining earlier and more timely results. With a 6-month rolling reference period, some data could theoretically be available after 12 months—assuming bounded interviews—and the data would be "centered" 3 months ago. For a 12-month reference period, 18 months would be required before data, comparably reliable, would be available and it would be centered 6 months ago. The sample size, however, for a 6-month reference period is twice that for a 12-month period.[13]

Another cited reason is that the actual month of occurrence was regarded as a critical data item in the national sample because the plans were to publish data on a quarterly basis.[14] This justification of a shorter reference period would appear to be supported by the finding in the San Jose study that the precision of respondents' reports of incidents declined as the time between incident and interview date increased; the exact month or quarter of the incident was more likely to be reported for incidents taking place up to 6 months previously than for those occurring 7–12 months previously.

Aside from technical considerations, the decision to base the NCS design on a 6-month reference period apparently was influenced by an interest in the timely publication of quarterly estimates. It is the opinion of the panel that the length of the reference period should be reassessed, from the vantage point of current experience and against criteria based on current program objectives.

In the reverse-record-check studies, reporting to interviewers of known incidents also varied according to type of crime. In general, reporting of burglary and robbery was greater than reporting of theft, and all three of these types of property crime were more likely to be mentioned to interviewers than were assaults. In the Washington,

[12]U.S. Department of Justice, LEAA. *San Jose Methods Test, op. cit.,* p. 7.
[13]*Ibid.,* p. 1.
[14]Turner, *op. cit.,* p. 5.

D.C., pretest, the proportions of recorded victimizations reported to interviewers were 91 percent for robberies, 88 percent for burglaries, and 77 percent for thefts. For assaults, the corresponding figure was only 65 percent. In the Baltimore study, combining 3-month-old and 6-month-old offenses, the proportions reported to interviewers were 86 percent for burglary, 76 percent for robbery, 75 percent for larceny, and only 36 percent for assault. In the case of assaults occurring 6 months before the interviews, only 17 out of 52 (or less than 33 percent) were reported to the interviewers. In the San Jose Methods Test, 90 percent of the burglaries, 81 percent of the larcenies, 76 percent of the robberies, and 67 percent of the rapes were mentioned to the interviewers. For assaults, the corresponding figure was only 48 percent. Thus, between one-third and two-thirds of the alleged assaults included in these reverse-record-check studies were not reported to the survey interviewers. Again, this must be regarded as a conservative estimate of the underenumeration of this type of crime. Although little detail was given in the pretest reports about the exact nature of circumstances of the assaults or about the degree of injury typically involved, it was found in the Baltimore study that simple assaults were slightly less likely to be mentioned to interviewers than aggravated ones.[15] This is important, since simple assaults and attempted assaults bulk fairly large in the LEAA national and city surveys data published to date.

NCS estimates (for particular cities or for the country as a whole) already suggest much more violence (in the sense of aggravated or simple assaults and attempts) than is shown in police statistics, such as the Uniform Crime Reports. Given the general level of public concern about violent crime, it would seem important that the NCS figures in this area be as accurate as possible.

One element of concern about violent crime relates to the possibility of attacks by strangers on wholly innocent victims who have not in any way invited or conduced the violence inflicted on them. In several of the NCS reports published to date, it is stated that in the majority of personal incidents involving violence the confrontation was between strangers; for example, in the national report for January–June 1973, it is stated that 60 percent of all assaults mentioned in the survey were committed by strangers.[16] There is reason to doubt the reliability of

[15]See Yost and Dodge, op. cit., p. 7: 67 percent of the 55 simple assaults were not reported, compared with 59 percent of the 44 aggravated assaults.
[16]See the following reports of the U.S. Department of Justice, Law Enforcement Assistance Administration (Washington, D.C.: U.S. Government Printing Office): Criminal Victimization in the United States: January-June 1973 (November 1974), p. 3; Crime in Eight American Cities: Advance Report (July 1974), p. 1; Crime in the Nation's Five Largest Cities: Advance Report (April 1974), p. 3.

this finding, however. For one thing, it is starkly at variance with the findings of several studies of victim–offender relationships, based on police records.[17] Also, the limited evidence available from Census pretests suggests that survey estimates may be seriously biased by underreporting to interviewers of incidents involving violent victimization in which the offender was not a stranger.[18] Among the 30 interviewed rape victims in the San Jose pretest, 11 of the 15 incidents of rape that were not mentioned to interviewers were cases involving an alleged offender who was known to the victim; four were "stranger" victimizations. More generally, in the San Jose study it was found that "violent crimes involving strangers were reported in the interview 75 percent of the time; those involving relatives were reported only 22 percent of the time; and those involving persons who knew each other (not kin) were reported with 58 percent frequency."[19] In other words, the closer the relationship between victim and offender in crimes of violence (other than robbery), the less likely the incident was to have been mentioned to the interviewer.

If these findings were used to adjust the NCS national or city-level data, stranger-attributed victimizations would constitute less than one-half of all NCS incidents involving violent victimizations, and not a majority. Moreover, any statement about the proportion of violent victimizations attributed to strangers should take into account the volume of incidents currently excluded from the main NCS count and tabulated separately as "series" offenses. According to Appendix A, Exhibit 8, p. 13, the proportion of violent personal victimizations

[17]See, for example, Marvin E. Wolfgang, *Patterns in Criminal Homicide* (Philadelphia: University of Pennsylvania Press, 1958); Hans von Hentig, *The Criminal and His Victim* (New Haven: Yale University Press, 1948); Donald J. Mulvihill and Melvin M. Tumin, *Crimes of Violence,* Vol. 11 (Staff report submitted to the National Commission on the Causes and Prevention of Violence) (Washington, D.C.: U.S. Government Printing Office, 1969), Chapter 5; since homicides are very likely to be reported to the police and recorded, these studies are likely to give a reasonably accurate picture of victim–offender relations for that crime.

[18]For violence not resulting in death, police statistics also are almost certainly biased by underreporting to police of crimes committed by family members. In a victim survey conducted in Minneapolis, it was found that not one of the 57 survey-reported violent incidents involving a family member had been reported to the police. See Paul Davidson Reynolds, *et al., Victimization in a Metropolitan Region* (Mimeo.) (Minneapolis: University of Minnesota Center for Sociological Research, October 1973), VI-13. Not only does this probable bias in police records need to be taken into account in the design and interpretation of reverse record checks for victim surveys, but also this study suggests how little is known of the effect of survey techniques on the eliciting of events for which the propensity to report (to either interviewers or police) may be affected by subjective definitions of crime.

[19]U.S. Department of Justice, LEAA, *San Jose Methods Test, op. cit.,* p. 9.

attributed to strangers is lower for the excluded "series" events, each of which must constitute three or more incidents, than is the case in the main NCS count of violent crimes. Clearly, differential reporting rates by victim–offender relationships require further exploration.

In addition, differential recall of victimization by other attributes of the respondent—such as age, race, sex, social class, or educational level—should be examined. It may be that the nonreporting of a victimization is mainly due to memory failure operating in a more or less random fashion and that little bias arises from differential recall among different subgroups. But this is not obvious, and the results of other surveys indicate that underreporting may be significantly higher among less-educated or less-fluent respondents.[20]

TELESCOPING

In victimization and other retrospective surveys, respondents typically are asked whether they have experienced an event and, if so, about the date of occurrence. Telescoping refers to the phenomenon whereby a respondent acknowledges an actual event to the interviewer but reports the date of its occurrence inaccurately. The phenomenon has been observed in many retrospective surveys, including victim surveys.[21]

Telescoping was among the important issues investigated in the pretest studies conducted by LEAA and the Bureau of the Census; several kinds of evidence were collected on this point. In the victimization supplement to the Quarterly Household Survey (QHS), which was implemented in January 1971, respondents were asked whether they experienced victimizations during calendar year 1970.[22] The results

[20]In victim surveys, Biderman, "Surveys of Population Samples," pp. 25–27. More generally, Sudman and Bradburn, *op. cit.,* Chapter 4; Marian Radke Yarrow, John D. Campbell, and Roger V. Burton, "Recollection of Childhood: A Study of the Retrospective Method," Monograph 5, *Society for Research in Child Development* 35 (August 1970), Ser. No. 138, University of Chicago: LB1103-S64, Reading Room 4.

[21]See, for example, Gray, *op. cit.,* p. 344; Biderman, "Surveys of Population Samples," pp. 22–23; John Neter and Joseph Waksberg, "A Study of Response Errors in Expenditures Data From Household Interviews," *Journal of the American Statistical Association* 59 (1964): 17–55; John Neter and Joseph Waksberg, *Response Errors in Collection of Expenditures Data by Household Interviews: An Experimental Study,* U.S. Department of Commerce, Bureau of the Census Technical Paper No. 11 (Washington, D.C.: U.S. Government Printing Office, 1965). For a more recent discussion, see Sudman and Bradburn, *op. cit.,* Chapter 3.

[22]Turner, *op. cit.,* p. 4.

show a greater concentration of victimization reported as having occurred in the second 6 months of the reference period than in the first 6 months. This may be due, of course, to greater memory losses in the first half of the year, as well as to the telescoping of incidents into the second half of the year. Data from the July 1971 QHS threw more light on the question of telescoping, since about half of the 12,000 interviews obtained in this survey were bounded by the January 1971 interviews. That is, those respondents who were interviewed in January 1971 were asked about victimizations during 1970. The reference period in the July 1971 survey was the first 6 months of 1971, and any incidents reported in both interviews by the same respondent could be deleted from the later reference period.

The results showed that "telescoping for household respondents is indeed a phenomenon to be contended with";[23] victimization rates for almost all categories of offenses were higher for the unbounded interviews than for the bounded ones—in the case of personal larceny, 2.33 times as high.

The issue of telescoping was directly investigated in the Washington, D.C., pretest by including a number of persons (approximately one-third of the sample) who had been victims of crimes that they had reported to the police 7 and 8 months and 13 and 14 months before the dates of the interview.[24] (It will be recalled that some of the interview schedules in this pretest used a 6-month reference period and some used a 12-month one.) Of these "out-of-scope" cases (those incidents in which the actual date of occurrence was prior to the initial point of the reference period), almost one-fifth reported that the victimization had taken place within the reference period—17 percent for the 6-month questionnaire and 21 percent for the 12-month questionnaire. (Because of the small numbers involved, the difference between reference periods was not statistically significant.) No "out-of-scope" cases were included in the Baltimore or in the San Jose studies, but the report on the latter does contain data that can be used to investigate effects of telescoping within the reference period.

Table 8, in this chapter, is based on Table 4 of the San Jose report; it shows incidents by recorded month of occurrence and by month of occurrence as reported (in January 1971) to interviewers.[25] The table has been partitioned in several ways, to indicate telescoping both forward and backward, especially within the last 6 months of the

---

[23]*Ibid.*, p. 9.
[24]"Victim Recall Pretest, Washington, D.C.," *op. cit.*, p. 1.
[25]U.S. Department of Justice, LEAA, *San Jose Methods Test, op. cit.*, p. 14.

TABLE 8 Incidents Reported to Interviewers in the San Jose Methods Test, by Month of Occurrences as Reported to Police and to Interviewers[a]

Reported to Police as Taking Place in:	Reported to Interviewer as Happening in:												
	Jan.	Feb.	Mar.	Apr.	May	June	July	Aug.	Sept.	Oct.	Nov.	Dec.	TOTAL
Jan.	**13**	1	1	—	1	1	—	—	1	—	—	—	18
Feb.	4	**3**	3	—	2	—	1	1	—	—	1	1	14
Mar.	2	4	**10**	1	—	2	1	—	1	1	1	—	21
Apr.	2	2	3	**11**	3	—	—	—	—	—	—	—	24
May	—	1	—	1	**11**	3	6	—	—	—	—	—	22
June	—	—	—	2	3	**13**	2	6	3	—	—	—	24
July	1	—	—	—	—	2	**14**	9	1	—	—	—	25
Aug.	—	—	—	—	2	1	2	**1**	4	3	1	—	21
Sept.	—	—	1	—	—	—	1	2	**12**	3	2	—	18
Oct.	—	—	1	—	—	—	—	1	3	**17**	4	—	24
Nov.	—	—	1	—	—	—	—	1	—	1	**19**	2	27
Dec.	—	1	—	—	—	—	—	—	—	—	3	**24**	27
TOTALS	22	11	18	15	22	22	27	20	27	28	26	27	265

[a]Based on Table 4, p. 14, of the report on the San Jose Methods Test, excluding cases not reported to interviewers (N = 102) and cases with month NA (N = 27).

reference period (i.e., July through December 1970). Cases falling on the diagonal are those which were accurately reported as having occurred within the correct month. Cases lying above the diagonal were telescoped forward, and those falling below it were telescoped backward. Of the 265 cases included in this table, 156 (or 59 percent) were reported as having occurred in the correct month, 49 (or about 18 percent) were telescoped backward, and 60 (or about 23 percent) were telescoped forward. Over the table as a whole, the average amount of forward telescoping is about 2.4 months, and the average amount of backward telescoping is about 1.7 months. Thus there appears to be a net forward telescoping effect, consistent with the results of most other studies of this type. The table also suggests that over 90 percent of the cases were reported to interviewers as having occurred within 2 months of their actual date of occurrence. This level was also indicated in the Baltimore study.[26]

Telescoping, however, does not necessarily affect estimates of victimization within a given reference period. Events may be telescoped *within* the reference period, as well as being telescoped *into* the reference period. In the first of these cases, the incident is wrongly placed in time, but this error does not affect an estimate of victimization within the reference period. For only the latter case would we expect telescoping to lead to inflated estimates. Of the 155 events reported to San Jose interviewers as having happened in the last 6 months of the reference period, 20 (or 12.9 percent) actually took place in the first half of the reference period; a further 22 incidents (or 14.2 percent) were telescoped forward 1 or more months within the reference period, and 18 incidents (or 11.6 percent) were telescoped backward within the reference period; but, based on this reverse record-check evidence, these errors would not have affected estimates of victimization for the last 6 months. (Of the 142 incidents reported to interviewers which actually took place in the last 6 months of the year, seven (or 4.9 percent) were telescoped backward out of the last 6 months.)

Inspection of the incidents occurring, and subsequently reported to interviewers as occurring, in the middle 6 months of the year covered by the San Jose record check shows that gains and losses from telescoping about balance out: Of 133 incidents reported to interviewers as having taken place in those months, nine (6.8 percent) had been telescoped forward into those months and seven (5.3 percent) had been telescoped backward into that period. Of 134 incidents that actually

[26]Yost and Dodge, *op. cit.*, p. 6.

happened in those middle 6 months, 8 (or 6 percent) had been telescoped forward into the last 3 months of the year and 9 (or 6.7 percent)
had been telescoped backward into the first 3 months of the year. Of
the 110 incidents reported as having taken place in the first 6 months of
the year, seven (or 6.4 percent) had actually taken place in the second
half of the year.

Further inspection of the San Jose data suggests that the probability
of an event's being reported but telescoped forward does not increase
much after about 5 months. In part this may be due, of course, to the
fact that the chance of an event's simply being forgotten increases the
further back it occurred from the interview. It thus might be the case
that the effect on total rates of forward telescoping, in terms of the
number of incidents projected into a given reference period, is not
much different whether the reference period is 6 months or 12 months.
This inference is consistent with the findings of the Washington, D.C.,
study, for which it was reported that 17 percent of the 7- and 8-month
cases were telescoped into the 6-month period and that 21 percent of
the 13- and 14-month cases were telescoped into the 12-month period.
If so, then the *relative error* introduced into survey estimates by
forward telescoping actually may be greater for a 6-month reference
period than for a 12-month one, if the total number of incidents covered
by the 6-month reference period is (approximately) one-half as great as
that covered by the 12-month period. In other words, if the relative
error in survey estimates due to forward telescoping be defined as the
number of cases wrongly telescoped into the reference period, divided
by the total number of incidents reported to interviewers, then the
error might be greater for the shorter reference period, because the
numerator of this error term may be about the same, but the denominator will be smaller than it would be if a longer reference period
were used. It should be emphasized that only one reference period—12
months—was used in the San Jose study. The inferences in this
discussion are based on time intervals within the actual reference
period used and, consequently, are at best tentative.

On the basis of the pretest evidence alone, we would draw the
following inferences: (1) Both forward and backward telescoping occur
in the reporting of victimizations, but the net effect appears to be in a
forward direction; (2) as in the case of memory decay, telescoping
varies by kind of victimization; (3) telescoping and memory decay bias
comparisons of estimates based on different reference periods,
whether bounded or unbounded; and (4) the interaction of telescoping
and memory decay has an unknown effect on victimization rates.
Given these inferences, there should be continuing examination of the

magnitude and effects on survey estimates of these phenomena in connection with current and planned research efforts.

QUESTIONNAIRE DESIGN

One main purpose of the Washington, D.C., Baltimore, and San Jose pretests was the development of the survey instruments. Comments in the reports on these studies indicate that several changes were made in the instruments as a result of pretest experience. The screen questionnaire is reported to have been "modified in wording and question order"[27] after the Washington, D.C., pretest. "Several improvements" were made in wording and order of the screen questions, which were asked to determine if an incident sheet should be completed, and general screen questions were replaced by more probing ones.[28] Alternate methods of obtaining details of victimizations, which are coded on *incident sheets*, were employed in Baltimore: In half of the cases, details were collected on "improved versions"[29] of the five specific incident sheets for different types of crime, but in the other half details were collected on a consolidated general incident sheet.

In the Dayton–San Jose pilot surveys,[30] a split-sample procedure was employed to compare differences in victimization rates reported by individual household members with those reported by one adult responding for all the members of each household. The basic conclusion of this experiment was that the self-respondent method is more productive in terms of number of reported victimizations than the household respondent procedure, a finding consistent with that of prior work.[31]

We commend LEAA and the Bureau of the Census personnel for conducting this questionnaire development effort. But since no published data are available on several aspects of the pretests (including the split-sample procedure used in Baltimore), we cannot comment on the effects of different forms of question and different question orders, nor on what biases the pretest results may indicate in the instruments currently in use.

This facet of pretesting is of special importance in the case of "attitude" questions such as those now being used in the city surveys.

[27]*Ibid.*, p. 1.
[28]*Ibid.*
[29]*Ibid.*, p. 3.
[30]Kalish, *op. cit.*, pp. 31, 34, and 36.
[31]Biderman, "Surveys of Population Samples," *op. cit.*, pp. 24–25.

An "attitude" questionnaire was first administered in the San Jose and Dayton pilot surveys, being given to one-half of the household respondents in each city. Comparison of the instrument used in San Jose and Dayton with the current one (NCS-6) shows quite a number of variations, although certainly not all of them are substantial. So far as can be gleaned from the San Jose–Dayton report, no split-sample or other systematic variations in these attitude questions were used.

While the NCS-6 "attitude" supplement has been used in the city-level surveys, it is not now a recurring part of the national component. It has been included once for a subsample of the national NCS household interviews. Although the decision to exclude regular attitude and behavior items from the national surveys may have been empirically grounded, we are aware of no pretest or pilot study results that support this possibility. In view of the recommendation in a separate section of this report to transfer city-level survey resources so as to augment the national effort, we especially would consider the absence of recurring attitude and behavior items in the national panel interview schedule to be a serious issue and one requiring continuing attention should this recommendation be adopted by LEAA.

4 The Need for Managerial and Technical Coordination

INTRODUCTION

Three major functions of the overall victimization survey activity are undernourished relative to the total program budget and to the scale of the NCS operation. These are (a) analysis of data, (b) program and policy coordination, and (c) methodological research and evaluation. This judgment stems partly from the small sizes of LEAA and other staffs who are assigned to these functions in relation to the magnitude of the tasks and partly from knowledge of federal surveys of comparable scope, even granted that the victimization surveys are still in their early stages of development.

In this chapter, we offer some suggestions for enhancing the first two of these three major functions, analysis of data, and program and policy coordination. Chapter 5 is devoted to discussion of increased and continued methodological research and evaluation.

ANALYSIS OF DATA

A small group (five professionals) of Census personnel is responsible for all official victimization survey data analysis and report writing. Our inspection, on request, of an analysis plan for these surveys revealed that an early publication schedule had specified periodic cross-tabulation of selected variables. These tabulations apparently are transmitted to Census personnel responsible for their analysis, the Crime Statistics Analysis Group. Without direct access to or control of computer resources, and without written analytic guidance from the sponsoring agency, this group is asked to write the victimization survey reports which in turn are to be published by LEAA.

In our interim reports, we have been quite critical of the quality, quantity, and scope of the victimization survey reports that have been published under the arrangement described above. An advance report has been released for the eight "impact" cities surveyed in 1972. For the five largest cities, also surveyed in 1972, both advance and final reports had been released as of April 1975. Advance reports on the national survey have been released covering the first half of 1973 and 1973 as a whole. An advance report on 13 cities surveyed in early 1974 was released in June 1975. There are to our knowledge no other released publications from the National Crime Panel nor from the city-level surveys; no final report on any calendar year of the national survey had been released as of March 1976.

One mechanism to augment analysis, as program objectives are determined, might be the establishment of a very small analysis contracting and monitoring unit within LEAA. Through this unit, LEAA might contract with individuals in academic and law enforcement organizations, and elsewhere, to do specific analyses that are part of LEAA's overall analysis plan. This suggestion presupposes that an in-house group exists to develop the overall analysis plan for the NCS. Hence, an analysis contracting and monitoring unit would become an extension of LEAA's analysis staff. Publication of results of contract research would be by LEAA, as a condition of the contract, with appropriate attribution to the individual authors.

We caution, however, that a new national survey is at once attractive and fragile. Outside scholars of demonstrated competence might have interests compatible with those of the sponsoring agency's, as exemplified by the laudable results of the National Center for Health Statistics' (NCHS) contract program, conducted under the conditions described above.[1] On the other hand, the sponsoring agency may be

[1]For example, see Howard W. Stoudt, Albert Damon, Ross McFarland, and Jean Roberts, "Skinfolds, Body Girths, Biacromial Diameter and Selected Anthropometric Indices of Adults, United States, 1960–1962," *Vital and Health Statistics,* Series 11, No. 35, U.S. National Center for Health Statistics (Washington, D.C.: U.S. Government Printing Office, August 1973). In the same series, see also Brian MacMahon and Jane Worcester, "Age at Menopause, United States, 1960–1962," No. 19 (October 1966); Aram Glorig and Jean Roberts, "Hearing Levels of Adults by Age and Sex, United States, 1960–1962," No. 11 (October 1965); Arnold Engel and Thomas A. Burch, "Osteoarthritis in Adults by Selected Demographic Characteristics, United States, 1960–1962," No. 20 (November 1966).

faced with decisions about release of data or modification of survey design at the request of researchers, whose goals overlap marginally, if at all, with those of survey. The fragility of a new statistical series—both in terms of the weight its design can carry and the organizational resources available to it—should be kept firmly in mind. Without this developmental orientation in regard to its victimization surveys, LEAA may find itself drawn into contractual agreements: (a) in the absence or in advance of survey documentation and sampling error publication; (b) in the absence or in advance of development of a public-use tape program and a program for provision of special tabulations, which require technical resources as well as resources for liaison with users and which require resolution of confidentiality issues; (c) without coordination of these contracting activities with the in-house analysis activities; (d) without rationalization of program objectives by the levels within LEAA above the National Criminal Justice Information and Statistics Service (NCJISS), the division administratively responsible for the NCS; and (e) without any mechanisms for weighting and coordinating the various claims of members of the scientific community to the resources of the NCS.

PROGRAM AND POLICY COORDINATION

LEAA is the sponsoring agency of the victimization surveys, and the Bureau of the Census is responsible for the planning and conducting of the field operation and data processing. The Bureau of Labor Statistics (BLS) stands in a similar relation to Census in the production of its monthly report on the labor force. This BLS effort and the victimization effort are supported by similar total budgets; however, the contrast in the number of their respective professional support staffs is striking. Whereas LEAA has only a few professionals assigned to the victimization project, BLS has the professional staff of three divisions working on labor-force statistics. In common with LEAA, the BLS professional staff monitors more than one survey operation. The BLS complement embraces economists, analytic statisticians, mathematical statisticians, and management personnel, including an assistant commissioner. Moreover, it receives significant amounts of time from the commissioner of BLS. This in-house group is active in every phase of the surveys. Both BLS and Census maintain an intensive and interactive surveillance of the course of affairs and engage in vigorous research and evaluation.

Another example is a smaller but analogous program in the health field. In this instance the National Center for Health Statistics (NCHS),

under the U.S. Department of Health, Education, and Welfare, is the
primary agency and is responsible for setting specifications, management, analysis, and publications. The Bureau of the Census conducts
most of its field operations. NCHS has assigned major parts of two
divisions, totaling about 30 professionals, and the full-time equivalent
of approximately six other professionals, not counting NCHS data-
processing personnel. Again, the assistant director and the Center
director give personal attention to the activities.

Although the NCS forms a new program, the contrasts with the two
above examples are striking. The LEAA unit charged with operating the
NCS is the Statistics Division, which is under the NCJISS. The Statistics
Division comprises fewer than nine professionals. Besides being
responsible for the NCS, the Statistics Division is charged with man-
aging research grants and with monitoring other LEAA-sponsored
surveys, including the Expenditure and Employment Data for the
Criminal Justice System survey, the Census of Jails, and the Census
of Prisoners.

An initial step toward coordination of program resources might be
the establishment of an NCJISS advisory committee. The concept of an
advisory committee is not new to LEAA. In 1974 its National Institute of
Law Enforcement and Criminal Justice formed an advisory committee.[2] One primary function of the NCJISS advisory committee would be
to assist LEAA in formulating long-range goals of the victimization
surveys and to provide guidance in their technical direction.

Should an advisory committee be formed by LEAA, it could be
expected to provide informed counsel only on major problems. Were
this group to be established and fully used, there still would remain
many essential and important activities needing the sustained attention
of a numerically and professionally adequate in-house professional
staff.

*We recommend that the staff providing managerial and analytic
support for the NCS be expanded to include the full-time efforts of at
least 30 to 40 professional employees. Without this expansion, the NCS
cannot be developed to achieve its potential for practical utility.*

A coordinated advisory committee and an expanded professional
staff could be instrumental in focusing goals of funded research towards those areas involving methodological and substantive issues
central to the objectives of the surveys. Besides helping to initiate
these studies, the advisory committee could play a role in monitoring

[2]U.S. Department of Justice, Law Enforcement Assistance Administration, *First Annual
Report of the National Institute of Law Enforcement and Criminal Justice* (Washington,
D.C.: U.S. Government Printing Office, 1975).

progress, but more importantly it could serve as an early recipient of the research findings and help NCJISS communicate research or policy implications of these findings to other areas of the Department of Justice, as well to the administration of LEAA, and foster interaction with scholarly groups and other user communities.

Here is one example of a technical problem that could be examined jointly by an advisory committee and an expanded professional staff. We have been provided with computer printouts of unweighted marginal tallies of NCS national household interview items by calendar quarter. These data files contain records only of victims. In reviewing the printouts, we find that at least 20 percent of the incidents recorded for each calendar quarter are taken from households not in the sample for the previous enumeration.

This raises several questions. Are the number and characteristics of victimizations reported by members of these households different from the number and types reported in households for which interviews actually are linked over time? How many of the substantive objectives of the National Crime Panel assume repeated observations for the same individuals? Are the methodological objectives of a panel design vitiated by an attrition rate, for adjacent interview periods, as high as 15 percent among households reporting NCS-related victim events?

Another technical question that could be examined jointly by an advisory committee and an expanded professional staff is that of producing quarterly data as an objective. Is this objective consistent with a field design that requires 8 months to produce estimates of victimizations for one calendar quarter? If the production of quarterly data were no longer an objective for the NCS, what modifications of field design would follow?

As administrators, academically oriented researchers in the criminal justice field, and other external consumers attempt to use the output of the victimization surveys, their commentaries should lead to modifications that will enhance the value of the survey. Yet we also emphasize that one of the most potentially fruitful sources for detection of weaknesses and suggestions for improvement is to be found in the emerging observations of individuals in the internal Census–LEAA analytic staff.

At the request of the panel's staff, representatives of the Crime Statistics Analysis Group of the Bureau of the Census presented and discussed a number of analytic problems at the August 14, 1975, plenary meeting of the panel. Supporting materials provided by the representatives of the Crime Statistics Analysis Group are attached to this report (see Appendix A).

In regard to decisions on the current victimization interview schedules, code procedures, and methods of file construction, we are concerned that suggestions and advice from the Crime Statistics Analysis Group have not been given more weight by the sponsor. While later in this report we assess broadly the concepts and measures in the victimization interview schedules (e.g., the choice of a victimization rate as the primary statistic and the corollary analysis of "victims only"), we are favorably impressed by the quality of advice on specific problems in the current data set readily available from the Census Crime Statistics Analysis Group.

We believe that LEAA can utilize better than it has the resource of knowledge that the Crime Statistics Analysis Group represents. In Chapter 7 we offer a specific recommendation for coordination of the analytic function—whether conducted in-house at LEAA or through a contractual arrangement with Census or some other organization. Our concern here is with managerial coordination of the NCS in general and not only with the analytic function. We see a definite need for better coordination *between* the Bureau of the Census and LEAA. *We recommend that a coordinator at Census be appointed whose responsibilities would crosscut the various Census operations that support the NCS.*

The Bureau of the Census has a long and excellent tradition in the design and operation of surveys, and its employees have contributed significantly to the development of this area. After questions and problems have been formulated by the sponsoring agency, Census can provide feasible alternatives, but it is the responsibility of LEAA as consumer and as agent for the communities of users to set both operational and research priorities. We would assign high operational priority to increased coordination within the Bureau of the Census of NCS-related activities, as well as to increased coordination between Census and LEAA. For LEAA's victimization surveys, we see a definite imbalance between the resources allocated to data collection compared with those allocated to analysis and management.[3]

We recommend that a substantially greater proportion of LEAA resources be allocated to planning and design, to delineation of product objectives, to managerial coordination, to data analysis and dissemination, and to a continuing program of methodological research and evaluation.

---

[3]The staff of the Statistics Division, NCJISS, estimates that approximately 90 percent of their total budget for the NCS is allocated to data collection. This estimate does not include funds expended independently on NCS-related activities by other divisions of LEAA, such as the National Institute of Law Enforcement and Criminal Justice.

INDEPENDENCE OF NATIONAL AND CITY-LEVEL VICTIMIZATION SURVEYS

In 1972 LEAA sponsored victimization surveys of a set of eight central cities to which monies would be awarded as part of the agency's crime control program. These cities were referred to as "impact" cities, anticipating that follow-up surveys would be conducted in 1975 and in 1977 with the objective of measuring change. Also in 1973, samples in the nation's five largest cities were surveyed by Census under LEAA sponsorship, with reenumeration planned and conducted in 1975. Samples in an additional, third set of 13 cities were enumerated in 1974. For 1976, a fourth and different set of 13 cities tentatively was scheduled to be surveyed. Beyond 1976, no plans have been formulated with the exception of a possible 1977 enumeration of the eight "impact" cities. The city surveys design, to date and anticipated, covers central cities only, has a reference (or recall) period of 12 months, and yields victimization data over time that are not bounded by interviewer reminders of prior answers. (For a listing of the tentatively scheduled 1976 cities and related correspondence, see Appendix B.)

Enumeration for the national component of the NCS also began in 1972 and has continued to the present. The panel design was intended to yield bounded interviews every 6 months for the 3 years in which members of the sampled dwelling unit participate in the survey.[4] One-sixth of the sampled dwelling units rotate into the panel each month.

The evaluation panel, recognizing the familiar tension between the need for national and for small area data, has considered carefully the advantages and disadvantages of independent victimization surveys, against both substantive and administrative criteria and has invited review of this issue by its parent, the Committee on National Statistics.

We recommend that resources now used for the nationwide survey and for the independent city surveys be consolidated and used for carrying out an integrated national program. The integrated effort could produce not only nationwide and regional data, but also, on the same timetable, estimates for separately identifiable major SMSA's and for at least the five largest central cities within them. For some purposes, it would be practicable and perhaps useful to combine data

---

[4]Addresses in each rotation group are interviewed once every 6 months for 3½ years, the initial interview being only for purposes of bounding, i.e., establishing a time frame to avoid duplicative reports on subsequent visits.

for 2 or more years and to show separate tabulations for a larger number of cities and metropolitan areas.[5]

This recommendation rests on three assumptions. First, it is assumed that at least five large metropolitan areas could be surveyed as indicated if resources are transferred that otherwise would be adequate to cover the 13 central cities referred to in Appendix B. A second assumption is that LEAA will support vigorously methodological research on the effects upon victimization rates of bounding techniques and of the length of the recall period as recommended in the following chapter. Should those results indicate either that a satisfactory screening technique using a longer recall period can be devised, or that its error can be adjusted, we assume that additional metropolitan areas, perhaps as many in total number as have been surveyed annually thus far, could be covered as part of the national effort, with the advantage of separate and identifiable estimates for central cities and for total SMSA's.

One major advantage of a merger of city-level and national victimization surveys is that comparisons may be made more directly between rates for a given metropolitan area and the national rates, both over time and annually. For field procedures, interviewer training and experience and procedures of estimation (e.g., poststratification by age, sex, and race) would become more nearly uniform.

As conducted thus far, relatively few cities have been surveyed within any given year, although cumulatively a substantial proportion of all cities with a population more than 250,000 could be covered within 4 to 5 years. But identifiable estimates for smaller cities and for suburban areas will not be available. Moreover, the residence-based design of the city surveys requires that a decision be made either to exclude or to tabulate separately those surveyed crimes reported to have occurred to respondents outside the central city jurisdiction. For some cities, notably San Diego, this decision may not be trivial.[6]

A design that simultaneously yields separate and identifiable esti-

---

[5]The intent of this recommendation is to increase specifically the urban coverage of the NCS. It is not implied by our use of the term "integrated effort" that the current city-level survey resources would be used to augment the NCS as a whole nor that the NCS sample design is inadequate for the purpose of producing national estimates.

[6]According to Mr. Robert Parkinson, Director of the Census Crime Statistics Analysis Group, preliminary tabulations indicated that as many as 25 percent of victimizations were reported by San Diego residents as having occurred when they were living or visiting outside the central city limits. For personal victimizations only, this San Diego proportion is estimated at 20 percent in U.S. Department of Justice, Law Enforcement Assistance Administration, *Criminal Victimization Surveys in 13 American Cities* (Washington, D.C.: U.S. Government Printing Office, 1975), p. 3.

mates for the nation, for a set of total SMSA's, and for major central cities within these SMSA's will have greater analytic potential, because it would be more consistent with the ecology of the types of crimes being surveyed.

The objectives of our recommendation to merge the separate city and national surveys are to increase both methodological consistency and analytic potential of the NCS as a whole. A decision to cover, say, 10 urban areas each year at the price of fewer sample cases per area than could be obtained if five areas were surveyed would be inconsistent with these objectives, although agency objectives that we have not considered might be served.

THE NEED FOR AREA VICTIMIZATION DATA

The administrative utility of LEAA's victimization surveys is of concern to Congress, to the agency, and to law enforcement administrators. Decisions must be made, however, at a policy level within LEAA on whether national estimates, estimates by region or state, metropolitan area estimates, county estimates, or central city estimates are most important to the goals of the NCS. The present sizes of the national surveys and the city-level surveys cannot provide all of these estimates, nor can any sample design for a size substantially less than a complete census, unless LEAA wants to obtain only aggregate victimization estimates for broad geographic units and has no interest in cross-classifying, for example, victim characteristics with the type of victimization.

If LEAA does want to provide information on victimization patterns in a local area, two distinct but coordinated strategies might be adopted. The first is to strengthen analysis capabilities so that answers to generic questions of interest to law enforcement officials and policymakers can be produced quickly from national data and in such detail that local officials can draw inferences applicable to their communities. Neither the city-level nor the national surveys are designed to yield precinct-level estimates. Few data tapes have been released to any cities surveyed thus far to enable them to do their own analyses. And, under present constraints of confidentiality, no data tapes can be released to local areas having under 250,000 population, were these areas to be independently surveyed.

As a first strategy, we recommend that the federal government produce reports on the NCS that contain detailed analyses of patterns and trends of victimization so as to allow law enforcement personnel,

*the public, and policymakers to draw inferences that might be appli-
cable to the issues with which they are concerned.*

*As a second strategy, we consider that the local interest in victimiza-
tion patterns could be addressed through* LEAA–*Census joint development of a manual of procedures for conducting victimization surveys.*
A survey kit might include a full set of planning materials and operations manuals that collectively would provide complete instructions for
conducting a local survey, using the same core protocol as in the
current national and city-level undertakings but allowing for supplementation of items of local concern.

Central to this recommendation is the assumption that the decision
to conduct a local survey would be made by local people, although the
interest might be stimulated by LEAA field personnel. It seems important to us that local officials and citizenry would want to have the
survey, would want to do the survey, and would want to use the
results. LEAA or Census, as appropriate, might offer technical advice,
and LEAA might provide part of the planning funds, but the local
interest in the survey should be made manifest by a commitment both
of local personnel and local financial support.

An alternate or supplementary approach might be the provision of
special tabulations to localities or to investigators who have interest in
small-area victimization data. We realize that issues of statistical
reliability and of confidentiality are involved in the production and
dissemination of tabulations, but we urge prompt attention to the tasks
of documenting and disseminating NCS procedures and limitations so
that these and related issues may be understood by users, whatever the
form in which data are released.

THE ISSUE OF CONFIDENTIALITY CONSTRAINTS

In December 1974, our staff received a copy of a letter to Dr. Charles
Kindermann, of LEAA, from Mr. Marvin M. Thompson, Assistant
Division Chief for Special Surveys, Bureau of the Census, informing
LEAA that most geographic identifier codes could not be included in the
national victimization data tape records because of confidentiality
requirements of the Bureau (see Appendix C).

These requirements, we agree, have substantial implications for the
administrative and research utility of the national and the city-level
data files. For they mean that geographically the national data can be
analyzed only by the 10 Office of Management and Budget regions, by
broad size-of-place categories that do not differentiate among areas

having populations of less than 250,000 or by a code that differentiates between types of places but not so that they may be identified. It also means that city-level data tapes would be released only in a form that masks any codes by which census tracts could be identified.

In view of these constraints, we strongly recommend that public-use tapes and LEAA tapes be adapted so that each record in any victimization survey contains a set of neighborhood characteristics obtained from the 1970 Census data tapes.[7] A neighborhood, which usually does not coincide with a census tract, contains on the average 4,000 to 5,000 people in a relatively compact and contiguous geographic area.[8] For each neighborhood, many characteristics are available from the 1970 Census tapes, including age, family size, ethnicity, education, mobility, employment, occupation, and income, as well as information on housing. To these could be added categorical information on the class of city or nonurban area of which the neighborhood is a part.

Without geographic information of this type, one cannot ask, for example, "Is there a difference in victimization rates of elderly persons who reside in predominantly young neighborhoods as compared with elderly persons who reside in senior-citizen neighborhoods?" Or, "Are victimization rates higher or lower in racially integrated neighborhoods than in racially segregated?" Or, "Are people more or less likely to be victimized in their own homes if the population density in their neighborhoods is high?"

We stress here that the mere addition of neighborhood characteristics to NCS public-use tapes would not be consistent with the broader intent of our recommendation. We also have in mind the inclusion of neighborhood variables in LEAA's own analyses and publications, a point to which we will return in Chapter 7.

OBJECTIVES OF THE COMMERCIAL SURVEYS

It has been alleged that the commercial victimization survey has been underfinanced—or alternatively that it is inadequate for currently voiced needs. Partly as a consequence of these views, a short-range sample expansion has been undertaken and was operational by mid-

[7]U.S. Department of Commerce, Bureau of the Census, *Public Use Samples of Basic Records from the 1970 Census: Description and Technical Documentation* (Washington, D.C.: U.S. Department of Commerce, April 1972).
[8]U.S. Department of Commerce, Bureau of the Census, Supplement No. 1 to *Public Use Samples of Basic Records from the 1970 Census: Description and Technical Documentation* (Washington, D.C.: U.S. Department of Commerce).

1975. But both Census and LEAA recognize that the new sample can do little more than provide a vehicle for adequate quarterly estimates of global victimization rates for robbery and burglary. The samples will still be too small to yield detail by geography, kind of business, or other sociological factors.[9] And the commercial inquiry still would offer data on only the two crimes of robbery and burglary, crimes that apparently are well reported to police, according to the results of the NCS itself.

The Bureau of the Census has proposed a longer-range overhaul of the commercial survey. We understand that proposals are under consideration at the present time. We support the investigations suggested by Census. However, it seems clear that the subject-matter scope of the survey should be widened if that is feasible—inventory shrinkage and vandalism are areas that merit attention.

We recommend that a review and restatement of the objectives of the commercial survey be conducted and that data collection be suspended except in support of experimental and exploratory review of these objectives.

The technical design and structure of some parts of the present commercial operation are impressive. There are questions, however, as to whether the present structure of the commercial survey faithfully reflects priorities that might today be assigned to objectives. An illustration in Chapter 7, based on data from the Houston commercial survey, indicates that 18 percent of surveyed retail establishments in 1972 accounted for 83 percent of surveyed crimes in the retail sector. This is an astounding finding. Yet, one cannot go beyond it and compare characteristics of these multiple-victim establishments with nonvictims in Houston in part because of sample size. Hence, the potential use of the commercial data for policy formulation is limited, whatever expansion of content coverage might be formulated.

We say that the commercial survey is too narrow in subject scope, that it probably covers crimes already known to police, and that it carries sampling errors that are too large. Wise decisions on both scope and precision can be made only when the specific objectives of the survey are clearer than they appear to us at the present time. In addition to a new determination of content, the review of objectives should produce answers to several questions. Since commercial robbery is a personal, as well as a property, crime, what are the arguments against accessing it through the household surveys? What specific objectives of the establishment effort would be vitiated by this strat-

---

[9]For example, a comparison of establishment victimization rates according both to time of day of occurrence of the incident and number of employees would be affected severely by the small number of cases in the table cells.

egy? Should business-loss aspects of property crimes be handled through a commercial survey and personal consequences of commercial crimes be handled through a household survey? What detail is required by geography and by kind of business? What specific cross-tabulations are needed? How frequently, for what time periods, and with what publication lags are expenditures justified? Is the commercial survey intended to be a part of a public-use tape program? If so, what sample design is dictated by confidentiality constraints?

There also are still a number of technical survey design questions that merit further study, e.g., can a list-sample of regional or national headquarters offices be used in conjunction with a mail inquiry for certain classes of topics? Can administrative statistics on crime rates be used to stratify the sample of establishments? Can the distribution of victimization rates indicated already by the NCS commercial surveys inform a design that departs from uniform sampling criteria so as to increase efficiency? Can the transportation industry be surveyed? Many of these technical questions will be clarified by a sharper delineation of objectives.

Chapter 5 considers methodological and analytic research, which has been and is needed if the potential of the NCS—in either its household or commercial component—is to be achieved.

5 Methodological Research

INTRODUCTION

The panel commends LEAA–Census for the developmental research and exploration that did precede the fielding of the NCS, finds the level of similar research during the first 2 years of survey operation to be inadequate, and strongly advocates that substantial resources be allocated to a continuing vigorous and coordinated program of research, development, and evaluation (RD&E) of victimization survey methodology. This theme is prominent throughout this report. Early research by LEAA–Census was reviewed in some detail in Chapter 3.

In this chapter, we take note of some recent RD&E efforts and some that have been planned and we offer suggestions for further investigations. Mention of specifics should not overshadow our conviction that personnel and resources should be assigned permanently to intensive analysis, evaluation, and improvement of the methodology of the survey.

In the listing that follows, some obscurity and lack of completeness are inevitable. It has been difficult to discover all that may be taking place, for projects have been conducted on a decentralized basis. The LEAA and Census staffs have been cooperative in discussing particular activities with us, and the panel staff has had access to internal memoranda (in some cases even to working notes). Yet there are almost no published accounts of these research activities, and many of the written materials are at present rough draft, working documents.

62

The panel's knowledge of details of current research is incomplete; findings from that research are not yet available to the public.

One of our suggestions is that LEAA–Census establish and distribute a running inventory of RD&E projects completed, projects in progress, and projects tentatively planned, including brief project abstracts. We are pleased to learn that steps in this direction are being taken. They will facilitate assignment of priorities and resources for future action.

CURRENT AND RECENT RD&E ACTIVITY

A few formal RD&E projects are currently in an operational stage. Perhaps the larger part of recent activity has been less formal in character—but not less meaningful. It consists usually of modest exploratory investigation, initiated by a particular LEAA or Census staff member in an attempt to shed light on some particular facet of the survey. Findings are typically preliminary and tentative and often serve only as background information for operations, rather than for use in modifying survey practice or in publication for the public.

REINTERVIEW

A principal ongoing evaluation and control activity is the reinterview program. This was described briefly in Chapter 2. Its objectives are to help control the interviewing process, to obtain some measure of interviewer variance and bias, and to understand response variability— good or bad—of specific questions. Results are tabulated regularly and made available to supervisors and analysts. Most tabulations relate to a 6-month period of interviewing. For each of a selection of items on the questionnaire and for consolidated classes of items, they show counts obtained by the original interviewer, first counts by the reinterviewer, and reconciled best-evidence counts. Data are compiled separately for each interviewer and for each Census region (i.e., supervisory district).

INTERVIEWER VARIANCE STUDY

Another effort to determine interviewer variance and some of its characteristics is a special study undertaken in connection with the most recent surveys of eight impact cities. The design and intended analysis of this study are similar to that employed by the Census Bureau in the 1960 and 1970 Population Censuses and in other sample surveys. Necessary data are secured through interpenetrating assignments of segments to paired interviewers. Within each assignment area, an estimate of total variance is obtained for a selected item from the squared difference of two mean values, an individual mean being the average over households assigned to one of the paired interviewers. An estimate of sampling variance is computed by averaging within-interviewer variance, for the selected item, over all interviews in the same city. The difference between estimated total variance and estimated sampling variance is judged to be a measure of interviewer variance. As of February 1976, fieldwork and data collection had been completed. Follow-up verification of fieldwork had been carried out in five of the eight cities. A preliminary report was scheduled for June 1976, and a final report for August 1976.

COMMERCIAL SURVEY SAMPLE

An investigation was undertaken of how best to increase the size of the national commercial survey with minimum cost and disruption of present procedures. An interim increase in sample was introduced in July 1975. The changes increased the number of primary sampling units from 34 to 58 and the number of sample segments from 1,000 to 2,469. It was estimated by Census technicians that the augmentation would reduce the coefficient of variation, i.e., the relative sampling error, for estimates of the total number of burglaries from the monthly sample from about 18 percent to 11 percent. Most observers agree that a further overhaul and updating of this sample are needed, and further comment on this matter is provided later in this chapter.

RECALL AND RELATED TOPICS

The complex of time-in-sample, distance between interview and event, and length of reference period is the subject of continuing investigations by Census staff. For example, one Census internal memorandum[1] demonstrates how spurious trends could be introduced into survey results prior to the time the survey matures in 1977, if there are increases in underreporting with increases in length of time a household has remained in the sample. A more substantial investigation of recall bias and telescoping is reported in another Census internal

[1]John Bushery, "Spurious Changes in Levels of Reported Crime in the NCS" (Memorandum of the U.S. Department of Commerce, Bureau of the Census, November 27, 1974).

memorandum.[2] This latter investigation uses data from the ongoing survey and a modification of a model suggested by Sudman and Bradburn in their book, *Response Effects in Surveys*.[3] The model is, however, of uncertain validity for the NCS problem, so the panel and the Census staff are doubtful that the initial calculations tell a correct story. They are but one attempt to study a complex situation. As noted below, this is an important matter, for which further work is essential.

CITY SURVEYS

Comparisons of estimates from the city-level surveys with those from the national survey for the same cities seemed an obvious step in assessing stability of the estimates and perhaps toward evaluating the merits of the two different procedures. Such a comparison was started early in 1974, but it was recognized that meaningful comparison would be more difficult than might appear because of the timing and different procedures of the two surveys. In fact, the comparative analysis has proven to be still more difficult than had been expected. Two different sets of tabulations now exist: One seeks to compare 1974 data from the two procedures for each of five cities and 1972 data from the city surveys with 1973 data from the national survey. The other is aimed at comparison of estimates for the reference period September 1974 through December 1974 for the two procedures. This latter set was chosen, because it is a period for which the distance between interview and reference period is most nearly identical for the two procedures. The unsatisfactory tabulations, and the lack of resources for analysis, have delayed reaching conclusions from this effort.

CONTINUITY OF SAMPLE HOUSEHOLDS

The panel has studied closely the bounding procedure and its meaning in LEAA publications. The Census Bureau noted in an internal report[4] that for collection in 1973 and 1974, 86 percent of the interviews came from the households in which at least one person was previously

[2] Henry Woltman, John Bushery, and Larry Carstensen, "Recall Bias and Telescoping in the NCS" (Memorandum of the U.S. Department of Commerce, Bureau of the Census, September 23, 1975).

[3] Seymour Sudman and Norman M. Bradburn, *Response Effects in Surveys* (Chicago: Aldine Publishing Co., 1974).

[4] Linda R. Murphy, "NCS National Sample: Extent of Correspondence of Households and Persons Between Enumeration Periods" (Memorandum of the U.S. Department of Commerce, Bureau of the Census, November 20, 1975).

interviewed at those same addresses, 9 percent came from entirely new households at old addresses, and about 5 percent were from households that were in the sample in the previous period but were nonrespondents. They noted further that, as might be expected, unbounded interviews showed a victimization rate about 35 percent higher than that for bounded interviews. They speculated that perhaps half the difference is due to the methodological difference of bounding and half due to real differences in victimization rates for movers and for nonmovers. As noted in Chapter 2, and again in the section "Basic Sampling Design" later in this chapter, this topic is closely interlocked with the issues of recall, telescoping, length of reference period, and length of retention of a household in the sample.

UNDERCOUNT

Differential undercount of certain age–sex–race categories in the NCS, as implied by the poststratification adjustment ratios, led to a comparison of experience between NCS and CPS (Current Population Survey). Both surveys tend toward relative undercounts in the same categories. But the NCS undercount is more severe for some groups, and especially for nonwhites in the age range 16–21 years. No proven cause has been established. It is speculated that some NCS interviewers may be reluctant to search with sufficient diligence for persons in this category. Census analysts are in the process of exploring the NCS undercount problem.

SOME SUGGESTIONS FOR FUTURE RD&E

RESEARCH COMMITMENT

In so major an undertaking as the NCS, the range of needed research and evaluation is great. It includes areas of purpose—especially the relationships between survey products and uses; of questionnaire content and manner of its presentation to respondents; of technical sample design and estimating procedures; of processing and editing operations; of analytic methods; of dissemination practices; and (very importantly) of overall management, administration, and coordination. In this section the panel offers some suggestions, but they are not presented as a complete and balanced program. The primary requirement is that there be a commitment to a continuing substantial program of RD&E and that the program be guided by a coordinated management.

This especially means fitting research activities to a sharper delineation of analytic objectives, and it means allocation of substantially greater resources of money and personnel on a continuing basis to RD&E effort in order to obtain a better product and one that is so recognized. A vigorous RD&E environment yields results with value far beyond the sum of its individual subprojects.

At least two broad objectives can be recognized. One is research and development that may lead to improvement in survey measurement. Occasionally a discovery results in immediate improvements, but more commonly there is time lag between formulation of a research effort and resultant improvement of published data. The reasons are legion. In the present instance they include the peculiar and complex relationship of date of interview to reference date of publication in the LEAA survey and the fact that the survey for the most part is dealing with counts of relatively rare phenomena.

The second type of research–investigation provides the analyst with a better understanding of results that are currently being produced. Here the task is to do the best possible job in making available both general and detailed descriptions of the obtained measures. These descriptions include both carefully prepared accounts of the designed undertaking and assessment of how faithful execution is to the design. The describing process should be both iterative—in the sense of continuous building on earlier findings—and interactive—in that there are continuing back and forth contributions between analysts of the data and the managers of data collection. One element of this communication is the proposed preparation, updating, and dissemination of the listing and abstract of all known RD&E projects in this program (completed, in progress, and about to be undertaken) referred to earlier.

BASIC SAMPLING DESIGN

The classic objective of survey designing is to secure estimates for a given budget of principal program targets, with acceptably small bias and maximum precision, within the prevailing environment. In simpler terms, one tries to maximize the quality of result for fixed cost (or to minimize cost for fixed quality). Toward this goal, high priority should be given in the NCS to additional research on the best combination of reference period, frequency of interview at an address, length of retention of an address in the sample, and bounding rules.

As noted earlier, there are *a priori* reasons, and some evidence, for believing that (1) there is a decrease in level of reporting as the distance between interview and event increases, (2) there is a net tendency for respondents to telescope forward in time the reporting of an event, and (3) there is a tendency for respondents to report more incidents the first time they are interviewed than on subsequent occasions. The unit cost of initial interview of a household is greater than that of subsequent interviews. If one focuses on sample size as household-months of experience, it follows that, for only slightly more than half the cost, a household provides more data if it is queried on a given occasion, say about 12 months of experience than about 6 months of experience, although the accuracy of the data may drop to unacceptable levels.

These are among the factors that should be further evaluated for their impact on mean square error at any given budget level. Evaluation and analysis should utilize both the empirical evidence and theoretical models. Many useful data already exist in raw form from the NCS and from pretests. But it would also be desirable to collect data for reference periods other than 6 months from a part of the sample of near-future respondents and, perhaps, some further data on telescoping. Objectives should be sharpened as the project takes place, but are likely to include answers to these questions:

1. Should the reference period be 3 months, 6 months, or 12 months (or possibly another interval)?

2. Should a household (address) be interviewed once, twice, three times, . . . seven times, or some other number?

3. Specifically, what are the shapes of the reporting decay, interview overload, and telescoping functions?

4. Is the bounding technique worth its cost, and does it introduce a new significant bias into results?

Part of the recommended research in this area should be a new reverse-record-check study—or possibly several interrelated studies. Such studies have weaknesses: They are expensive and difficult to execute without operational bias; they do not measure overreporting; and in the victimization field they deal only with those crimes that have been recorded by the police and thus shed no light on other criminal events. Yet they are valuable as one input toward resolution of difficult issues. A study should contribute to knowledge of general underreporting (and thus overall levels of estimates), but its main purposes should be to shed light on:

1. Differential degrees of reporting for differing types of victimizations and different classes of respondents (or victims). This is signifi-

cant because measures of relationships may be highly sensitive to different degrees of underreporting.

2. The telescoping and decay problems, as well as the effectiveness of current procedures for eliciting reports of victim events.

3. Biases in the misreporting of facts.

The study might be conducted in several of the same PSU's as the national panel—ranging from large metropolitan areas to low-population-density PSU's. The record-check cases should be drawn from all police jurisdictions within the selected PSU's. Neighboring households of check cases could be assembled for interviewing into loose clusters around the check cases in order to camouflage the key households. It might be possible thus to present the study to interviewers as a test of costs and variance between two different types of clustering: the loose clusters of this experiment and the ordinary clusters of the regular survey.

Interpretation of data from reverse-record-check studies is not easy. It is likely that raw data should be refined, at least for nonmatched cases, by return to the police—and just possibly to households—to seek explanation for nonmatching data.

A small study would almost certainly be unproductive. Uncommon situations would be improperly represented. And the primary focus should be on differential impacts for what should be fairly uncommon events in the total of households interviewed. Thus, the sample of check cases needs to be large, and overall costs likely would be several hundred thousand dollars.

One aspect of design that cannot be much illuminated by record checking is the consistency of population undercount. As the program matures, the measurement of trend will become more important, and levels, although not unimportant, may receive somewhat less emphasis. This in turn means that some degree of undercounting can be tolerated, if it is fairly consistent over time. It should not be assumed without supporting evidence that degree of undercounting is consistent over time. And, certainly, efforts to secure better levels should not be abandoned, since the determinations for approximating correct levels for each year would yield approximately correct year-to-year trends.

Almost every facet of sampling or estimation has some impact on the efficiency of the basic design. While not every facet can be studied in depth, a continuing research effort should include investigations of selected features, with reasonable expectation that some of those investigations might lead to improvements. For example, examination of cluster-size effects could be undertaken at modest cost and possibly pay substantial dividends. Rather typically, to measure rare events, clusters containing an average of more than four households would be chosen. Investigation of comparative variances and costs for clusters of sizes four, eight, twelve, and twenty-four households for the victimization survey might confirm the four-household cluster as best. Alternately, it might indicate that a larger cluster would be more efficient.

On a quite different level, we suggest a longer-range exploration of the feasibility and utility of a more radical design modification. At present, stratification and probabilities of selection are keyed to the geographic distribution of the human population. A good bit of information on the distribution of crime exists in publications from the Uniform Crime Reports (UCR) and from other sources, including the NCS. Is it possible that these data could be organized in such a manner that they could be used directly or in conjunction with simple population counts as covariables in sampling and estimation? The answer may be "no." But if the answer should be "yes," the benefits might be substantial.

THE COMMERCIAL SURVEY

There is doubt that the commercial survey, as operated thus far, justifies its cost. Output of the survey is restricted largely to counts of burglary and robbery in commercial establishments, classified by kind of business. Sampling errors for subnational totals and for estimates by kind of business are large. Sampling is less efficient than desirable, being based on limited and outdated universe data that in some instances refer to the commercial structure of the nation as of 1948. The value of even the global estimates of robbery and burglary is reduced by the availability of UCR data for those crimes, since early NCS results indicate these to be well reported to the police.

Pretesting for the commercial effort envisaged coverage of a broader spectrum of crime than robbery and burglary. Yet attempts to collect other information were discouraging, perhaps because of attempts to parallel too closely the UCR. Trials with new questionnaires might yield data that are more descriptive and explanatory on robbery and burglary. New tests, and possibly new collection techniques, might produce usable data on other topics, such as inventory shrinkage, vandalism, and the costs of protective devices. Presumably, many establishments have records of these latter items. This suggests, too, that the use of mail inquiry to headquarters or district offices of multiestablishment concerns might lead to valuable information at relatively low cost. Differential sampling of different kinds of business might be desirable. The panel would like to see the commercial survey survive in a more productive form, and research is needed to determine what that format should be.

TELEPHONE INTERVIEWING

Person information in the household survey, as noted in Chapter 2, is secured in large part through direct interview of the individual persons. Proxy respondents have proved unsatisfactory, and the necessary call-backs make the procedure expensive. After a first direct contact with the household, telephone interviews are permitted for persons not present at the initial visit. Data for about 25 percent of all persons are secured by telephone. Several proposals have been suggested for increasing the use of telephone interviewing and thereby reducing costs. The panel encourages testing of telephone methods to determine whether acceptable data can be secured at lower cost or whether telephone interviewing should be minimized. It is not suggested that sampling or initial household contact necessarily be by telephone, but only that study be made of the utility of telephone follow-up. The use of mail questionnaires, perhaps combined with face-to-face and telephone techniques, deserves exploration in the household component of the survey.

MIGRANT HOUSEHOLDS

Households that move out of sample addresses between interviews pose several problems for the execution of the national survey design, including the realization of bounding objectives. Substantively, there is a question as to whether the experiences of out-migrants are different from those of nonmigratory households. It would be costly to follow the out-migrant households, but the national sample contains a comparable group of in-migrants who were out-migrants from other places. Additional questions to these in-migrants, and careful analysis of the responses, might provide much of the desired information. In any event, such an investigation would provide a basis for help in deciding whether it would be worth the cost of a subsidiary survey to follow up out-migrant persons.

TIME REFERENCE FOR PUBLISHED DATA

Time series analysis of reported data by month of reporting, month of reference, quarter of reference, and year of reference should aid in choosing the best format for regular release in publications. Such analysis may be persuasive in deciding to use moving averages, relatively long reference periods, preliminary reports from completed subsamples, or all. Devices of these kinds can help to dampen the effects of sampling error and episodic irregularities. For many items it is likely that change is rather gradual and that allocation of counts to an exact time is not critical.

USE OF DESCRIPTIVE OPERATIONAL STATISTICS

We advocate a practice that should be termed a standard procedure rather than an RD&E project. The Census Bureau compiles extensive descriptive records of the conduct of the survey, the editing actions, and the statistical features of estimating steps. Even more features of data collection and processing might be recorded and tabulated: for example, length of interview and its major sections, day of event, time of day of the interview, percent of imputation by items, and age–sex distribution of household respondents. Routine communication of this technical and administrative information to LEAA analysts, and through them into publications, will enrich the output and contribute to public understanding.

ANALYTIC FEEDBACK

Earlier in this chapter, the desirability of continuing interaction between analysts and data collectors was stressed. The feedback from analysts who discover gaps, peculiarities, inconsistencies, and other questionable evidence in tabulations of survey data can be a valuable catalyst for survey improvements. A somewhat more systematic transmission and use of such information might be considered by LEAA–Census.

STANDBY PROCEDURES FOR LOCAL SURVEYS

The panel has recommended that resources used in the past for the city surveys might better be transferred to augmentation of the national survey. Such local data as the program is able to produce would come from tabulation of the national sample reports for selected SMSA's and for the groups of SMSA's, with separate figures for the largest central cities or for groups of central cities and for outlying areas. That course will not provide data for specific police jurisdictions, nor for smaller metropolitan areas or cities. To facilitate meeting the demand for statistics for particular local areas, we have recommended the development and assembly of a "Standard Procedural Kit for Conducting

Local Victimization Surveys." The kit would include a full set of planning materials and operations manuals that collectively would provide a standby blueprint and complete guidelines for conducting a local survey, using the core protocol of the national survey, but allowing for modification or supplementation to meet local objectives. Successful surveys require motivated sponsors and management by skilled survey statisticians in addition to a blueprint. We would see use of the kit in a particular instance being initiated by local interests and financed outside the regular NCS program. Operational management of a survey should be contracted to an experienced survey organization, which might be the Census Bureau or another competent group.

RANDOMIZED INQUIRY

The pretests indicated that assault is underreported in the NCS, especially when the offender is known to the victim. Underreporting of assault might have several different causes. Respondents might not recognize some assaults as reportable. There might be fear of retaliation if the offender should learn that an assault had been reported. The principal reason, however, for underreporting may be embarrassment or sensitivity to admitting assault by someone closely associated with the respondent. A number of theoreticians and survey practicioners have proposed or experimented with variations of a method for securing relatively unbiased replies to sensitive questions. This general method is coming to be known as the "Randomized Response" or "Randomized Inquiry" technique. The essence of the method is to ask this sensitive question in such a manner that no one (including the interviewer) other than the respondent knows how the respondent replied to the sensitive issue. Yet, overall estimates of the proportion of persons who have the sensitive attribute can be calculated from the survey results.[5]

[5]The idea of randomized response methods was first introduced by Stanley L. Warner in "Randomized Responses: A Survey Technique for Eliminating Evasive Answer Bias," *Journal of the American Statistical Association* 60(1965): 63–69. A considerable number of papers have been written on a variety of modifications of the Warner concept, some dealing with theoretical development and others reporting on field trials. Useful procedural suggestions can be found, for example, in these articles: R. E. Folsom *et al.*, "The Two Alternate Questions Randomized Response Model for Human Surveys" (Paper presented at the Biometric Society Meeting, Ames, Iowa, April 26, 1972); B. G. Greenberg, A. A. Abul-Ela, W. R. Simmons, and D. G. Horowitz, "The Unrelated Question Randomized Response Model: Theoretical Framework," *Journal of the American Statistical Association* 64(1969): 520–39; J. J. A. Moors, "Optimization of the Unrelated Question Randomized Response Model," *Journal of the American Statistical Association*, 66(1971): 627–29. Each of the referenced papers includes a relevant bibliography.

We recommend that an experiment be conducted to discover if the Randomized Inquiry technique has value in eliciting reporting of assault. Two randomized half-samples could be selected. One half-sample is given the regular interview. In the other half-sample, two features are introduced. The first of these is to exclude in the main interview inquiry about assaults by relatives or close acquaintances. The second is to cover these assaults at the end of the interview with the Randomized Inquiry technique. The immediate objective is to discover the direction and magnitude of assault rate differences by the two methods.

It seems unlikely that Randomized Inquiry would ever become a regular part of the ongoing survey. Rather the intention is to attempt an assessment of the nature of underreporting in the normal procedure.[6]

PUBLIC-USE TAPES

It was mentioned earlier that some of the analyses of NCS data will be performed by investigators using public-use tapes. Valid inferences from such analyses require sampling errors of calculated statistics, and research is needed to discover adequate methods for estimating those sampling errors that are sufficiently simple and usable. This is not easy, but is necessary; it should be coordinated with the work on public-use tapes in other fields. One elementary approach was suggested in Chapter 2. But the methodology for drawing inferences from data from complex surveys is not well developed and deserves more attention than it has received.

ANALYTIC RESEARCH ON EXISTING DATA

We recommend in this section several kinds of analytic research that could be performed on the NCS data now available. Except where the

[6]One member of the panel strongly feels it inadvisable for the Bureau of the Census to engage in field operations that might imply that the public cannot rely upon Census interviewers to be affectively neutral and to safeguard confidentiality. For the survey profession as a whole, this member would be concerned that, while Randomized Response techniques may improve the data for a given study, its general use might decrease the value and increase the cost of interview surveys as an institutionalized procedure to the extent that a suspension of trust between interviews and respondents is implied. While this member does not dissent from the specific experiment outlined above and is entirely supportive of the objective of investigating interview methodology, he thinks inquiries of the type proposed here should be conducted by contractual arrangement with a private research organization.

contrary is noted, the proposed analyses of existing data could be done on both the national panel and city data; indeed, it is clear that certain of the issues we raise can be investigated by comparing the findings for particular questions in the two different data sets. The analyses suggested here are restricted to the household component of the NCS.

Two preliminary points must be made about the organization of the NCS data. First, the NCS publications to date have generally presented findings in the form of population estimates of victimization rates in which the data have been weighted. This is an entirely appropriate publication procedure and one that exploits the potential of the survey design. But for some analyses—in particular those aimed at investigating the internal validity of the data—it would be better to use unweighted sample data, at least in the first instance. Second, the data files from both national and city surveys are at present victimization files, i.e., each case in the file corresponds to one victimization, with the appropriate household and personal characteristics appended. Since more than one victimization can be reported in an interview, and not infrequently is, both personal and household characteristics can be counted more than once in a victim-only file, and, obviously, those persons who did not report any victimizations are excluded. A number of the issues discussed below require analyses based on a file that includes both victims and nonvictims. While the use of the full file obviously would increase the cost of analysis, the alternative is to leave many crucial questions unanswered and thus, in effect, simply to throw away data.

INTERNAL VALIDITY AND RESPONSE BIAS

A high priority in examining the existing NCS data is to try to obtain some idea of the extent to which the sample data, and population estimates based on them, may be biased by differential reporting of incidents by different groups in the sample. It may be that the reporting of incidents, and other responses, in an interview are related to verbal fluency and to educational attainment, which in turn are related to social class; responses in this context may also be related to cultural differences in the perception of criminal violence.

An initial step in investigating these hypotheses would be to look at victimizations reported by family income, education, and possibly occupation (as an indicator of social class) within categories of sex and race. At first, one would examine types of victimization separately and distinguish between attempted and completed crimes. For each type of victimization, the table specification would be: Income *by* number of victimizations *within* sex by race categories; similarly, highest grade of school ever attended (and, separately, occupation) *by* number of victimizations *within* categories of sex *within* categories of race. Such an analysis will permit estimates of the effects of each of the separate variables (e.g., education or income, sex and race) and any interactions among them.[7] One would then be in a better position to consider whether changes in interviewing procedures were needed to help elicit better reports from possibly unresponsive groups.

HOUSEHOLD VICTIMIZATION REPORTS

A substantial proportion of the household informants in the NCS have been under 19 years of age, but it is not known how the choice of household informant affects victimization reporting.[8] A table is needed, therefore, on numbers of household victimizations reported by age, household status, and sex of household informant, again preferably within categories of race. It is reasonable to assume that younger members of the household may be less likely to know about or to have reported to police, say, attempted burglaries or household thefts and

---

[7]In their mid-sixties pilot victimization study, Biderman *et al.* examined the distribution of numbers of respondents reporting on incidents to determine whether there were implausibly few respondents with more than one incident, given the number reporting zero or one incident. See especially Biderman *et al., Report on a Pilot Study in the District of Columbia on Victimization and Attitudes toward Law Enforcement* (Report of the President's Commission on Law Enforcement and Administration of Justice), Field Surveys I (Washington, D.C.: U.S. Government Printing Office, 1967), pp. 52–57.

[8]The evidence is persuasive from earlier victimization studies that household informants underestimate the incidence of personal victimizations that would be obtained directly from individual household members. The evidence is suggestive that reports on household-level victimizations also may vary according to which member of the household serves as informant. One objective of the analytic research recommended above is to approximate an experimental design in which household, screen, and incident questions are administered to each respondent. We think it very likely that this procedure is preferable to the current practice of designating a household informant to report on all household-level victimizations. If the results of the research recommended above are ambiguous, we would suggest further exploration of the issue by means of an experimental design. (See especially, Albert D. Biderman *et. al., op. cit.;* Philip H. Ennis, *Criminal Victimization in the United States: A Report of a National Survey* (Report of the U.S. President's Commission on Law Enforcement and Administration of Justice), Field Surveys II (Washington, D.C.: U.S. Government Printing Office, 1967), pp. 101–6; Albert D. Biderman, "Surveys of Population Samples for Crime Incidence," *Annals of the American Academy of Political and Social Science,* 374 (November 1967): 24–25; Carol B. Kalish, *Crimes and Victims: A Report on the Dayton–San Jose Pilot Survey of Victimization* (Washington, D.C.: U.S. Department of Justice, Law Enforcement Assistance Administration, June 1974), pp. 33–36.

that household heads may be more likely to know about or to have reported thefts from motor vehicles.[9]

MONTH OF INCIDENT AND MONTH OF INTERVIEW

Further evidence on selective underreporting of incidents could come from an examination of the distributions of time elapsed between incident and interview for different groups. Thus it could be hypothesized that persons of relatively low educational attainment tend to report only the more recent events that happened to them, whereas better-educated respondents are more likely to report incidents happening throughout the reference period. The table specification for this type of analysis might be: education (income, occupation, and so forth) by numbers of incidents reported (1, 2, . . . 6 months back in the national sample; 1, 2, . . . 12 months back in the city-level surveys) *within* categories of race. A further control variable in the national sample could be rotation group, i.e., length of time in panel. Use of this control would throw some additional light on the question of "time-in-sample" bias.

MULTIPLE VICTIMIZATION AND SERIES OFFENSES

The structure of the NCS data files at present do not enable any investigation of multiple victimization. A number of other victim surveys have found evidence that the numbers of persons reporting more than one victimization in any given time period is greater than would be expected by chance.

Conceptual problems with multiple victimization in the NCS are related to problems of codification of the so-called series victimizations (i.e., those cases in which the respondent says he was victimized three or more times but cannot give certain details of the individual incidents). It appears from our analysis of 1973 NCS data that each personal series report accounts, on the average, for between six and seven victimizations. These victimizations are not included in present population estimates of rates of personal victimization. To include them

---

[9]The age of household informants also may affect the reliability of data on household characteristics. Inspection of unweighted marginals supplied to us by Census indicates that data on family income are missing for approximately 25 percent of all surveyed households (i.e., victim and nonvictim files) in a typical collection quarter. We suspect that household informants who are not heads of households or spouses of heads may have either no information on family income or information that is less reliable than that obtained from informants in these categories.

would increase those rates by about 35 percent in certain incident categories (and by over 75 percent in the case of simple assault).

Recommendations for exploratory work towards revised procedures for collection, tabulation, and analysis of these series data are presented in Chapter 6. Here, we recommend preliminary investigation of how the count of events in series reports is related to the counts reported by the same respondents of "nonseries" victimizations. Separate tables should be constructed for different types of victimizations. Further, it would be useful to examine the distribution of series reports within the reference period, i.e., to see what proportion were reported in the first season falling in the 6- or 12-month period and what proportion in the season(s) falling near the end. It may be that for incidents occurring 5 or 6 months back, respondents cannot remember details (and, so, the incidents are treated as a "series"); whereas for more recent multiple victimizations, details can be recalled, so that one or more of the series would appear as discrete counts in the present estimates of victimization rates.

A further analytic question, which can be answered partially from existing data, is this: For those "multiple victims" who report separate incidents (not "series" events), who was the offender? For example, if a female respondent reports being assaulted on two, three, or more occasions, was the person who assaulted her in each case her husband? Did each assault occur in her home? And so on. It would seem that the best method of carrying out such an analysis would not be (at least in the first instance) the construction of tables (e.g., showing offender at last reported victimization by offender at subsequent victimization). Rather, it would be to recode existing file data to permit distinguishing between those multiple victims who mentioned the same type of victimization (e.g., assault) and the same category of offender (e.g., spouse) and those who did not.

MISCELLANEOUS VICTIMIZATIONS

A related question, which bears both on the issue of differential "productivity" of respondents and on the issue of multiple victimization, concerns the responses to miscellaneous, catchall questions, such as "Other than any incidents you've already mentioned. . . ." (For example, see Questions 45–48, Appendix D.) It appears that in pretests for the current series of surveys, a substantial proportion of all victimizations reported were in response to catchall questions: Is the same thing true for the ongoing national and city-level surveys? If so, responses from these questions should be analyzed, first in relation to educational level, income, and so on, by sex and race and second in relation to multiple victimization as measured by responses to other, more specific screen questions. What types of incidents are being mentioned here—and by what types of respondents?

ATTITUDE DATA

For one-half of the 1975 city-level survey households (and for a part of the national panel data from 1975 on), a separate questionnaire relating to attitudes has been administered. For the city samples, the relevant questionnaire is designated NCS-6. At the present time, so far as we are aware, no data from this questionnaire have been published by Census or LEAA. Neither have any results from the San Jose–Dayton pretest (in which most, although not all, of these attitude items were pretested) been made available, except in a brief description.

We suggest constructing tables of responses to each NCS-6 question, by victimization (0, 1, 2, 3+) and by sex and race. An analysis by income and education, along the lines discussed earlier, also would be desirable. Two of the questions on NCS-6 seem especially important in relation to victimization. Question 1 asks, "How long have you lived at this address?" Since there is reason to suspect that geographic mobility is positively related to victimization, an analysis of responses to this question in relation to victimizations of different types would be useful. This analysis should be based on data files relating to nonvictims as well as to one-time and multiple victims. Question 8a—"How often do you go out in the evening for entertainment . . . ?"—may be interpreted as a (crude) measure of exposure to the risk of victimization and thus also should be analyzed in relation to reporting of victimizations of different types. If such behavioral questions were to be included on a continuing basis in the national survey, it would be possible to examine changes in reported behavior patterns, perceptions, and the like, in relation to victimizations reported in earlier time periods.

Finally, if questions like those in NCS-6 continue to be asked, an analysis of interrelationships between the various items should be conducted, in order to eliminate redundant or contradictory questions. A corollary objective of this component of the analysis should be the exploration of possible effects on victimization rates from item ordering. Specifically, for the 1975 city-level surveys, one could compare victimization rates obtained from respondents who were asked questions on the NCS-6 attitude supplement with those respondents to whom only the standard interview schedule was administered. It may be that recall of specific incidents is stimulated by preliminary questions related to crime. If so, one would predict a higher average victimization level for the one-half of respondents in the 1975 city-level surveys who responded to NCS-6 questions before being asked about their victim experiences.

6 Assessment of NCS Collection Instruments and Procedures

INTRODUCTION

With so much analysis needed before the existing NCS data can be fully evaluated, it may seem premature to make recommendations for modification of the existing questionnaires. But, in fact, there are indicated changes and additions to the survey that do seem important from both a methodological and a substantive point of view and certain types of analysis that are needed for interpreting both existing and future NCS data.

Many of the recommended changes and additions are related to basic issues of questionnaire design. The reports on the pretests for the NCS show little systematic research on the effects of such factors as question order and question wording. Yet plainly these may be important, not only for attitude data of the NCS-6 variety but also for household and individual screen questions on victimization. *Given the very large samples involved in the NCS, we recommend that 5 percent of those cases in future surveys be available to interview with different forms of questionnaire in order to study different forms and ordering of questions and for pretesting possible new questions.*

THE SCREEN QUESTIONS AND FINAL CLASSIFICATION

The most crucial part of the entire NCS operation is the set of procedures by which respondents' experiences with victim-events are elicited, screened, and classified.[1] In our view, these procedures are defective in that they reflect a carry-over of a mistaken original belief that by having the NCS screen questions correspond to UCR categories, they would yield directly tabulable UCR-classed crime counts. Although the view that one could and should use screen responses for classifying incidents was abandoned, the NCS has not abandoned altogether the idea of wording screen questions so that each would correspond to one UCR Index class. We fail to appreciate the purpose served by aspects of NCS screen procedures, and we suspect much mischief is created by complicating and confusing the mental task set for respondents by imposing on the questionnaire categories of logic that interfere with collection and analysis.

The function of the screen questions should be to facilitate, in ways convenient for the interviewer, the ofttimes difficult recall and reporting by the respondent of happenings that fall within the scope of the survey. The usefulness as data of screen responses themselves is restricted to their use in analyses of the effectiveness of the screen questions. The (wise) operating rule is that the data for final tabulations come from the detailed exploration of the pertinent events by the use of subsidiary (incident) forms.

For the interviewer to know that something has happened to the respondent requiring detailed exploration by an incident form, it is sufficient for the respondent to say that someone, with apparent criminal intent, has done any one of the following things to him/her:

Basic Elements

    A. physically injured, or attempted to;

    B. forced, or threatened force;

    C. entered household (or commercial establishment), or attempted to; and/or,

    D. took property.

If any one or more of these four things have occurred, one of the seven *crimes* of interest to the NCS (that is, recordable in accordance with the *Uniform Crime Reporting Handbook*[2]) has occurred. Any combination of A or B with D involves the crime of robbery (with or without injury). Certain subsidiary elements in addition to the basic

[1]The NCS interview schedule and classification scheme are reproduced in Appendix D. Readers who are unfamiliar with the NCS might find it helpful to review Appendix D at this point, as well as the Glossary, which follows the appendixes.

[2]U.S. Department of Justice, Federal Bureau of Investigation, *Uniform Crime Reporting Handbook* (Washington, D.C.: U.S. Government Printing Office, 1966).

four must be ascertained to permit specific classification of crime into UCR Index offenses:

Subsidiary Elements

1. if A, whether or not offender used a dangerous weapon;
2. if A, whether or not a serious or aggravated injury was intended or suffered;
3. if A or B, whether or not sexual penetration ("carnal knowledge" is the UCR delicacy) occurred or was attempted (A or B precedes 3); and
4. if D, whether or not property taken was an automobile.

There are some additional distinctions that figure in UCR analyses— i.e., subcategories of the major offense classes on police reporting forms:

Detail Elements

1. types of dangerous weapons as subclasses of assaults;
2. forcible versus unlawful entry for burglaries;
3. pocket-picking, purse snatching, thefts from vehicles, thefts of vehicle parts and accessories, and thefts from buildings in the case of larcenies; and
4. armed or not for robberies.

None of the subsidiary or detail elements of information, however, is needed for the purpose of screening. No decisions of the interviewer hinge on this information. Yet most of these items do figure currently in the screen questions. The result is a long list of fairly complex, compound questions. Some features of the priority code of the UCR classification system are reflected also in the question order of the screener. If these details of the screener are not needed for deciding whether an incident form should be administered, why are they there? The borrowings of the *Uniform Crime Reporting Handbook* by the screener do serve the purposes of the screener in two ways:

1. They serve as specific cues to jog the memory of the respondent. But what reason is there for thinking that these are optimum or even particularly good cues for jogging respondents' memories? Are the particular bundles of elements that figure in the UCR classes the best ones in terms of their fit to events or memories of events? Are cues put in the best sequence?
2. Some of the UCR features are used to divide up crimes into

household or personal for separate administration in accordance with
the two different respondent selection procedures for the two types.
However, as Richard W. Dodge's data indicate, they do this on the
basis of assumptions about victimization phenomena that are often
incorrect.[3] Elements that frequently occur in association with personal
crimes appear only in the household screen and *vice versa*.

The screen questions represent an inappropriate application of principles of the UCR classification system to the victimization survey
method. This is true even if one accepts the decision to restrict the NCS
to data on victimizations involving UCR offenses.

The NCS screener is, moreover, unnecessarily constrained by limitations of the UCR reporting system. The UCR uses manually recorded,
preaggregated response forms. It perforce must establish a very restricted number of categories, each of which represents a combination
of quite distinct elements that figure in offenses, which are listed
above. In addition, the UCR system imposes a priority code.

The priority coding dictates that when a certain element or combination is present, other elements that would otherwise figure in classification are to be ignored. The result is a UCR offense-reporting form with 7
major classes divided into a total of 19 subclasses. Omitting homicide,
which is outside of the NCS scope, there are 6 major and 15 subclasses.
None of the four basic elements and the four subsidiary elements listed
above excludes the possibility of the other occurring in the same event,
except for the element "serious or aggravated injury," which is dependent on some injury having occurred and which is mutually exclusive
of a "nonaggravated injury" having occurred. Ignoring distinctions
between actual, attempted and threatened events, then, we have seven
independent elements and one dependent element. Each independent
element might be a separate "count" of an indictment, as might be
various of the combinations. There are 190 possible combinations of
these elements that can be found in incidents. This number must be
multiplied manyfold if we take pertinent threatened and unsuccessful
crimes into account or any of the detail elements.

A set of well-designed screen questions must recognize that there are
not just seven crimes in which one is interested and regarding which
one must jog the respondent's memory (or his recognition that something he can remember is pertinent to the interviewer), but many times
this number of possible crimes. The screener can be a cue to any of the

---

[3]Richard W. Dodge, "Analysis of Screen Questions on National Crime Survey"
(Internal memorandum of U.S. Department of Commerce, Bureau of the Census,
Washington, D.C., December 1, 1975).

elements, as well as to various combinations, that may be effective in jogging memory or in otherwise increasing the chances a respondent will mention an eligible event. The screen questions also can be a cue to some element of place or some other circumstance of the victimization that may help bring about mention of an incident, whether or not this is a pertinent item of information for UCR classification. The NCS screener need not be restricted to any of the limited combinations of elements that figure in the UCR classification system.

The current NCS screener:

1. involves unnecessarily difficult, complex screening questions;

2. confuses the functions of question elements as cues for recall with criteria for classification, with the result that some cues appear only in specific combinations that are not exhaustive and not always the most important uses of these cues;

3. adopts a priority ordering that results in key screen questions never being posed at all to certain respondents, particularly because of divisions between household and individual parts;

4. incorrectly assumes a discrete dramatic unity of person, place, time, and action in the meaning of the word "incident" for the respondent;

5. illogically assumes that mutual exclusivity of the applicability of certain screen questions to incidents will follow from the question order (as is evidenced by the questions to which the phrase "other than any incidents already mentioned" is added) and adopts an undesirable procedure that rests on the assumption of a one-to-one correspondence between "yes" responses elicited by screen questions and discrete incidents; and,

6. may have self-confirming properties that lead to thinking the screener or its individual items work well because each yields a large portion of the incidents eventually classified in a particular way.

Recommendations for a completely redesigned screener follow from the above considerations. Given the central importance of the screen-question procedure to the NCS, there has been deplorably scant research and analysis of the survey's data for the purposes of developing, evaluating, and improving the measurement of incidents. The following suggestions might figure in efforts to identify questions that might yield a more effective screener:

1. The screen questions should follow the principles of simple sentence construction. Questions should ask about one thing at a time and ask about a very different thing (if only by instructions for an

interviewer pause between questions) only after the previous question has been answered. Instead of the present first screen question (Question 29), one might ask, for example, "Did anyone break into your apartment?" "Yes" or "No" [Pause] Followed by, "Did anyone break into your garage?" "Yes" or "No" [Pause] Then, "Did anyone break into some other building you own?" "Yes" or "No." (Note, for example, that with the present screener someone answering "Yes, someone broke into my house" is thereupon asked "How many times?" and may answer thinking only about other times someone broke into the house and not be thinking about the break-in of a garage, and so on.)

2. A UCR distinction by itself provides no justification for having an information element in a question, for example, the phrase "by using force" in Individual Screen Question 37. This question illustrates the possible importance of permutations of elements. Property can be taken stealthily, and force used to effect a getaway when the offender is caught in the act. The answer to Question 37 would be "No," but the offense would be "robbery."

3. Cues relating to locales and other circumstances of victimization should be used for their mnemonic value so that the respondent is free to associate with that circumstance or locale any pertinent victimization event. Such questions should be grouped together, so that when the respondent is thinking "automobile," he can be asked economically about auto theft, theft of parts, thefts from, and possibly even assaults in automobiles. Bicycle theft should form a separate Individual Screen Question, rather than appearing only as one item on a list as in Household Screen Question 31. (We suspect the NCS erroneously records a disproportionate number of bicycle thefts as from the residence and misses many of which the household informant is not aware.)

Home, street, school, work, recreation, public transportation, restaurants, and gathering places could all be subject to a separate question sequence appropriate to the victimizations likely in each. Attacks and specific weapons cues can remain very much as they now stand in Individual Screen Questions 38 to 42 (although the exclusion of telephone threats in Question 41 is a distraction that saves less than it costs and should be deleted).

The principle should be to use a variety of cues in constructing questions on the assumptions that different minds work differently and that different features of crime events may be the salient ones in a given interview. For example: "Did anyone try to force you or frighten you to make you give them money or anything else [Pause] . . . use force or frighten you so they could get into your house [Pause] . . . to do something sexually?" "At school, has anyone hurt you physically, or tried to hurt you on purpose [Pause] . . . has anything been stolen from you at school . . . have things disappeared from your desk or locker?"

4. The household-informant section should be limited to questions on breaking and entering and to household property items (tools and toys might figure as specific cues). The household informant should not be the available teenager, but someone who regularly has responsibility for "taking care of the house." Alternately, for research purposes, everyone who is interviewed within the household should be asked about household, as well as personal, crimes. Interviewers and schedule format should assume the burden of eliminating separate mentions by different household members of identical incidents, including thefts of jointly owned property such as automobiles.

5. Screening procedure should reflect less worry about redundancy and about eliminating ineligible incidents than about unnecessarily cluttering up discrete questions and the respondent's thinking. For example, the recent bound should be eliminated from the reference period question. "When was that?" can substitute for "Was it between ____, 197__ and ____, 197_?" (Answer "Yes" or "No.") The interviewer can determine which incidents are too recent to take. (Indeed, perhaps all incidents to date of interview should be taken at time of interview. Burdens are being put on the weak link—the respondent—that are better assumed by data processors.)

6. The work of screening might be aided by explaining the screen procedure to the respondent. A system for separating incidents is needed other than the "Yes—How many times?" or "No." The respondent should be allowed to think about each screen question separately. For those that apply to him, he should be asked "When did that happen?" and, only if needed for clarification of his reply, "Was that part of (an/the) incident you told me about?" (Replies will sometimes be, "No, but it was connected to it" or "I don't know.") He thereupon should be asked whether there was some other time that sort of thing happened (repeating the screen item words), with the probing continuing until the respondent has nothing further to mention in response to the screen question.

This kind of procedure involves much more logical redundancy of questioning than the current one, but it recognizes that there is a need for redundancy if one is to be sure that nonredundant potential information is not excluded. Logical and psychological redundancy are not necessarily equivalent.

THE SCREENING AND CLASSIFICATION OF
EVENTS AS "SERIES"

The screen questions should take account of the large volume of incidents now classed as "series." At present, an estimated 20–30 percent of reported personal "victimizations" are treated as series and are excluded from the personal incidence count. More importantly, these series victimizations are treated in the Census–LEAA publications of the NCS data as anomalies to be relegated to an appendix rather than as the extraordinary findings that they probably are.

Currently, a separation of events into series and discrete incidents is done in the field by interviewers. If the respondent can specify details of events, such as the month of occurrence, a separate crime-incident report is filled out for the located event, even though the same crime elements may be involved for one or more other incidents reported to interviewers, the same offender may be involved in them, and the incidents may have occurred at the same location and at the same time of day. Conversely, if the respondent can recall "3 or more similar incidents" occurring in the past 6 months, interviewers in the field may code, as a last resort according to the interviewer manual, events as "series." Determinations, as to the similarity of events in the set are made by interviewers, and details are recorded only for "this/the most recent" event. (See Appendix D, especially Crime Incident Question 1(a, b, and c) and the interviewer instruction preceding Crime Incident Question 2.)

This procedure, which arbitrarily splits events in the field, seems to be related to an early interest in producing quarterly data. For the purpose of producing quarterly data, one might wish to aggregate all incidents according to specific temporal characteristics of those incidents, such as the calendar month in which the event occurred.

Yet, clearly, the current procedure involves designation by the respondent of "Spring, Summer, Fall, Winter" for any "3 or more similar events which the respondent cannot recall separately." These seasonal designations are obtained in the field. But they have not been used in the incident counts for a calendar quarter nor a calendar year, partly because they do not correspond to these time units. "Winter," for example, is defined as "December, January, February."

Another reason that the series events may not enter the incident count is that the respondent himself is asked to recode a set of incidents into a "series" and to estimate for each series the number of incidents involved. This number is recorded on the current interview form as "Three or four, Five to ten, Eleven or more, Don't know.") Then, for only the most "recent" incident in the series (which, presumably, the respondent decides), details are asked of time and place of occurrence, offender characteristics, harm or loss sustained, and all other questions that are asked for nonseries incidents.

It seems to us that there are two problems implicit in this procedure:

1. An unknown number of events that are repetitive in one or more respects are now disaggregated into discrete counts, depending on interviewer persistence[4] and/or respondent ability to distinguish among events according to details deemed important at the field stage.

2. An unknown number of events that are distinct in terms of time and place of occurrence, characteristics of offender, degree of loss or injury, and so forth, are defined as serial in nature and are aggregated.

The extent to which events are similar is determined in the field by interviewers. It seems to us that it would be far more consistent with standard canons of survey methodology to have judgments on the similarity of complex events made by data analysts rather than by interviewers.

Were the incident reports altered so as to make "month of occurrence" only one among many descriptive variables associated with an incident, the data analyst subsequently would have the flexibility to:

1. obtain a baseline count of reported incidence that included both series and discrete incidents;

2. partition the baseline incidence count according to type of offense;

3. partition the baseline incidence count by subgroups of the surveyed population;

4. partition the baseline incidence count by characteristics of the event;

5. partition the baseline incidence count for each type of offense by subgroups of the surveyed population;

6. partition the baseline incidence count for each type of offense by characteristics of the event;

7. partition the baseline incidence count according to the number of occurrences within the reference period for each member of the surveyed population (e.g., 0, 1, 2, 3, 4, . . .);

---

[4]Early evidence from the Census reinterview program suggests an interviewer effect on the proportion of events classified as "series." This proportion apparently is declining as interviewers gain more experience with NCS procedures.

8. partition the baseline incidence count, by type of offense, according to the number of occurrences within the reference period for each member of the surveyed population (e.g., 0, 1, 2, 3, . . . counts of robbery);

9. partition the baseline incidence count, by type of offense, according to the number of occurrences within the reference period for subgroups of the surveyed population (e.g., 0, 1, 2, 3, . . . counts of burglary for whites, for blacks, for individuals whose homes are occupied during the day, for individuals whose homes are unoccupied during the day); and,

10. partition the baseline incidence count into clusters of offenses (e.g., personal incidents only, household offenses only, robbery and assault), according to the number of occurrences within the reference period for each member of the surveyed population (e.g., 0, 1, 2, 3, . . .).

The above list is illustrative and nonexhaustive. What we mean to convey is that the current handling of both discrete and series victimizations obscures and precludes satisfactory measurement of the surveyed crimes. It seems to us that "series" victimizations are but a special case of the phenomenon of multiple victimization, including cases of time-extended victimization.[5] The NCS might tap these phenomena, but the current data are not analyzable, mainly because of field and tabulation procedures.

Multiple victimization is a global concept, theoretically subsuming numerous components. Field and tabulation procedures should allow the widest flexibility for exploration of these components. A procedure that arbitrarily excludes a subset of reported offenses not only limits exploration of multiple victimization but also affects the validity and reliability of every numerator and denominator based upon nonseries counts. Specifically, a ratio that purports to show the proportion of violent (surveyed) crimes attributed by respondents to strangers cannot legitimately exclude from the base all reported violent crimes for which the respondent was unable to assign a month of occurrence. This exclusion obviously affects the denominator, because with the current field procedure the count of stranger-attributed offenses is based on a subset of reports. Less obviously, it affects the numerator, because no information is obtained from respondents on offender characteristics for any event in a series except the "most recent" if no month was

[5]Examples of time-extended victimizations are continuing terrorization by threats or assaults, shakedowns, nonsupport of dependent children, violations of building codes, or embezzlement.

assigned to the events. (This discussion leaves aside the issues of selective reporting to interviewers and selective coverage of respondents, as these may affect the validity and reliability of results. These issues are considered elsewhere in the report.)

Fundamental to the concept of multiple victimization is the establishment of a time frame. Ideally, in view of the rarity of events surveyed by the NCS, one wants counts of incidents to be based on a broad time frame. Operationally, one wants to take advantage of the panel rotation design of the NCS and hence aggregate across repeated interviews so as to tap multiple victimization for 6 months, 12 months, 18 months, . . . up to 3 years. This is possible in a technical sense.

The point at which the mobility of the population biases seriously the incidence count is unknown. Preliminary review by Census, however, indicates that for adjacent 6-month intervals, 86 percent of sampled dwelling units have the same occupants, and 95 percent of these previous occupants are reinterviewed at least once. No information is available yet on the number of first-interview respondents who are reinterviewed for the full 3 years their dwelling unit remains in the sample. (This also means that no information is available on the extent to which interviews, in fact, are bounded for the time period designated households remain in the sample.)

For a 6- or 12-month reference period, it is possible to describe multiple victimization according to:

1. What proportion of the surveyed population accounts for what proportion of the total offenses reported to interviewers as having occurred within the reference period?

2. What proportion of the surveyed population accounts for what proportion of each of the specific offenses reported to interviewers as having occurred within the reference period?

A victimization survey should be able to answer these questions. Were it not for constraints imposed by field and tabulation procedures, the current LEAA version could answer them. A requirement is that "month of occurrence" of the event not be used as a device to separate series from discrete events. Clearly, the respondent who cannot assign an event to a calendar month within the reference period is assigning the event to the reference period.

Another dimension of multiple victimization is that of the clustering of the types of offenses that individuals experience. Exploration of this dimension would involve grouping of offenses and arranging of these clusters according to the frequency of their occurrence for each respondent. Offenses can be grouped by whatever variables are measured to describe them. They can be grouped according to specific types of offenses—e.g., personal only, property only, or both property and personal. Or, respondents can be described according to whether they experienced only personal offenses, only household offenses, or both household and personal offenses for the reference period. This line of analysis implies not only some reprogramming, but also some reconceptualization. For, it is far from obvious to us that a resident of a house that is burglarized has not experienced victimization in a very personal sense.[6] With current tabulation procedures, the event of burglary can be counted over a base of households surveyed, but no analysis specification we have seen allows for a total count of offenses experienced where the unit of analysis is the victim.

In addition to clusters of offenses experienced by individuals within a time frame, multiple victimization can refer to social, spatial, or temporal characteristics of the event—both within and across offense categories. A respondent may experience one or more assaults within a reference period. With current field and tabulation procedures, one cannot determine the actual number reported. Moreover, even if the offender was observed, one cannot determine whether the same offender was involved in each event or whether the only commonality was, in fact, the type of offense. While it is now mechanically possible to aggregate some subset (i.e., "nonseries") reported offenses by time and place of occurrence, degree of loss or injury, and the like, in order to explore commonalities of events, it is not possible to determine whether the same offender is involved in multiple personal contact offenses simply because the respondent is not asked.

Statements like "Fifty percent of crimes of personal violence were committed by (attributed to) blacks" or "Sixty-five percent of crimes of personal violence were committed by (attributable to) strangers" cannot legitimately be made with the current data set as long as series victimizations are excluded from the denominator and numerator of the ratio. What is required is modification of these statements to the effect that they "refer only to surveyed crimes of personal violence, reported to interviewers, in which interviewers could distinguish among specific characteristics of these events, exclude all 'similar' offenses that contained three or more events for which specific characteristics were

---

[6]Albert D. Biderman et al., Report on a Pilot Study in the District of Columbia in Victimization and Attitudes Toward Law Enforcement (Report of the President's Commission on Law Enforcement and Administration of Justice), Field Surveys I (Washington, D.C.: U.S. Government Printing Office, 1967).

not obtained, and include an unknown number of 'similar' events for which the attributed characteristics of the offender also have counted in connection with another victimization of the same respondent.''[7]

THE NEED FOR INDEPENDENT VARIABLES

The central argument in the preceding section is that the interview schedule for the NCS should allow wide analytic flexibility for exploration of the commonalities of incidents and for assessment of the distribution of incidents among the entire surveyed population.

Hence we do not offer a definition of series events, but we do suggest one minor short-run change pending field studies on screen questions and procedures. The question in NCS-2, "How many incidents were involved in this series?", now formats responses into four categories: Three or four; Five to ten; Eleven or more; Don't know. This format makes difficult the inclusion of series incidents into any aggregate, for each series either must count as one incident or a weight for an interval must be arbitrarily assigned. A solution would be to instruct interviewers to obtain a number and subsequently to treat the variable, "number of incidents," as integral rather than grouped data.

The above recommendation is not a solution to the larger question of estimation of incidence and distribution of those victimizations within the scope and capability of the NCS. Understanding the incidence and distribution of criminal victimization will require exploration of characteristics of events in order to determine to what degree the events are uniformly distributed across population subgroups of interest. This exploration presupposes that data are gathered with this objective in view, and it is on this larger problem that we have focused our attention.

[7]This statement should be accompanied by discussion of the probable bias in offender characteristics data that stems from selective reporting to interviewers of events. This caveat could and should be applied to any rate discussed in NCS reports and not be limited to descriptions of characteristics of events. But while the degree of underreporting of events to interviewers is not known, the pilot and pretest studies clearly indicate that both type of offense and relationship with offender are factors. Hence, the direction of bias in the numerator of ratios of attributed characteristics to reported events is known, albeit the magnitude of the bias is not. To be sure, every rate is affected in terms of level by underreporting to interviewers and, perhaps, crucially affected by differential underreporting by or undercoverage of subgroups of the sampled population, but it should not be the case that biases on which evidence exists are ignored in official reports simply because biases for which no evidence exists reasonably can be assumed. The essence of scientific reporting, it seems to us, is provision to the reader of information on the known limitations of the data.

Individuals who experience repeated victimizations may well differ from those who experience either no victimizations or isolated victimizations in one fundamental respect—degree of vulnerability. If there exists among the population a set of individuals whose experience with victimization is rare or nonexistent and another set for whom victimization is repetitive, it follows that the latter may be exposed to crime-correlated circumstances that represent conditions of existence. Linking the concepts of vulnerability and conditions, one might distinguish among three broad categories—ecological vulnerability, status vulnerability, and role vulnerability. Each of these types of vulnerability will be discussed below.

ECOLOGICAL VULNERABILITY

Ecological vulnerability refers to social contexts that are relatively durable conditions in the life of an individual. Examples might include: living in a high- or low-income area; how many windows and doors of one's dwelling unit are directly accessible from ground level; whether one lives in a high- or low-crime area; whether one's neighborhood is homogeneous or heterogeneous with respect to land use (i.e., primarily residential, mixed, primarily commercial) or with respect to the age structure or racial composition; whether one lives in rural, suburban, or urban areas; whether one's neighborhood is densely or sparsely populated; whether one's street (or apartment building) is often or rarely frequented; whether interviewers are reluctant to go into one's neighborhood; or whether one's neighborhood is or is not contiguous to a sharply contrasting social area.[8]

STATUS VULNERABILITY

Status vulnerability refers to a social category or class to which an individual belongs that is relatively or absolutely fixed. Attributes of individuals, such as race or sex, would be included here. While gender probably would be considered by most social scientists to be the only "true" attribute—barring surgical alterations—we also would include categories from which migration or mobility is either relatively low or relatively slow, such as occupation, age, and social class. Thus, women may be vulnerable to some types of victimization because they

[8]High rates for such offenses as burglary have been found in police statistics for upper-income census tracts contiguous to very low-income ones. See Sarah L. Boggs, "Urban Crime Patterns," *American Sociological Review 30* (December 1965): 899–909.

are women; police officers, prostitutes, or Presidents may be vulnerable to victimization because they *are* police officers, prostitutes, or Presidents; those with more wealth may be vulnerable to victimization because they have more objects to steal or because they can afford to pay ransoms if people are taken from them. Where class and race are highly correlated, whites may be more vulnerable to victimization because they are white and more affluent; where the age distribution is correlated with race, blacks may be more vulnerable to victimization because they are black and members of a population group characterized by a (relatively) young age structure; where the age structure is correlated with employment status, the young may be more vulnerable to victimization because they are young and members of a group where unemployment is highest, assuming unemployment is more highly correlated with street exposure than employment.

ROLE VULNERABILITY

Role vulnerability refers to specific and relatively durable social relationships from which an individual cannot readily withdraw. Typically, this would refer to primary relationships, such as husband–wife or parent–child. It also can refer to secondary relationships under the condition that a reinforcement exists between the individuals that defines role durability in ways that can be enforced by external sanctions (i.e., landlord–tenant, high school student–classmate, jailer–prisoner) or backed by internal calculations of penalties for withdrawal (i.e., blackmailer–blackmailee; lawyer–client). Hence, some men and women may experience assault only in connection with spousal role partners and not experience it as a function of ecological or status vulnerabilities.

Role vulnerabilities may be correlated with other types of vulnerabilities. Palpably, women who are beaten by husbands may be more likely than women who are not beaten by husbands to be married, but also they are more likely to be (a) residents of low-security buildings who (b) commute to public-contact jobs by (c) public transit.

What is desired is a measuring instrument that leads to estimates of the unique and combined effects of several types of vulnerabilities on the probability of individual victimization for any specific type of surveyed incident. While the categories of vulnerability discussed here clearly are broad and nonexhaustive, the current interview schedule in the household component of the NCS is inadequate for the objective of assessing vulnerability. The combination of instrument deficiencies and tabulation deficiencies radically reduces the potential of the NCS to tap the effects of vulnerabilities on either individual or subgroup risks of victimization.

A national survey of victimization should tell us the incidence among the surveyed population of events selected for coverage. It should tell us what proportion of the population is affected by experience with the surveyed crime at all (once or more) within a given time period, what proportion accounts for what proportion of the total reported crime incidents, and what proportion accounts for recorded experience with each of the crime categories surveyed. Unless current screen and tabulation procedures are changed, the NCS official reports cannot address these questions.

We also hold that a descriptive survey of victimization should yield information on risk and its correlates. As presently tabulated, the NCS will not do this because of the exclusion of series events and because of the exclusion of nonvictims from the analysis. Attempts have been made in Census–LEAA reorts published to date to approximate risk probabilities by reporting the rate per 1,000 of victimizations for subgroups of the population. This measure of risk overestimates the probability that members of a subgroup were victimized during the time period of interest unless each respondent reporting an incident reported one and only one incident for the time period. With present tabulation procedures (and leaving aside the issue of series count), one cannot legitimately state, for example, "Blacks were more likely (less likely) than whites to have been robbed," or "Young people were more likely (less likely) than older people to have been assaulted." Current tabulation procedures and recommendations for modification are discussed more fully elsewhere in this report. We emphasize the effect of tabulation procedures on estimates of risk in this discussion in order to show that the concept of risk operationalized in the current household interview schedule is narrowly limited to a few aspects of only one dimension of vulnerability—what we have termed status vulnerability. Hence, data analysts are restricted in describing the distribution and the correlates of risk.

We recommend that the current interview schedule be revised and expanded so as to illuminate more clearly the dimensions of vulnerability. Status vulnerabilities, by definition, are relatively immutable attributes or conditions. They are of interest, to be sure, because they help describe the distribution of victimization across some demographic categories. From a policy perspective, however, one wants to know whether correlates of victim experience represent changeable or fixed conditions of life. A baseline count, for example, of robbery incidents is needed to learn whether robbery is an isolated and rare event experienced at the hand of an unknown assailant or whether it is a function of vulnerabilities that might be amenable to either collective or individual control. Answering this fundamental kind of question should be the principal objective of a nationwide, publicly funded, statistical series on victimization.

It may well be that very few of the victim experiences tapped by the NCS can be prevented by either government or private action. But the present interview schedule does not allow the survey to shed light on this question.

We strongly urge that the NCS interview schedules and public-use tapes be augmented by adding measures that will illuminate ecological, status, and role vulnerabilities. We recommend that the official publications of results from the NCS present data that analyze victimization probabilities along these dimensions for all surveyed respondents. Finally, we recommend that items intended to measure these vulnerabilities be formulated by considering separately each surveyed category of crime. For example, we do not expect ecological vulnerabilities that would distinguish victims and nonvictims of burglary necessarily to be the same vulnerabilities that distinguish victims and nonvictims of rape. To describe the distribution and risk of victimization, we hope that revision to the interview schedule is made with an eye toward all surveyed respondents and toward each surveyed crime.

OPPORTUNITY AS A PREDICTOR OF VICTIM EXPERIENCE

Although relatively fixed conditions of life might correlate positively and negatively with repetitive experiences of victimization, experiences doubtless also depend on the actions taken to minimize risk. From a policy perspective, the first step is to learn to what extent vulnerabilities and victim experience are connected. The second step is to learn to what extent individual actions may alter that connection.

In the model we propose, the concept of opportunity is interpreted as a set of variables that intervene between vulnerabilities and victim experience. With one exception, we find nothing in the current NCS household interview schedule that appears related to the concept of opportunity as defined here. That exception is the Incident Question 10 (a and b), which asks any respondent reporting a personal contact victimization whether resistance was attempted. Resistance to an attack may increase or decrease injury. No tables have been published by Census–LEAA to date that cross-tabulate resistance by degree of loss or injury sustained. No tables have been published indicating who resists and under what circumstances and with what effect. Are men more likely than women to offer resistance? Are unarmed assailants more or less likely to meet with resistance than armed assailants? Are acquaintances more or less likely to meet with resistance than unknown assailants? The conventional wisdom is that it is safer not to resist: No tables that we have seen from the NCS shed light on whether or how opportunity for injury or loss is affected by victim reaction.

The one exceptional variable noted is observed only if a respondent reports a personal-contact victim experience. Hence, it cannot aid in understanding actions that might reduce the probability of an event occurring in the first place. We think that correlates of victim reactions are important to measure, but from a policy perspective it is at least as important to measure actions of victims and nonvictims that might affect the opportunity for the event to have occurred at all. The household component of the current interview schedule is not constructed to yield information on opportunity for victimization.[9]

We recommend that items be added to the interview schedule as indicators of opportunity for victimization, and that the official reports on the NCS routinely include tables that show incidence by vulnerability and opportunity.

We offer an illustrative and nonexhaustive list of possible indicators of opportunity that individuals or household units might exhibit to potential offenders: Examples would include the presence or absence of: bars on windows; of a security guard; of a burglar alarm system; of double-bolt locks and chains; of item identification stickers on windows or doors; of a watch dog; of a handgun or rifle; of timers for the lamps; of neighbors who can be relied on to provide surveillance when the dwelling unit is empty; of a garage which can be locked for storage of automobile, bicycle, or lawn implements; and, whether a telephone number for police is posted by a telephone.

For some of the above items, we also would ask whether use is always, often, sporadically, or rarely made of the protection measure—for example, whether the garage is locked, whether lamp timers are used, and whether neighbors are asked to provide surveil-

---

[9]For general discussions relevant to the idea of standardizing victimization rates for differential opportunities or vulnerabilities, see Leslie T. Wilkins, *Social Deviance* (London: Tavistock, 1964), pp. 53–55; Albert J. Reiss, Jr., *Studies in Crime and Law Enforcement in Major Metropolitan Areas*, Vol. I (Report of the President's Commission on Law Enforcement and Criminal Justice), Field Surveys III (Washington, D.C.: U.S. Government Printing Office, 1967), pp. 10–12 and 18–23.

lance, and so forth. Drivers of automobiles should be asked individually whether their car is always, often, sporadically, or never locked when empty and whether doors are locked when occupied.

Discretionary exposure to public places could be measured in the NCS. For example, how often in the past month one was out at night other than for work after 6 p.m., 10 p.m., or 12 p.m.; whether the frequency reported was high, low, or about average; whether one was unaccompanied (never, sometimes, mostly) between home and destination; whether one traveled by foot, by public transportation, by private automobile; how many times one left the immediate neighborhood after dark in the past month; how many times one went to commercial establishments after dark is contrasted with either trips to private homes or to church or fraternal meetings; in how many places frequented were alcoholic beverages served or available; what was the largest amount of cash carried at any time; for each "exposure" mentioned, was there someone at home who knew where the respondent could be reached in case of emergency and/or who would notice a prolonged absence.

These indicators are merely illustrative, and, obviously, no interview schedule would include each and every type on a regular basis. If the objective were to distinguish between dwelling units that were and were not burglarized in a given time period, one might ask whether the unit is occupied during the time of day evidence suggests most burglaries occur. Similarly, if the focus were on robbery, one might ask each respondent whether he gets to work (or school or errands) by private automobile or by walking to bus or subway stops. We point out, also, that a number of the indicators of vulnerability and opportunity discussed here could be measured by interviewer observation or could be taken from Census files on neighborhood characteristics and are not necessarily candidates for either regular or periodic inclusion in the interview schedule itself.

Theoretically, most of the indicators mentioned thus far could be divided according to whether a collective or an individual action is implied in order to deter opportunity for victimization. In practice, even actions taken for collective protection, such as installation of burglar alarm systems, typically require individual monitoring on behalf of the unit. Someone has to see that alarm systems are operative, that windows and doors are bolted, and so forth. The point here is that the usefulness of a "household informant–individual respondent" interviewing model would depend on the specific question being asked. Each of the illustrative questions is aimed at distinguishing between people who take more or less care for their safety. For some forms of protection, this care can be delegated or assumed. For other forms, unilateral or uniform action is required of each individual.

The preceding discussion pertains to measuring opportunity at the individual or household level for crimes that fall within the scope of the NCS. One might also include actions at the level of neighborhoods or communities, such as levied payment for a private security force.

For victim experiences to which a people might be vulnerable because of their involvement with the offender in a primary or quasi-primary role relationship (e.g., marriages or consensual unions), deterrence of opportunity may be indicated less by physical or behavioral measures than by psychological ones. Attitudes toward physical discipline of children and toward physical violence between husband and wife may vary among and within social classes. Across social classes, we might expect different norms to operate with regard to family beating and to correlate with the incidence of family beating by class level.

Clearly, whether there is more variation in tolerance for interpersonal violence among than within social classes (geographic regions or any number of other social constructs, for that matter) is an empirical question. The NCS could address it and, more important, it could explore systematically the link between tolerance for violence and victim experience that criminologists and police administrators have pondered historically.

We do not recommend acceptance of our illustrative model of victimization. Rather, our global recommendation is that LEAA should recognize that its model is implicitly and unduly restricted to the link between a few specific components of vulnerability and one specific, and we believe faulty, definition of risk. Moreover, neither in-house nor outside analysts can use the LEAA results to explore the modifiability of risk, however incidents are tabulated, because no measures are taken of ways in which individuals or households increase or decrease the opportunity for victimization.

We recognize that the illustrations offered here, if taken literally as recommendations and implemented simultaneously, would yield an interview schedule so lengthy as to be unadministrable, even in a pretest phase. We further recognize that selection of items for inclusion in a large-scale national survey is a very difficult task.

In an earlier chapter, we emphasized the need for a sharper delineation of objectives for the NCS, and we believe that this sharpening should serve as a basis for decisions on what the annual and special Census–LEAA reports will contain. The first step is to specify what this survey is expected to produce in the way of new or complementary information on victim experiences of the U.S. public. The second step is to explore through pretests and analytic research which of those expectations are realistic, given the potential and the limitations of the state of the art of surveying, in general, and of victim surveying, in particular. For example, some types of victimization may be measured reliably, but may occur so infrequently among the population that little or no analysis can be done of the events, by either in-house or outside analysts. Other and more frequent events may merit an annual report devoted to distinguishing between victims and nonvictims and for which a special supplement of independent variables was added to all interview schedules. Some sets of items might be added to the last interview conducted before the sampled dwelling unit rotates out of the panel, while other sets may be asked at the first- and last-scheduled interview only. For some objectives, substitution of items can serve as well as addition of items.

We do not recommend a single strategy for defining the scope of the NCS interview schedule, because we think that a mixed strategy is appropriate. The NCS is new. It is ground-breaking. It is complex.

If we were limited to only one recommendation on the structuring of the NCS interview schedule, it would be to justify explicitly each and every item in terms of its use for analysis or estimation. The process of justification forces the specification of agency objectives and of implicit models. It aids in the formulation of analysis schedules and in the outlining and production of reports. It guides decisions on what tasks must be coordinated between the sponsoring agency and the data collection arm and what tasks reasonably might be delegatable to an outside contractor, within the bounds of currency and confidentiality constraints.

Within a very short time, the NCS has demonstrated enormous potential utility. The question now is whether resources can be allocated and coordinated so as to transform potential into practical utility.

7   NCS Findings: Analysis, Publication, and Dissemination

INTRODUCTION

The Bureau of the Census, the NCS data-collection agent, routinely produces several kinds of NCS output. Initially, responses to most items on individual questionnaires are recorded on magnetic tape. Next, basic survey tapes are used by Census to generate official survey-data tabulations, according to specifications approved by LEAA. Available to the public at a nominal cost are versions of these microdata tapes, called public-use tapes, in a format such that individual identities cannot be determined.

Data tapes and tabulations have been produced on a periodic basis for each city-level survey and for the national component of the NCS. Tabulations include victimization rates and incident counts by victimization category and by variables such as victim characteristics and event characteristics (e.g., degree of injury, number of offenders, whether weapons were involved, and time of day of occurrence). Special tabulations are distributed to LEAA's Statistics Division, to local officials in surveyed cities, to us, and to other groups, as time and resources permit.

The public-use tapes are intended to provide NCS data to persons and organizations with an interest in the criminal justice field, especially individuals whose work is supported by research grants awarded by NCJISS. The NCS grant program has three objectives: to support basic research on topics related to victimization surveys in general, to investigate issues related to the NCS operation, and to inform consumers about NCS concepts and operations. More information on the grant program is included here in Appendix E.

A judgment on the potential contribution of the grant activities to NCS analysis and dissemination efforts would be premature at this time. The panel agrees, however, that the contributions to the NCS program would be enhanced if the objectives of individual grants were linked more closely to those of the NCS. Furthermore, arrangements should be made with at least some grantees to publish selected results of their work as official LEAA reports. Otherwise, the prospect exists that the primary audience for analyses done under grants will be readers of dissertations and of professional journals.

Of the NCS-related grants awarded by the NCJISS, two are related directly to dissemination goals. While NCS public-use tapes are available from the Bureau of the Census, the LEAA has given a grant to an independent organization, Data Use and Access Laboratories (DUALabs), to furnish tape users with information and custom services tailored to their needs. DUALabs' tasks include the reformating of data tapes, producing of technical documentation, conducting a series of user seminars, and furnishing consultation services to users. Work began in October 1975. At present, the grant is being renegotiated to accommodate the complexity and scope of the tasks.

The second grant related to dissemination was awarded to the Criminal Justice Research Center, Inc. (CJRC) (The expected products of this grant are summarized in Appendix E.) The grantee, CJRC, is holding a series of seminars in order to acquaint researchers and operating agency staffs with NCS methods and procedures, available data, and current research based on the NCS. Other objectives of CJRC seminars are to create a forum for the exchange of ideas among researchers and to facilitate communication between researchers and the LEAA.

Although efforts of outside researchers are essential to the long-term health and data utilization of large, continuing surveys such as the NCS, these efforts alone cannot provide results in a form suitable for distribution to the general public and to policymaking officials. It is the panel's view that the interests of the public and their policymakers are best served by the distribution of findings through the mechanism of official LEAA publications, although in some cases these may contain analysis conducted by outside researchers. Hence, the remainder of this chapter on dissemination of NCS results is devoted to LEAA's own analysis and publication efforts.

REPORTS ISSUED AS OF MARCH 1976.

The practice of LEAA has been to issue two kinds of documents containing NCS results. The first is a preliminary report designed to release basic survey results soon after collection, processing, tabulation, and initial analysis have been completed. These reports are brief; these texts highlight gross survey findings and are supported by a small number of tables. Final reports, the second category, are more detailed with respect to the number of topics discussed and, in some cases, with respect to the depth of the analysis.

A third (anticipated) kind of publication will describe change over time in NCS victimization levels. Both annual change in national levels as derived from the NCS and estimated change based on city-level surveys conducted at different time points will be presented. No documents of this third type have been issued as of March 1976, although such reports are in preparation.

A complete list of released NCS reports follows:

Preliminary reports

Crime in Eight American Cities: Advance Report, July 1974 (September 1974)

Crime in the Nation's Five Largest Cities: Advance Report, April 1974 (April 1973)

Criminal Victimization in the United States: Advance Report January–June 1973, November 1974 (December 1973)

Criminal Victimization in the United States: Advance Report 1973, May 1975 (June 1974)

Criminal Victimization Surveys in 13 American Cities, June 1975 (April 1974)

Final Reports

Criminal Victimization Surveys in the Nation's Five Largest Cities, April 1975 (April 1973)

A report is classified as preliminary either if it is titled "advance" or if, according to the document, there will be a more detailed publication on the same survey issued later. Two dates are given with each report. The first is the date of publication, which is an approximate release date. The date in parentheses is that by which the field interviewing for the data therein had been completed.

For the city-level surveys, data produced through all field collection activities completed by December 1974 have been reported in at least one publication, either a preliminary or final report. The five largest-cities surveys are the only ones for which both a preliminary and a final report have been issued.

Two preliminary reports on the national component of the NCS have been released, one for the first half of 1973 and one for that entire year. No final or detailed report for the nation has been issued, but a final document for 1973 is in preparation, together with one on change in levels of NCS victimization from 1973 to 1974.

DISTRIBUTION OF NCS REPORTS

Approximate numbers of copies printed for five of the six released reports follow:

Crime in Eight American Cities: Advance Report	40,000
Crime in the Nation's Five Largest Cities: Advance Report	41,000
Criminal Victimization in the United States: Advance Report	
January–June 1973	13,000
Criminal Victimization in the United States: 1973 Advance Report	17,000
Criminal Victimization Surveys in the Nation's Five	
Largest Cities (Final Report)	11,000

As for future publications, LEAA currently plans to print approximately 10,000 copies of each document. Publications are distributed through three mechanisms. LEAA's NCJISS maintains a list of persons to whom copies are forwarded soon after the release date. Second, some reports, including *Five Largest Cities* (Final Report) and *Criminal Victimization in the United States: Advance Report January–June 1973*, are available through the U.S. Government Printing Office. And, all NCS publications are distributed by the National Criminal Justice Reference Service (NCJRS), a separate organization operating under contractual arrangements with LEAA.

NCJRS maintains files of individuals and institutions having interest in criminal justice and related topics. Announcements of various publications, including NCS reports, are mailed to those on the file, and they in turn can order copies of these NCS reports from NCJRS, free of charge. To illustrate the magnitude of this operation, summary statistics for distribution of *Criminal Victimization in the United States: January–June 1973* and *Criminal Victimization Surveys in 13 American Cities* are presented in Table 9. Note that the distribution list includes parties at all levels of government.

REVIEW OF NCS REPORTS

During our evaluation, we have observed an evolution in the quality of scientific reporting in NCS documents. Initial publications fell below standards reflected in documents produced by established government statistical agencies; more recent NCS reports, however, show a

TABLE 9   NCJRS Statistics[a] on Announcing and Distributing Two NCS Reports: *Criminal Victimization in the United States: Advance Report January–June 1973* and *Criminal Victimization Surveys in 13 American Cities*[b]

Class of Interested Parties	Number Receiving Announcements		Copies Ordered	
	U.S.	13 Cities	U.S.	13 Cities
LEAA headquarters	160	160	24	26
LEAA regional office	160	161	26	21
SPA (state planning agency)	793	784	147	168
Regional SPA office	662	659	255	216
College/university	4,309	4,309	1,719	1,665
Commercial/industrial	1,295	1,239	301	271
Citizen groups	571	569	121	103
Police				
Federal	1,497	1,493	433	365
State	1,328	1,331	365	296
City	2,317	2,325	636	500
Local	8,089	8,105	2,399	2,007
Courts				
Federal	369	371	79	63
State	1,398	1,404	269	223
City	1,253	1,253	230	193
Local	307	308	85	70
Correctional agency				
Federal	315	323	66	60
State	2,375	2,383	712	555
City	782	781	285	240
Local	291	290	101	77
Legislative body				
Federal	26	27	7	4
State	93	95	25	21
City	21	21	2	3
Local	42	42	8	9
Other government agency				
Federal	839	838	93	86
State	741	737	130	97
City	335	334	69	50
Local	347	345	89	73

TABLE 9 *Continued*

Class of Interested Parties	Number Receiving Announcements		Copies Ordered	
	U.S.	13 Cities	U.S.	13 Cities
Professional association				
Federal	191	189	59	51
State	159	158	42	30
City	68	68	8	17
Local	164	164	21	28
Crime prevention group				
Federal	43	43	9	14
State	77	80	11	23
City	89	89	19	22
Local	137	136	22	39
Other	—	—	857	233
TOTAL	31,563	31,614	9,724	7,920

[a]Current as of early 1976
[b]SOURCE: Staff of Statistics Division, NCJISS, LEAA.

considerable improvement over earlier ones. In fact, readers of, for example, *Criminal Victimization in the United States*[1] are provided with much of the background information that is essential for the reader to appreciate the basis of the data and findings. We hope that this trend will continue and that it will result in a series of quality publications in balance with the complexity and cost of NCS field operations.

Our review of NCS publications is in two parts. The first is devoted to the initial NCS reports issued by the LEAA: *Crime in the Nation's Five Largest Cities: Advance Report*[2] and *Crime in Eight American Cities: Advance Report,*[3] and it includes an evaluation of the LEAA press release[4] announcing *Five Largest Cities: Advance Report.* The second part of our review covers the remaining NCS publications issued by the LEAA, as of March 1976.

[1]U.S. Department of Justice, Law Enforcement Assistance Administration, *Criminal Victimization in the United States: 1973 Advance Report*, Vol. 1 (Washington, D.C.: U.S. Government Printing Office, May 1975).
[2]U.S. Department of Justice, Law Enforcement Assistance Administration, *Crime in the Nation's Five Largest Cities: Advance Report* (Washington, D.C.: U.S. Government Printing Office, April 1974).
[3]U.S. Department of Justice, Law Enforcement Assistance Administration, *Crime in Eight American Cities: Advance Report* (Washington, D.C.: U.S. Department of Justice, July 1974).
[4]U.S. Department of Justice, Law Enforcement Assistance Administration, Public Information Office, *News Release* April 15, 1974.

Our review focuses on the general content of NCS publications and on the way in which the NCS concept is presented. No detailed assessment of the treatment of particular substantive topics is contained in this chapter; however, a supporting illustration is included in Appendix F.

The panel reiterates here that NCS reports are written by members of the Crime Statistics Analysis Group, a unit administratively located within the Bureau of the Census. Ultimate control of the data-collection mechanism rests with the LEAA, and no changes in the basic sample design, field procedures, survey instruments, or tabulation specifications can be instituted without LEAA approval. LEAA is the sponsoring agency, and its staff would be expected to be more familiar than Census personnel with agency policy objectives for the NCS and to have administrative responsibility for the implementation of these objectives. Nonetheless, we have observed an unusual administrative distance between the Census professionals who write NCS reports and the responsible LEAA staff. We believe that some of the deficiencies in the NCS publication program, to which we refer in this chapter, are a consequence of this administrative distance.[5]

INITIAL REPORTS AND ANNOUNCEMENT

The first NCS report released by the LEAA was *Crime in the Nation's Five Largest Cities: Advance Report*. This document was announced by LEAA in a *News Release*, dated April 15, 1974. Because victimization surveys are a relatively new concept and because the *News Release* represented the first communication of NCS findings to the general public, this announcement merits attention.

In general, we conclude that the LEAA *News Release* did not do justice to the *Five Largest Cities: Advance Report*, on which it was based, and that the report itself did not do justice to the innovative survey effort on which it was based. For instance, the *News Release* contrasted "actual crimes" with crimes known to police in Chicago, Detroit, New York, Los Angeles, and Philadelphia.[6] The scope of the events covered in these surveys is not stated explicitly. Contrast should have been drawn between selected events reported to interviewers and selected events recorded by police. The use of the term "actual crime" is misleading and ignores both sampling and nonsampling constraints known to responsible Census–LEAA staff. Further-

[5]A recommendation concerning these administrative arrangements is provided later in this chapter.
[6]U.S. Department of Justice, LEAA, *News Release, op. cit.*, p. 1.

more, the use of the term implies that the NCS operational definition of crime is an accepted and accurate standard. Quite apart from our position that no such unique standard exists, we caution LEAA against equating NCS crimes with "actual" or "true" crimes.

The panel does not consider the misleading characterization in the *News Release* to be an aberration from the overall thrust of the document. The paragraphs below illustrate that the consistency with the scope and methodology behind the survey estimates are ignored:

According to the panel, about 45 percent of the 3.1 million criminal acts that occurred in the surveyed cities in 1972 were carried out against individuals, 40 percent against households and 15 percent against businesses.[7]

Crimes of theft constituted a majority of all incidents against persons, while about one-third of all personal incidents involved violence. In at least three-fourths of the personal incidents involving or threatening violence, the confrontation was between stangers. Burglary was the most common household and business crime.[8]

From the *News Release,* one reasonably could infer that burglary is more common among commercial establishments in the five largest cities than shoplifting, that 3.1 million criminal acts occurred in these cities in 1972, that a panel design was used in surveying these cities,[9] and that "For the first time we have in our hands reliable data relating to crime as seen by its victims."[10] These official expositions are not sufficiently consistent with the report to which they refer.

Moreover, the statement, "For example, these data tell us that there is a general feeling of apathy among citizens in reporting crime,"[11] implies that "apathy" measurements were taken on three categories of citizens:

1. citizens who experienced none of the crimes surveyed;

2. citizens who experienced one or more of the crimes surveyed and did report these experiences to the police; and

3. citizens who experienced a surveyed crime, reported it to interviewers, and stated that it was not made known to police. (A fourth

---

[7]*Ibid.*, p. 3.

[8]*Ibid.*

[9]The word "panel," a technical term, does not apply to the data-collection procedures used in the city-level surveys. Yet, it appears in reference to the cross-sectional data seven times in the 6-page *News Release:* page 2, paragraph 7, line 4, paragraph 8, line 3, paragraph 9, line 1; page 3, paragraph 1, line 5, paragraph 8, line 1; page 4, paragraph 3, line 1, paragraph 4, line 2.

[10]*Ibid.*, p. 2.

[11]*Ibid.*, p. 3.

logical category is that of citizens who reported to police one or more but not all crimes experienced.)

In the *Five Largest Cities: Advance Report*, data are presented only for the third (and residual fourth) category of citizens. It is worthwhile to illustrate the significance of the interview screening process used to produce this data.

The *Five Largest Cities: Advance Report*[12] indicates that household and commercial burglaries were reported to police, according to interviews, for a majority of victimizations. If the respondent reported no victimization to the interviewer for this and other surveyed crimes, no measurement was taken of the respondent's attitude toward reporting events to police. According to the Table 3 series in that document, a majority of individuals and households reported no NCS victimization for the crimes and time period surveyed. If those reporting the experience of victimization also reported to the interviewer that the crime was made known to police, no measurement of "apathy" was taken.

Personal larceny without contact was reported to interviewers as affecting in 1972 no more than 7.3 percent of the over-12 population in any of the five largest cities.[13] It is for this small (estimated) number of incidents that respondents were asked by interviewers if the crime was made known to the police, and, for approximately 75 percent of the incidents, respondents said, "No."[14] It is this set of respondents that were asked why they did not report it. That is, respondents acknowledged personal larceny incidents to interviewers at an average rate of less than 7.3 percent, and, for three-fourths of these incidents, respondents were asked why the incident was not reported to the police.

Another personal crime surveyed, robbery and attempted robbery with injury, was reported to interviewers by less than 8 per 1,000 of the over-12 residents in the five largest cities. Fifty percent or more of these incidents, according to survey interviewers, were known to police.[15]

For robbery and attempted robbery with serious assault, the range of NCS victimizations reported to police is from 58 to 73 percent

[12]U.S. Department of Justice, LEAA, *Five Largest Cities: Advance Report, op. cit.,* Table 8.
[13]*Ibid.,* Table 2.
[14]*Ibid.,* Table 8.
[15]*Ibid.,* Tables 2 and 8.

across the five cities. The survey-estimated over-12 population rate for this crime is between 3 and 5 per 1,000 for 1973 in the five cities.[16] Because individual respondents can and often do report to interviewers more than one victimization, one cannot conclude that between 3 and 5 per 1,000 of eligible respondents acknowledged a robbery victimization. If one equates the average robbery rate to the fraction of respondents reporting robberies to the survey, the fraction is overestimated. Moreover, "apathy" measurements can be counted more than once for respondents reporting to the survey more than one robbery victimization. Apart from these considerations, the fraction of respondents for whom "apathy" measures were taken for this crime plausibly must be small; an overestimate derived from victimization rate statistics ranges between one-sixth of 1 percent and one-fourth of 1 percent of the cities' over-12 populations, assuming conservatively 50 percent as the rate of nonreporting to police. The derivation of this range is illustrated in Table 10.

As Table 10 suggests, more than 99 percent of the surveyed population in Detroit reported to interviewers no robbery and attempted robbery with serious assault victimization during the reference period. The approximate fraction of 1 percent who reported this type of victimization to interviewers were asked if they also reported it to the police. For 28 percent of the incidents, respondents said that they did not. Only these respondents then were asked their attitudes toward reporting this particular crime to police. No attitude measurements were taken for the (estimated) 72 percent of victimizations that were coded as having been known to police, and no measurements of attitudes toward reporting this crime to police were taken for the (estimated) 99 percent who reported no victimization for the reference period surveyed.

TABLE 10 "Apathy" Measurement for Detroit Robbery and Attempted Robbery with Serious Assault

Interviewers:	"One (or more) victimization(s)?"		
Respondents:	"Yes" (0.5%)[a]→	*I:* "Reported to police?"	
	"No" (99.5%)	*R:* "No" (28% of 0.5%)→ *I:*	"Reason(s)
		"Yes" (72% of 0.5%)	for not
			reporting?"

[a]Percentages in this chart are based on victimization rates. not fractions of individual respondents. and thus the figures are overestimates of fractions of respondents.

[16]*Ibid.*

Without commenting here upon the reliability of these estimates, or upon the validity of the measure referred to in the *News Release* as "apathy," we agree that the *News Release* statement on the "general feeling of apathy among citizens in reporting crime" was not based on the city-level victimization survey data available to the LEAA Public Information Office.

Our criticisms of the *News Release* have been of two main types: (a) the limitations of the referent data base were not acknowledged, and (b) some important factual portions of the *News Release* were not faithful to the report being summarized. We conclude that many of these problems could have been avoided if the members of the Crime Statistics Analysis Group were not so far removed from those responsible for writing the *News Releases*. In the following paragraphs, we consider the extent to which the *Five Largest Cities* and *Eight American Cities* advance reports might have been made less susceptible to misunderstanding prior to their public release.

One statement on the opening page of the *Eight American Cities* report is that "approximately 44 percent of the recorded criminal acts were carried out against individuals, a comparable proportion was committed against households, and roughly 12 percent were directed against commercial establishmetns."[17] This statement is highly susceptible to misinterpretation. A reader of this report may not know that the cited statement refers only to events detected by the survey of residents of these cities. It seems reasonable to have in each forthcoming publication a statement about the crimes that are not surveyed and a rationale for the choice of those that are.

For any future reports on city-level surveys, we recommend that a discussion be included of implications of the omission of events committed against nonresidents and the inclusion of those committed against residents but occurring outside the city. Consideration might be given to excluding the latter from some tables or at least to indicating their magnitude. Otherwise, much of the rationale for conducting the studies in central cities is obscured.

Both the *Five Largest Cities* and *Eight American Cities* advance reports suffer from a lack of technical review. The possibility of sampling error is alluded to in the text, but the possibility of measurement error is not mentioned. It is stated in the "Foreword" of each report that subsequent and more comprehensive reports will include data on sampling errors and response rates, as well as technical details about the surveys.

[17]U.S. Department of Justice, LEAA, *Eight American Cities, op. cit.,* p. 1.

We recommend that subsequent reports on national and city-level victimization surveys, whether preliminary or detailed, routinely include technical notes on survey design, sampling and estimating methods, sampling and measurement error, response rates, evaluation materials, and other qualifications of the data.

The recently revised Circular A-46 on standards and guidelines for federal statistics, issued by the Office of Management and Budget, states, "A description of the survey plan, an assessment of the accuracy of the data published, and a statement explaining any limitations should be available to users of the data."[18] This statement is amplified in Exhibit B of the Circular, where it is further noted that these matters should be treated in reports in which the data are presented or referenced in those reports to other sources available to users of the data.

This standard presentation of supporting technical materials has been followed for some time by the principal statistical agencies, notably in reports released by the Census Bureau. These technical reports have differing degrees of coverage, depending upon the nature of the parent publication. For example, a most comprehensive technical description of the Current Population Survey (CPS) appears in the Census Bureau Technical Paper No. 7;[19] an intermediate, non-mathematical, less theoretically oriented version has been published and widely distributed in *Concepts and Methods Used in Manpower Statistics from the Current Population Survey*,[20] a joint publication of the Census Bureau and the Bureau of Labor Statistics (BLS). A further significant guideline in this area is the recently published Census Technical Paper No. 32,[21] entitled *Standards for Discussion and Presentation of Error in Data*.

Another good example of a technical appendix in a monthly periodical is the material in *Employment and Earnings*,[22] published by the

---

[18]Executive Office of the President, Office of Management and Budget, "Standards and Guidelines for Federal Statistics," Revised Circular A-46, May 3, 1974.

[19]U.S. Department of Commerce, Bureau of the Census, *The Current Population Survey: A Report on Methodology*, Technical Paper No. 7 (Washington, D.C.: U.S. Government Printing Office, 1963).

[20]U.S. Department of Commerce, Bureau of the Census, *Concepts and Methods Used in Manpower Statistics from the Current Population Survey*, Current Population Reports, Series P-23, No. 22 (Washington, D.C.: U.S. Government Printing Office, June 1967).

[21]Census Technical Paper No. 32 was published in the *Journal of the American Statistical Association*, Vol. 70(Part II), No. 351, September 1975.

[22]For example, see U.S. Department of Labor, Bureau of Labor Statistics, *Employment and Earnings*, Vol. 22, No. 9 (Washington, D.C.: U.S. Government Printing Office, March 1976).

BLS. The National Center for Health Statistics (NCHS) regularly issues descriptive technical materials with rather extensive separate reports[23] and lesser technical appendices in each of its substantive reports.[24]

It is recognized that the LEAA *Five Largest Cities* and *Eight American Cities* advance reports are preliminary releases, but even a preliminary release should carry a brief description of the survey methodology and offer at least modest information on sampling error and other known qualifications on the substantive data.

Insofar as the victimization estimates are dependent on memory, these estimates are subject to errors of memory decay and of forward and backward telescoping. According to LEAA's pretest results, for victimizations reported to police, victims are better able subsequently to recall robbery than burglary, burglary than theft, and theft than assault. The accuracy of recall, defined as the ability to match an incident in time with the police record of the same event, is reported in the LEAA pretest results as varying by type of crime and as varying appreciably by length of time elapsing from the event.

NCS reports should include some discussion of the best suppositions as to measurement error, pending more rigorous methodological checks.

We agree that the questions addressed in the *Five Largest Cities* and *Eight American Cities* advance reports were not stated in such a way as to link text and tables. The introductory remarks in each report refer to a range of topics that might be addressed by victimization surveys, but the reader is not informed as to the organization of topics in these particular reports. We consider the "Table of Contents" in *Crimes and Victims*[25] to be an adequate model of substantive organization, ranging logically over surveys, cities, crimes, vic-

---

[23]For example, see National Center for Health Statistics, "Health Survey Procedure: Concepts, Questionnaire Development, and Definitions in the Health Interview Survey," *Vital and Health Statistics*, Series 1, No. 2 (Washington, D.C.: U.S. Government Printing Office, May 1964).

[24]For example, see National Center for Health Statistics, *Current Estimates from the Health Interview Survey, United States 1969*, Series 10, No. 63 (Washington, D.C.: U.S. Government Printing Office, April 1973); and *Body Weight, Stature, and Sitting Height: White and Negro Youth 12–17 Years*, Series 11, No. 126 (Washington, D.C.: U.S. Government Printing Office, August 1973).

[25]Kalish, Carol B., *Crimes and Victims: A Report on the Dayton–San Jose Pilot Survey of Victimization* (Washington, D.C.: U.S. Department of Justice, Law Enforcement Assistance Administration, 1974). Note: This is a report on NCS pretest activities and, therefore, it is not considered to be part of the routine NCS publication series.

tims, offenders, and community attitudes. A clear initial statement, in subsequent advance and detailed reports, of the topics to be covered in the report, along with the generous use of subheadings and transitional sentences, would give the reader a clearer impression of highlighted findings.

The inclusion of definitions in each of the two preliminary reports is helpful but the distinctions among victims, incidents, victimization, victimization rate, and victim rate are not sufficiently clear.

Although the *Five Largest Cities* and *Eight American Cities* advance reports are the initial publications in a series, an effort should be made to be more precise in the distinction among victims, victimizations, and incidents.[26]

Thus far, we have reviewed only the preliminary NCS publications, as of September 30, 1974, and the early public announcement of this series. In numerical, and possibly in political, terms, the major consumers of this series are likely to be the readers of news releases and press accounts and the audiences of newscasts. If LEAA's official releases continue to highlight the ratios of survey to police statistics for the crimes covered, significant victim-based findings that now cannot be derived from administrative statistics may not be brought to the attention of the public.

For example, scrutiny has been deflected from the finding that, in terms of disposition to report NCS victimizations to police,[27] the LEAA data reveal a startling degree of uniformity in the five largest cities in the nation—ranging across these cities from 33 to 39 percent for personal crimes, 44 to 49 percent for household crimes, and 73 to 80 percent for commercial crimes surveyed (i.e., percent of victimizations that respondents claim were known to police). Why would residents of Chicago, Los Angeles, New York, Philadelphia, and Detroit—who may differ markedly with respect to variables assumed to be associated with victimization—exhibit this degree of uniformity in their dispositions to report those victimizations to the responsible officials of their cities? This, it seems to us, is the type of finding that argues for the continuation of LEAA's new statistical series. We agree that the space devoted to Federal Bureau of Investigation (FBI)

---

[26]For an excellent discussion of the choice rates for calculating crime statistics, see Albert J. Reiss, Jr., "Measurement of the Nature and Amount of Crime," in *Studies in Crime and Law Enforcement in Major Metropolitan Areas*, Vol. 1 (Report of the President's Commission on Law Enforcement and Administration of Justice), Field Surveys III (Washington, D.C.: U.S. Government Printing Office, 1967).

[27]U.S. Department of Justice, LEAA, *Five Largest Cities: Advance Report, op. cit.,* Table 8.

comparisons in the early *News Release* did not promote the new series and, indeed, may have served it poorly.[28]

The victim-based crime counts and the FBI counts are noncomparable in some known respects. For example, LEAA-sponsored city surveys include crimes reported to have been experienced while residents were outside their central city jurisdictions, balanced to an unknown extent by crimes against nonresidents in these cities. Some of the former crimes would be excluded from FBI counts for the same jurisdictions, while the latter could be included. Until the magnitude of this and other points of noncomparability between the two series is assessed, we recommend on methodological grounds alone that LEAA not provide for the public its own comparison of the two series.

MORE RECENT REPORTS

NCS documents issued after the *Five Largest Cities* and *Eight American Cities* advance reports show a substantial improvement in quality. We commend LEAA and the Crime Statistics Analysis Group for the improved quality of the later reports, especially given the pressures of time and the lack of analytic resources that have plagued this fledgling statistical series.

The "Preface" of *Criminal Victimization in the United States: 1973 Advance Report*[29] contains an abbreviated description of the NCS concept. The body of the report comprises approximately a dozen pages of descriptive text, together with several tables, highlighting some basic survey findings. There are 12 tables in an appendix intended to provide supporting evidence for statements in the text; about one-half of these tables present NCS personal victimization rates cross-classified by sex, race, age, marital status, or family income. Other appendix material includes definitions of crimes surveyed and terms used, some information on sources of data, estimation procedures, the treatment of series victimizations, and comment on the variability of data.

The listing above illustrates that the recent publications address the essential elements necessary to indicate the quality of the NCS data. These elements, however, need to be expanded in order to attain the

[28]Aside from the April *News Release,* a table comparing counts based on the victimization surveys and those derived from FBI statistics appears in the *LEAA Newsletter,* Vol. 4, No. 6, December 1974, p. 5.
[29]U.S. Department of Justice, LEAA, *Criminal Victimization in the United States: 1973 Advance Report, op. cit.,* pp. iii–vii.

standards reflected in more established government report series, a number of which are cited in the previous section. This is especially the case because none of the reports released to date contains references to methodological documents to which the reader can turn for more information.

As for information presented in the reports, inaccurate and imprecise statements persist. The following example appears in the advance report on the national survey:

a criminal act began as a burglary would be classified as robbery if the burglar was surprised by members of the household and, in turn, threatened them.[30]

Under current NCS classification procedures, unlawful or forcible entry of a home, whether or not attended by theft, is an act of burglary. If the burglar either harmed or demonstrated an intent to harm any household member through, for example, a verbal threat, then the event would be classified as assault or attempted assault. The act would be classified as robbery only if theft or attempted theft was accompanied by force or the threat of force. This, the event described in the quoted statement would be coded, according to NCS classification procedures, as burglary, not robbery, because a necessary element to classify it as a robbery is absent.

Another area of continuing imprecision concerns the exposition of victimization rates. We argue in this chapter and throughout this report against statements equating victimization rates with probabilities of being victimized. We find statements of the following type throughout the recently released NCS reports:

Often viewed as an indicator of the probability of being victimized, victimization rates for selected groups. . . .[31]

One clear improvement shown by more recent NCS publications is the inclusion of tables of sampling errors. The presentation in Appendix II of the *Five Largest Cities* (Final Report) is an adequate introduction to the use of standard errors, but the discussion of statistical significance in the preface of the report is flawed. For example:

Analytical statements in this report involving comparisons have met the test

[30]*Ibid.*, p. v.
[31]U.S. Department of Justice, Law Enforcement Assistance Administration, *Criminal Victimization Surveys in the Nation's Five Largest Cities* (Final Report) (Washington, D.C.: U.S. Government Printing Office, April 1975), p. 22.

that the differences are equal to or greater than two standard errors or, in other words, the chances are at least 95 out of 100 that the difference reported is a true one and not due to sampling variability.[32]

The referenced test is at the 5 percent level. That is, if there is no difference (i.e., the two statistics being contrasted have the same expected value), then the probability is 0.95 that the estimated magnitude of the difference will not exceed two standard errors. Of course, if one selects the largest pairwise difference from a set of more than two estimates, the noted probability that the difference will be less than two standard errors is less than 95 percent (under the hypothesis that the expected values of all estimates in the set are the same). In the statement above, there is confusion between the level of the test and its power. The power is the probability that the observed difference will exceed two standard errors when the expected difference is in fact not zero. In general, the power of this test, which depends on the magnitude of the expected difference, can be as small as 5 percent and is not necessarily 95 percent, as asserted in the cited statement. Moreover, without any prior information, one cannot make a probabilistic statement about the actual difference given the outcome of this test.

Another problem with the quoted passage is that the outcome of the statistical test by implication is attributed to a *true* difference. In victimization surveys, as with all surveys, reality is merely tapped through the measurement process. We hold that victim experiences are reported to interviewers with differential biases across subgroups of respondents, across categories of victimizations, and across different elapsed times from the event and the interview. Assumptions concerning the inferential process should be made as explicit as possible in NCS official reports.

Consider, for example, that Detroit victimization rates for robbery and assault are estimated 32 and 33 per 1,000 for residents ages 12 and over, respectively.[33] These rates are offered as evidence in support of the following inference: Robberies and assaults were experienced at approximately equal rates by the surveyed population. This inference would be discredited if one knew that there is a differential bias in respondent reports to interviewers of robbery and assault experiences. We maintain that it is LEAA's and Census' responsibility in conveying NCS results to go beyond merely testing for statistical

---

[32]*Ibid.*, p. iv.
[33]*Ibid.*, p. 69, Table 8b.

significance. The assumptions on which such tests are based should be examined within the context of what is known about victimization surveys, in general, and what has been indicated by pretest and pilot studies for the NCS, in particular.

The above illustration is an example of a more general issue: the treatment of nonsampling errors in NCS publications. In the more recent reports, one finds brief discussions of probable sources of nonsampling errors in victimization surveys. Such discussions, which are in the introductory and appendix sections, contain no quantitative information, and qualitative relationships seldom are mentioned. The discussion remains isolated in peripheral parts of the reports and is not cited nor taken into explicit account in analytical sections of the documents. No references enable the reader to review for himself what is known about nonsampling errors in the NCS or in other victimization surveys.

With regard to nonsampling errors, there is one area about which we consistently have been concerned: inferences on relationships between victims and offenders. Evidence produced through pretests sponsored by LEAA suggests that there exists differential reporting of events by victim–offender relationship. In particular, pretest findings indicate that, given an event was recorded by police officials, it is more likely to be detected by the survey in the case that the offender was a stranger to the victim than if the offender was not a stranger, implying that the measurement process is biased in this respect. Albeit the evidence is derived from small samples, it is consistent with findings derived from other victim surveys. Moreover, it is consistent with expectations based on our experience with the interview process.

As for substantive considerations, it is our opinion that violence among persons who are acquainted is at least as common as that among strangers. This opinion is in agreement with conclusions of the 1966 President's Commission on Law Enforcement and Administration of Justice[34] and with findings of individual researchers cited in Chapter 3 of this report. The extent to and circumstances under which violence is perceived as criminal in nature remains a major empirical question, to be sure.

Proportions of violent events in which the assailant was said to be a stranger have been reported consistently in NCS publications without

[34]The President's Commission on Law Enforcement and Administration of Justice, *Task Force Report: Crime and Its Impact—An Assessment* (Washington, D.C.: U.S. Government Printing Office, 1967), pp. 81–82.

caveats as to the probable bias of the quotients.[35] For example, one finds the following assertion in *Criminal Victimization in the United States: 1973 Advance Report:*

For 1973, about two-thirds of all personal crimes of violence involved a confrontation between strangers. Table B gives the percent of victimizations committed by strangers for crimes of rape, robbery, and assault.[36]

The fraction, two-thirds, surfaced in a speech delivered by President Ford in his June 1975 Message to Congress,[37] an illustration of the importance attached to crime statistics at the highest policy levels of government. NCS results on comparative levels of stranger and nonstranger violence have and can be expected to receive wide attention. For instance, an NCS table showing victimization rates, by type of crime and by relationship of victim and offender, appears in the 1975 *Statistical Abstract of the United States.*[38]

We are not concerned that there might exist a small bias in this stranger-violence quotient; we are not quibbling over whether 60 or 70 percent of violent crimes reported to NCS interviewers are attributed to strangers. Rather, we are concerned that a more appropriate figure, adjusted for differential reporting of victimizations according to relationship between victim and offender, could be less than one-half; if so, the policy implications would appear to be quite different.

Another topic that merits attention here is the treatment in NCS publications of "series" victimizations. A set of victimizations recounted by a respondent during a household interview is classified as one series victimization in case:

1. there are at least three separate events in the set;
2. each event is considered similar in nature; and,
3. the respondent is unable to recall details, such as the month of occurrence of the individual events.

One incident report is completed for each series victimization, and the details on the form, according to interviewer instructions, refer only

---

[35]For example, see U.S. Department of Justice, LEAA, *Five Largest Cities* (Final Report), *op. cit.,* pp. 13–14.

[36]U.S. Department of Justice, LEAA, *Criminal Victimization in the United States: 1973 Advance Report,* p. 2.

[37]The speech is reproduced in full in the *LEAA Newsletter,* Vol. 5, No. 1.

[38]U.S. Department of Commerce, Bureau of the Census, *Statistical Abstract of the United States: 1975* (Washington, D.C.: U.S. Government Printing Office, 1975), pp. 152–53.

to the most recent event in the set. Events within series are not included in general NCS victimization counts, but are relegated to special tabulations reserved exclusively for series victimizations.

We discussed this procedure in Chapter 6; our purpose here is to examine the manner in which the significant finding of large numbers of victimizations within series has been presented in published NCS documents.

In the introductory sections of more recent NCS publications, series victimizations are discussed briefly,[39] but they are excluded from the main analysis. In *Criminal Victmization in the United States: 1973 Advance Report,* series events are dismissed as being "usually minor."[40] This assertion is contradicted by data in the same document, as illustrated in Table 11.

Recall that each series victimization accounts for at least three individual victim-events whereas each nonseries victimization accounts for exactly one victim-event. Almost half the personal series victimizations fall in the violent category, as contrasted with the slightly more than one-fourth of nonseries events classified as violent. The relation is even more pronounced for NCS city-level survey results, as illustrated by Chicago data presented in Table 12. Note that according to the Chicago table about two-thirds of personal series victimizations are placed in the violent category, as compared with about one-third of the nonseries.

There is a procedural factor that might have an effect on the apparent degree of seriousness of series victimizations. When an interviewer is recording the details of a set of events classed as a series, the respondent is asked to recount only details of the most recent event in the series. Perhaps some respondents are inclined to recall details of the most violent event as opposed to the last event. If so, this would tend to bias series victimizations in the more serious direction, at least within the personal crime category. In any case, it does not appear to us that events reported as series are "usually minor." In fact, they would seem to be serious relative to those recorded in the NCS as nonseries victimizations.

The importance of series victimizations also is discounted in NCS publications by the observation that the number of series events is

---

[39]See, for example, U.S. Department of Justice, LEAA, *Five Largest Cities* (Final Report), *op. cit.,* p. 4, and *Criminal Victimization in the United States: 1973 Advance Report, op. cit.,* p. iv.

[40]U.S. Department of Justice, LEAA, *Criminal Victimization in the United States: 1973 Advance Report, op. cit.,* p. iv.

TABLE 11   Percent Distribution of Personal Series Victimizations and Victimizations Not in Series: United States[a]

Victimization	Series		Nonseries	
Violent	46.3		27.1	
Rape	0.8		0.8	
Robbery	4.9		5.5	
Assault	40.6		20.8	
Aggravated		12.8		8.3
Simple		27.9		12.5
Theft	53.7		72.9	
TOTAL	100		100	

[a]SOURCE: U.S. Department of Justice, LEAA, *Criminal Victimization in the United States: 1973 Advance Report,* Appendix Table 1.

small relative to NCS counts of nonseries victimizations. For instance, in the 1973 national report, one finds:

In 1973 series victimizations comprised about 5 percent of all victimizations reported in the survey.[41]

In the above sense series victimizations are small in number, but that is not to say they are unimportant. Aggravated assault victimization rates would be increased by as much as 70 percent if individual aggravated assaults now aggregated in series counts were included in the main tally. Readers of NCS publications are not likely to be aware of this, however, because there are no statistics published to date on the number of events within series. The apparent existence of substantial numbers of entities—be they persons, households, or commercial establishments—that are victimized on repeated occasions is one of the most significant findings yet to emerge from the NCS operation. No comparable data on the important phenomenon of multiple victimization are available from other sources. Therefore, we urge LEAA to devote more attention to this general topic in future NCS publications.

SUMMARY AND GENERAL CONCLUSIONS

The general quality of scientific reporting reflected by the first six NCS publications has shown a substantial improvement during the 2-year period of our evaluation work. More recent publications contain all the necessary elements to enable a reader to assess in a generic sense

[41]*Ibid.*

the quality of the data contained therein. Although these elements are now included in NCS reports, they should be brought into sharper focus to provide a basis for a reader to make informed inferences and judgments on the quality of particular measures.

Because the victimization survey is a new technique, it is incumbent upon LEAA and Census to go a step beyond including general background information in NCS documents. Qualitative and, wherever possible, quantitative information on the victimization survey process should be integrated into descriptive and analytical discussions in the text. As to the presentation of tabular materials, elements bearing on their reliability and validity should be either reiterated or referenced in table headings or in footnotes. Caveats should address important factors such as the universe of events surveyed and the probable differential reporting across victimization categories and across population subgroups. In regard to NCS incident counts, phrases such as "actual crimes" and "all crimes" should be avoided.

We recognize that it is not feasible to cover many topics in any one NCS report and, therefore, that compromises must be made in the selection of topics and in the tabulation of supporting evidence. Together with the importance of a given topic to criminal justice policy and to the public, the strengths and weaknesses of the NCS survey method should weigh heavily in decisions on what to highlight in routine publications.

Once a topic has been selected for inclusion as a standard item in the NCS publication series or as an item for special exposition in a single report, specific tables or analyses should be available readily to in-house analysts in order for them to address particular subhypotheses related to a topic. There should be definitive links between

TABLE 12   Percent Distribution of Personal Series Victimizations and Victimizations Not in Series: Chicago[a]

Victimization	Series	Nonseries
Violent	64.1	35.7
Rape	—	1.8
Robbery	21.0	16.8
Assault	42.5	17.0
Aggravated	16.4	7.4
Simple	26.6	9.6
Theft	35.9	64.2
TOTAL	100	100

[a]SOURCE: U.S. Department of Justice, LEAA, *Five Largest Cities* (Final Report). Table 1 and Appendix V, Table VII.

questions asked and available evidence, and the evidence should be appropriate to investigate the given area. The presence or absence of statistical significance should not be used as a sole criterion for including or highlighting a data subset. Furthermore, since all questions that could be asked about a given topic obviously cannot be exhausted in a single NCS document, data should be presented in a form suitable for secondary analysis. For example, no table of percentages should appear unless the base of the percentages is available in the same document.

We contend that the perfunctory application of statistical significance tests in itself is not sufficient either to support or to refute a hypothesis. Indeed, we would much prefer to see five tables on a topic in which the NCS data consistently fall in the direction of a predicted result, but at the 80–90 percent significance level, than to see five pairwise comparisons included only because they each met an arbitrary level of significance. We think most students of crime statistics, in particular, and of survey methodology, in general, would agree with this position.

VICTIMIZATION RATES AS A BASIS FOR REPORTING AND INTERPRETING NCS RESULTS

NCS data are transmitted by the Bureau of the Census to LEAA and to the Crime Statistics Analysis Group by means of a set of standard tabulations, as referenced in survey documentation.[42] With a few minor exceptions, the variables in these tables are either victimization counts, victimization rates, and incident counts or functions of counts or rates. Transmission media are computer printouts and microfilm; no data in a form suitable for computer input, such as magnetic tape, are provided routinely to LEAA or to the analysis group. Official analyses are based directly on the tables. The operational implication of this arrangement is that if a substantive or methodological question is formulated that cannot be addressed with data already specified or tabulated it often goes unanswered. This arrangement is unsatisfactory to support analysis of survey results, especially in the case of a large-scale and relatively new operation like the NCS.

One important objective of the NCS is to explore multiple victimization. There are numerous important questions within this area. For

---

[42]See, for example, U.S. Department of Commerce, Bureau of the Census, *National Crime Survey Documentation* (Washington, D.C.: U.S. Government Printing Office, 1976).

example, consider the set of persons who were victims of robbery during a given time period. What is the probability that a random person will be a victim of robbery or some other crime during a subsequent time period? Is this probability greater or less than that for the entire population at risk? Given an arbitrary person in the same set, what is the probability that he will be assaulted during the same or subsequent time period? To what degree is a household victimization event an indicator of whether its members will be victims of other crimes? To what extent are the experiences of a given household member associated with other members of the same household? None of these questions can be addressed with available tabulations.

Quite apart from reducing LEAA's capability to satisfy its own objectives, the concentration on victimization and incident counts limits the utility of the NCS enterprise. Interested persons, whether criminologists, administrators, or members of the public at large, cannot obtain from official reports answers to elementary and obvious questions about victims of crime. For instance, an administrator in New York City will not find any statistics on the number of city households that were or were not victims of burglary during 1973 in the NCS tables,[43] nor in published reports. Answers to these and similar questions are central to understanding crime as it affects victims. A victimization survey is an excellent vehicle for producing data to address these issues, and, were the data tabulated appropriately, the NCS could address them.

The Crime Statistics Analysis Group staff is aware of many of the problems discussed here and elsewhere in this report, but, under current administrative arrangements, it is exceedingly difficult for that staff to initiate or effect changes required to alleviate them. Therefore, for substantive reasons, we urge LEAA and Census to reexamine the administrative structure within which official NCS reports are being produced.

We recommend that the staff that performs NCS analysis and report writing functions, whether LEAA employees or otherwise, have an active role in the management of the NCS. Specifically, the analytic staff should participate in the development of objectives for substantive reports and publication schedules. Once analytic plans are formulated, the analytic staff should have autonomy in specifying tabulations to be used in support of the analysis, and they should have direct access to complete NCS data files and to data processing

---

[43]U.S. Department of Commerce, Bureau of the Census, *National Crime Survey, Central Cities Sample Survey Documentation* (Washington, D.C.: U.S. Department of Commerce, May 1974).

resources. It should be the analytic staff's responsibility to formulate statistical or other criteria used in hypothesis testing. Finally, a feedback mechanism should be instituted through which the staff can influence decisions on the content of survey instruments, on field and code procedures, and on analytic and methodological research to be undertaken.

Second, the panel recommends that routine NCS tabulations include results on risk of victimization, particularly of multiple and series victimization, and that analysis of risk be part of NCS publications on a recurring basis.

The principal data in NCS publications to date are victimization rates and total counts of incidents. The NCS definition of victimization rate is the aggregate number of times (not counting events in series) individual units were victims of a specified crime during a given time period, divided by the number of units in the sampled universe. Units are either persons, households, or commercial establishments, and the universe is determined by the survey target population. An incident is a victim-event within the scope of the surveys that directly affects at least one member of the target population. Both incident counts and victimization rates are measures of the volume of NCS crimes. The incident count is the total number of events affecting the survey population, and the victimization rate is the average number of times a member of the target population is affected by an event. Both measures are defined in terms of a time period of interest.

Victimization rates and incident counts are similar to offense counts employed by the Federal Bureau of Investigation and published in its Uniform Crime Reports. Important facets of the impact of certain crimes on victims can be investigated with data collected through a population survey that cannot be examined with data currently available from Uniform Crime Reports and other sources. These questions, however, cannot be addressed with NCS data if these are limited either to statistics of the form of victimization rates, to total incidents, or to statistics that are functions of these quantities.

As noted earlier in this chapter, a reasonable measure of risk is the proportion of a population that are victims of a given crime or a set of crimes per time period. The victimization rate has been treated erroneously in the NCS publications as if it were that proportion. For example, LEAA's estimates of commercial burglary and robbery victimization rates for a 12-month period in Houston, Texas, appear in *Criminal Victimization in 13 American Cities*.[44] Survey estimates of

---

[44]U.S. Department of Justice, Law Enforcement Assistance Administration, *Criminal Victimization Surveys in 13 American Cities* (Washington, D.C.: U.S. Government Printing Office June 1975), p. 82.

burglary and robbery rates for retail establishments are 0.939 (coefficient of variation: 12.8 percent) and 0.339 (coefficient of variation: 20.1 percent), respectively. One might be tempted to interpret from the victimization rate that 93.9 percent of the Houston retail establishments, according to the survey, were burglary victims during the appropriate 12-month reference period. Quite aside from sampling variation, the interpretation would be wrong, because the victimization rate estimates the total number of times members of the population were victims of burglary, divided by the total population. That is, the rate estimates the average number of times a retail establishment selected at random from the population was victimized during the 12 months. The average value can be a substantial overestimate of risk, if defined as the proportion of the population victimized at least once.

For Houston, the combined survey victimization rate for burglary and robbery among retail establishments is 1.278 (not presented explicitly in the report). One can infer from the combined rate that the average number of times a firm was a victim of either burglary or robbery is 1.278; one also can infer that a substantial number of firms were victimized more than once.

Although the victimization rate is a reasonable summary statistic, more information is contained in a tabulation by number of times victimized than in the aggregate rate. Consider the estimates in Table 13 for retail establishments taken from the Houston Commercial Survey.

From Table 13 one would estimate the percentage of Houston retail establishments not victimized by either burglary or robbery to be 59 percent. To put it differently, some 41 percent of these establishments were either burglary or robbery victims at least once during the 12-month period of interest. These simple indicators of aggregate risk are more informative than is the average victimization rate (of 1.278 for burglary and robbery); simple arithmetic based on table entries and the aggregate rate of 1.278 will show that some 18 percent of retail establishments in Houston were victimized at least twice and that these 18 percent account for approximately 83 percent of the volume of burglary and robbery incidents detected by the survey among Houston's retail establishments. The average risk, as measured by the proportion victimized, is high, but the victimization rate gives a misleadingly inflated impression of risk unless it is qualified repeatedly in a text and is accompanied by other summary statistics.

Findings such as those in the above example have implications for other kinds of analyses. For instance, one set of statistics found in NCS publications is the percentage of victimizations detected by the surveys that were made known to police. The base of the percent is

TABLE 13 Number of Commercial Establishments Victimized by Robbery and Burglary, by Number of Times (1973): Houston Retail Establishments[a]

Number Victimized	Number Not Victimized	Burglary Only[b]				Robbery Only				Both Burglary and Robbery		
		1	2	3	4+	1	2	3	4+	2	3	4+
4,184	6,146	1,664	644	187	305	639	0	34	85	270	102	154

[a]SOURCE: NCS Tabulation 2A provided by the Statistics Division staff, NCJISS, LEAA. These survey estimates have been inflated to reflect the entire population of Houston retail establishments and have large sampling errors. Similar statistics are not available for persons or households surveyed in the NCS.

[b]Number victimized n times for n = 1, 2, 3, and 4 or more.

TABLE 14   Number of Persons Victimized by Robbery and Assault, by Number of Times (1970): Dayton[a]

Victims of Robbery and/or Assault	Total No. of Persons Victimized[b]	Persons Victimized Once	Persons Victimized Twice	Persons Victimized Three or More Times
Victims of robbery[c] (only)	2,530	2,490	d	d
Victims of robbery with assault (only)	1,740	1,710	d	d
Victims of robbery without assault (only)	800	780	d	d
Victims of assault (only)	11,610	9,320	1,530	760
TOTAL	14,600	11,810	1,870	910

[a]SOURCE: Kalish, *Crimes and Victims*, Table 18.
[b]"Victims of robbery with assault (only)" and "Victims of robbery without assault (only)" will not add to the total in most cases because of persons who were victims of both robbery with assault and robbery without assault.
[c]An incident of crime involving both robbery and assault is classified as a robbery.
[d]See table and explanation of statistically reliable numbers in Introduction to Appendix III of Kalish, *Crimes and Victims*.

the victimization, as opposed to the population unit; therefore, data on police awareness is linked to the event and not to population members. When a small fraction of victimized entities account for a large portion of incidents, as in the Houston example, the percentage known to police is weighted heavily by the characteristics of this small fraction and does not reflect the characteristics of the population of victims detected by the survey.

The Houston illustration was taken from the NCS city-level commercial survey data for which both the victimization rate and the percentage of population units victimized is large. We expect the same pattern to exist in the household surveys with regard to personal and to household victimizations. Table 14 is taken from the report on the Dayton pilot survey.[45] Among those persons victimized by either robbery or assault, approximately 18 percent were victimized at least twice and some 6 percent were involved in three or more events. Had the Dayton results been presented in terms of a victimization rate, as opposed to a *victim rate*, the implied risk would have increased by more than 30 percent, although only about 4 in 1,000 respondents in the Dayton survey recounted one or more assault or robbery victimizations.

These two illustrations suggest that substantial degrees of multiple victimization are being tapped by the NCS method and that multiple victimizations have a significant impact on the utility of a victimization rate. The rate can overestimate aggregate risk, measured at the

[45]Kalish, *op. cit.*

population-unit level, and it can mask the phenomenon of multiple victimization, an important finding in itself. Consequently, we urge that more appropriate measures than the victimization rate be used in NCS tabulations and publications for the objective of describing risk and that caution be applied to interpretation of the rate when it is used for objectives for which it may be better suited.

Although we are critical of some of the interpretations in NCS publications of victimization rates and incident counts, we do not intend to imply that these statistics have no place in the analysis of NCS data. These statistics are reasonable measures of, for example, total volume of events surveyed and of the proportion of total NCS events known to police. Moreover, we recognize that the decision to tabulate victimizations and incidents was made before the NCS field operations began and, hence, before anyone had experience with large-scale victimization surveys. Victimization rates were then attractive measures for the following reasons: Similar indicators are used in the Uniform Crime Reports, victimization rates are simple to compute, the combined rate for several crimes is the sum of the rates for the individual categories, and summed rates for adjacent time periods produce the rate for the combined time period. Too, when all tabulated statistics are in the form of victimizations and incidents, the magnitude of data processing is relatively small because the only files that must be maintained are those in which the victimization is the basic unit. Persons, households, and commercial establishments reporting no victimizations for the reference period can be eliminated from the files at early stages of processing, thus reducing the size of the files by several orders of magnitude.

Albeit these statistics offer considerable economy in producing data tabulations, we conclude that the potential of the NCS will not be exploited unless agency analysts have access to data in a more complete and suitable form.

Statistics provided in the Uniform Crime Reports are an important part of our national information system, but these administrative statistics provide little or no information on many elementary and basic questions in the area of victimization. The victimization survey method potentially offers new and complementary and supplementary information on the incidence and distribution of certain crimes and on their effects on the public. We agree that using procedures reflected in the Uniform Crime Reports as a model for NCS tabulations and official analyses is a disservice to the potential of the NCS.

For example, the Uniform Crime Reports by necessity treat the event, which is an offense, as the basic unit of analysis. The outstanding feature of the victimization survey method, however, is that it is based on the observation of population members—victims and nonvictims—and their characteristics. This fundamental feature allows for the population member to be the unit of analysis, as illustrated in this section. We contend that the expansion of the dimensions of the NCS tabulations and official analyses into this broad terrain will be a major step towards establishing the NCS as a fundamental component of policy formulation in the criminal justice area.

8   Assessment of Objectives of the National Crime Surveys

INTRODUCTION

The purposes of this chapter are to set out a list of NCS objectives, advanced by LEAA and Census staff involved in the development phase and to summarize briefly some aspects of the design and analysis of the NCS that appear to impinge upon the achievement of those objectives.

The list of objectives has been culled from a number of papers written over the past 4 years or so; the principal sources are the following:

Richard W. Dodge and Anthony G. Turner, "Methodological Foundations for Establishing a National Survey of Victimization," a paper presented at the 1971 meeting of the American Statistical Association, August 23–26, Fort Collins, Colorado (henceforth cited as Dodge and Turner).

George E. Hall, "The Program of the Statistics Division of the Law Enforcement Asistance Administration," a paper presented at the 1971 meeting of the American Statistical Association, August 23–26, Fort Collins, Colorado (henceforth cited as Hall).

Anthony G. Turner and Richard W. Dodge, "Surveys of Personal and Organizational Victimization," a paper presented at the Symposium on Studies of Public Experience, Knowledge and Opinion of Crime and Justice, March 16–18, 1972, Washington, D.C. (henceforth cited as Turner and Dodge).

Charles R. Work, "Objectives of the NCS and of Victimization Surveys," part of an internal document prepared for Mr. Work, dated March 7, 1975 (see Charles

Kindermann's letter dated April 1, 1975, addressed by Bettye Penick) (hereafter cited as Work). (Internal statement of objectives, see Appendix G.)

Crime Statistics Analysis Group, Bureau of the Census, "Presentation on Analytical Issues," a paper prepared for the panel meeting on August 14, 1975 (hereafter cited as Appendix A).

Wesley G. Skogan, "The Use of Victimization Surveys in Criminal Justice Planning," published in *Quantitative Tools for Criminal Justice Planning,* ed. by Leonard Oberlander (Washington, D.C.: U.S. Government Printing Office, 1975), Chapter 2, p. 13 (hereafter cited as Skogan).

Naturally the objectives mentioned in these papers overlap, even though they may be stated in different ways. We have therefore tried to group together those statements that seem to deal with broadly similar points, giving references in each case to the source of the particular statement quoted.

Our review here is of initial objectives that have been suggested by some of the people directly responsible for the NCS. But it is important to note that only one of these six papers—that written for Charles R. Work by Charles Kindermann—can be regarded as giving, in any sense, an official statement of those objectives. Skogan's paper, in particular, deals for the most part with possible uses of victimization surveys in general and not with the NCS in its present form. It was, however, written while Skogan, who is a professor of political science at Northwestern University, was a Visiting Fellow at the National Institute of Law Enforcement and Criminal Justice. It thus draws on his knowledge of the present series and its development, and it gives clear statements of many points made by others in connection with the NCS.

These objectives are mostly ones claimed for the NCS at its inception: They are not the only objectives that publicly funded victimization surveys might have or that the NCS itself might have in the future. Since those initial objectives can be said to have provided at least part of the motivation for the NCS, it seems reasonable to assess the surveys to date by the corresponding yardstick, although other yardsticks might also be used. An interim report of the panel (First Quarter, 1975, "Progress Report," p. 64) pointed out, "After the survey has been underway for a period, there may well be second thoughts on a number of points. New or modified objectives may emerge; new evidence or understanding may indicate need for design changes." In Chapter 9, therefore, we describe some important objectives for the future of the NCS, and we sketch the shift in perspective that would underlie those new objectives.

MEASUREMENT IN THE INCIDENCE OF CRIME
AND CHANGES IN CRIME RATES OVER TIME

It has been argued that the NCS can "provide measures of the incidence of serious crime. . . ." (Dodge and Turner, p. 1); that it can "provide a reliable statistical series on the amount of dangerous crime in the United States. . . ." (Work, p. 1); and that—in combination with UCR data—victimization survey findings could provide "statistical indicators as comprehensive as the ones reported by the federal government in labor and agricultural statistics" (Turner and Dodge, p. 3; see also Hall, p. 1).

The basic aim of measuring crime—of counting or at least estimating the numbers of criminal acts committed in different places and times—has, of course, a long history. More recently, it provided part of the rationale for the development of the present UCR system. Indeed, a major claim made for the victim survey method is that it overcomes the deficiencies of the UCR as a measuring instrument—that many crimes are never reported to the police, or, if reported, are not recorded by them so as to be reflected in the official statistics that comprise the UCR.

The validity of this objective of measuring serious crime will be considered further below. Here, we point out that the present NCS fails to attain this primary objective, for at least five separate reasons.

1. First, the NCS survey results can at best be used to estimate some crime rates (or crime frequencies). The NCS in its present form does not measure some of the most frequent (e.g., so-called white-collar crime, thefts from workplaces, shoplifting, vandalism, and so on) and some of the most serious (e.g., homicide and child molestation). But there are many forms of crime that can, in principle, be measured by a victimization survey, but that are not included in either the NCS or the *Uniform Crime Reports:* Examples include vandalism, obscene telephone calls, and possibly certain forms of fraud and public disorder. To the extent that these kinds of crime are objects of public concern, they should certainly be included in the surveys: A measuring instrument should be used to measure what it can measure and not just those things that are already being measured (even if inaccurately) by another instrument.

2. There is some emerging evidence that data from the NCS can be used, in conjuction with the UCR, to provide fuller information about certain trends in crime. For example, a perennial question is the extent to which observed changes in the levels of crime as measured

by the UCR are due to an increase in the proportions of incidents reported to the police or due to an increase in the recording by the police of crimes reported or known to them. Table 15, which is based on both NCS and UCR data, suggests wide variation across cities in the proportion of crimes reported to NCS interviewers that also are recorded by police, at least for robbery.

Table 15 is not, strictly speaking, an example of using the NCS itself as a measure of crime *per se,* and the comparison in this table probably is legitimate only for particular kinds of offenses that are reasonably well-reported to survey interviewers. The results of the pretests carried out by the Census Bureau before the NCS began (discussed in Chapter 3 of this report) strongly suggest that certain sorts of assaults, and some types of personal thefts, are seriously undercounted in the current NCS. The amount of bias (in terms of victim–offender relationships, time and place of occurrence of incidents, and so forth) introduced by this understatement is at present unknown, as is the magnitude of the understatement itself. Unfortunately, there is some reason to think that both may be serious. At the present time it is unclear how far the underreporting to interviewers of certain incidents is due to memory failure or to other forms of response bias in the narrow sense of that term and how far it is due to differences between respondents in the definition of particular types of incidents (for example, a subcultural tendency in certain groups to regard some physical violence as permissible or, at any rate, non-deviant rather than as an "assault").

Underreporting in itself deserves much further investigation, as indicated by Figure 1.

Figure 1 shows the relationship between the levels of aggravated assault reported to NCS interviewers in 26 cities and the levels of the same type of crime recorded by police in those same cities. It will be seen that these two measures of aggravated assault are negatively correlated: Those cities with relatively high UCR rates tend to have relatively low NCS rates, and *vice versa.* Many factors—including patterns of response bias, demographic characteristics of the 26 cities, reporting to police and recording by police—may be involved in the explanation of this curious finding. But until findings of this type are explained—and, in particular, until the impact of underreporting to NCS interviewers is better understood—comparisons of the NCS with the UCR for other than methodological purposes would appear to be highly suspect.

3. Another limitation on comparison of NCS and UCR data stems from the jurisdictional base of the latter's data set. So far as the

TABLE 15 Comparison of Survey-Estimated Robberies and UCR Robbery Statistics for 26 Cities

City	(1) Survey-Estimated Robberies	(2) Estimated Percent Reported to Police	(3) "Reported" Survey Robberies: (1) × (2)	(4) UCR Robberies	(5) UCR as Percent of Survey "Reported" Robberies, 100 × (4)/(3)
Newark	8,000	55.9	4,472	5,158	115.0
Washington, D.C.	10,070	73.0	7,351	7,171	97.6
St. Louis	7,800	66.0	5,148	4,900	95.2
Cleveland	13,200	59.9	7,906	5,813	73.5
Detroit	36,100	65.5	23,645	17,170	72.6
Los Angeles	36,400	55.1	20,056	14,241	71.0
Baltimore	20,400	65.8	13,423	9,532	71.0
New York	191,400	59.5	113,883	78,202	68.7
Miami	4,890	76.0	3,716	2,389	64.3
Chicago	64,100	57.5	36,858	23,531	63.8
Boston	15,162	65.0	9,855	5,969	60.6

	(1)	(2)			(4)
Pittsburgh	6.331	69.9	4.425	2.647	59.8
Portland	5.700	52.4	2.986	1.756	58.8
Buffalo	5.590	58.5	3.270	1.924	58.8
Dallas	7.600	63.8	4.848	2.738	56.5
Oakland	7.899	65.8	5.197	2.879	55.4
Houston	18.244	62.5	11.402	6.265	54.9
New Orleans	9.808	61.0	5.982	3.033	50.7
San Francisco	18.034	52.8	9.522	4.817	50.6
Denver	7.400	57.4	4.247	2.090	49.2
Atlanta	8.000	71.2	5.696	2.640	46.3
Minneapolis	7.245	61.9	4.484	1.928	44.2
San Diego	6.339	56.6	3.587	1.422	39.6
Cincinnati	6.082	58.0	3.527	1.386	39.4
Philadelphia	44.000	58.9	25.916	9.710	37.5
Milwaukee	9.302	61.1	5.684	1.085	19.1

SOURCES: Household and commercial robbery incident totals [column (1)] are taken from NCS city advance reports. Column (2) gives percentages of incidents mentioned to interviewers that were said by respondents to have been reported to police. UCR robbery statistics [column (4)] are taken from the appropriate UCR data. Note that estimates based on NCS data are subject to sampling errors of unknown magnitude. The rates shown in this table and in Figure 1 were calculated by Wesley Skogan, of Northwestern University, while a Visiting Fellow of the National Institute of Law Enforcement and Criminal Justice at LEAA. Both will appear in Wesley G. Skogan, "Crime and Crimes Rates," in Sample Surveys of the Victims of Crime, ed. by Wesley G. Skogan (Cambridge, Mass.: Ballinger Publishing Co., 1976), and are reproduced here with permission.

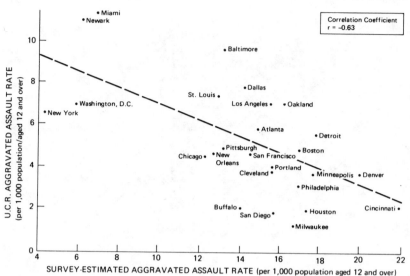

FIGURE 1 Relationship between survey and official aggravated assault rates for 26 cities.

national component of the NCS is concerned, the domain of the surveys is not (indeed, was not meant to be) identical with any single jurisdiction or set of jurisdictions. But most law enforcement in this country is locally organized, and the relevant "jurisdictions" (states, counties, cities, or police beats) do not correspond with, and at present cannot easily be related to, the present design of the NCS. In principle, it would be possible to disaggregate the NCS results so as to produce estimates of certain crime rates for certain jurisdictions or combinations of jurisdictions (e.g., states or regions); in practice, however, questions of sampling error and issues of confidentiality now make this impracticable.

The city-level surveys conducted as part of the NCS come closer, of course, to the ideal of providing estimated crime rates for a jurisdiction. Even they, however, fall short of this ideal for several reasons. To begin with, these surveys ask respondents to report all crimes committed against them, whether or not they were committed within their city of residence (the only crimes excluded at present are those committed against the respondent while he was outside the United States or stationed on a military base or institutionalized). Second, the city-level surveys do not measure victimization within cities of persons residing outside those cities (i.e., not only suburban residents but tourists or other visitors). In some cities, victimization of nonresidents constitutes an important fraction of all the crime with which the police deal; but that kind of "crime in a jurisdiction" is not now measurable by the NCS city-level surveys.

Some of the uses of area-specific victimization data could be met through attachment of the Census neighborhood characteristics data to victimization files; and it may well be that local organizations (e.g., state law enforcement planning agencies) will begin or continue to carry out their own victim surveys, within their own jurisdictions or other areas of special interest. This seems to us a reasonable solution to the need for area data on victimization, as discussed in Chapter 4.

4. The present NCS count of incidents is affected, especially in the case of assault and personal theft, by the exclusion of so-called "series" offenses from the published aggregate rates. In the case of assaults, the inclusion of these offenses probably would increase published victimization rates by about 70 percent. We do not suggest that the mechanical inclusion of an estimated number of these incidents in the survey rates is necessarily the best solution. It is arguable that many of these "series" incidents really reflect something more akin to a chronic personal condition than a set of discrete events. Clearly, however, their complete exclusion is not the answer either. Until more is known about these "series" cases and their relationship to other reported victimization, no realistic decision as to the best way to treat them can be made; meanwhile, the victimization rates for certain crimes may be seriously misleading.

5. Finally, the NCS in its present form is limited in its accuracy of measurement by numerous problems of sampling and response. For one thing, there is evidence that certain groups (e.g., young black males) are underenumerated by the NCS; for another, about 14 percent of the households in the NCS sample to date have been "replacement" households, whose interviews are not bounded in the way that the panel design provides.

There also appears to be some reasonable doubt about the knowledgeability of some of the household informants in the sample (a not insubstantial proportion of whom have been under 20 years old). And, it is likely that certain victimization rates for male respondents are seriously understated, since almost a third of their interviews were conducted by telephone, which apparently yields substantially lower rates of victimization than personal interviews. (NCS tabulations, for example Table SA1, show that, for 1974 annual totals, 31.5 percent of interviews with males were by telephone. The telephone interviews yielded an overall rate of 2.96 personal crimes per 100, 20 percent lower than the rate of 3.76 per 100 resulting from personal interviews).[1]

In summary, the NCS in its present form may provide a measure of crime incidence that is complementary or supplementary to the UCR and other police statistics. Some of its shortcomings in this respect—those relating to underreporting of offenses and underenumeration and estimation of "series" offenses—might in theory be overcome by further research and development. Other limitations, however, such as the types of crime covered and the coverage of particular jurisdictions or areas, are intrinsic to the present design and scope of the NCS.

PROVISION OF DETAILED INFORMATION ABOUT CRIME

An objective often claimed for victim surveys in general is that they can "be used to study the details of . . . crimes" (Skogan, p. 3); that they can study the part which the victim plays in crime, his role in potential prevention, and his characteristics (Turner and Dodge, p. 4); that they can be used to explore such things as the outcome of a criminal incident (e.g., whether it was an attempted or a completed crime—see Appendix A, Exhibit 12, Paragraph G); the characteristics of offenders, and victim–offender relationships (Dodge and Turner, p. 1). Specifically, it was anticipated that the NCS surveys in particular would "examine the circumstances surrounding the victimization event to be able to quantify those situations that the public considers extenuating circumstances" (Hall, p. 107; cf., Turner and Dodge, p. 29).

Certainly the exploration of the details of criminal events is an important objective, and most administrative statistics on crime give only limited information about related topics, such as victim–offender relationships. Depending on the adequacy of police case records, it may be possible to investigate these details by means of *ad hoc* studies; *Patterns in Criminal Homicide*[2] is an example of this kind of research. It might also be possible for more information of this kind to

---

[1]Table series SA1, titled "Personal Victimization by Type of Interview by Age by Sex," is part of the standard NCS tabulations discussed in Chapter 6.

[2]Marvin E. Wolfgang, *Patterns in Criminal Homicide* (Philadelphia: University of Pennsylvania Press, 1958).

be included in published police statistics. In several jurisdictions, such data already are collected routinely and processed by police information systems. But it undoubtedly would be valuable to have data on these subjects from the NCS, including data on crimes not reported to the police. Data on the characteristics of criminal events could well have an important impact on public perceptions of "the crime problem."

There are, to be sure, some inherent limitations on the utility of surveys for this purpose, and there are special limitations stemming from the present design and execution of the NCS.

To begin, many of the questions studied by criminologists under the heading of "victimology" are microsociological in character. They concern, for example, the "precipitation" of an assault by one or more parties to an argument, or of sexual attack after some sort of quasi-seductive preliminaries.[3] It is very difficult to obtain valid information on recriminatory situations through interviewing of the kind entailed by a large-scale sample survey, perhaps especially for offenses that were not voluntarily made known to the police at the time of their occurrence. Even asking victims if they had been drinking before an incident involving alleged assault might be dubious, on both ethical and administrative grounds, although one might ask, "Did drinking play a part in what happened?" Similarly, certain associations between victim and offender(s)—e.g., with prostitutes— are unlikely to be mentioned in interviews. Finally, of course, the victim's description of what happened in an incident is almost certainly an account, in the justificatory sense of that term.[4] Only by interviewing all parties involved in an incident, including the offender, could one hope to reconstruct a full description of the matter, and even that would often not be sufficient (as the police and courts know all too well). In short, victim surveys can provide very little detailed

[3]See, for example, Hans von Hentig, *The Criminal and His Victim* (New Haven: Yale University Press, 1948); M. E. Wolfgang, *op. cit.*, Chapter 14; E. Gibson and K. Klein, *Murder, 1957–68* (A Home Office Research Report) (London: Her Majesty's Stationery Office, 1970); F. H. McClintock, *Crimes of Violence* (London: Macmillan & Co., 1963), pp. 36–45; K. Svalastoga, "Homicide and Social Contact in Denmark," *American Journal of Sociology* 62(1956):37–41; D. J. Pittman and W. F. Handy, "Patterns in Criminal Aggravated Assault," *Journal of Criminal Law and Political Science* 55(1964): 462–70; Amir Menachim, *Patterns in Forcible Rape* (Chicago: University of Chicago Press, 1971).

[4]See Marvin B. Scott and Stanford M. Lyman, "Accounts, Deviance and Social Order," in Jack D. Douglas (ed.), *Deviance and Respectability* (New York: Basic Books, 1970), pp. 89, 93–94; *idem*, "Accounts," *American Sociological Review* 33 (1968):46–62.

information on the transactions that may take place between victim and offender, and the NCS is further limited by constraints of interview time that can be allocated to exploration of any one aspect of victimization.

Victim surveys can, however, be used to obtain information about the attributes of victims and incidents, and, in some cases, offenders: that is, such things as the age, sex, and race of both parties; the location of the incident in physical and social space; and, within limits, the nature of prior relationships between the victim and offender. The evidence now available, however, indicates that the present NCS version is not particularly successful in providing this information, for several reasons:

1. As we pointed out in Chapter 3, evidence from the San Jose pretest strongly suggests that assaults involving nonstrangers may be seriously underreported to interviewers; if so, the picture of violent victimization emerging from the surveys is thus likely to be seriously biased.

2. Persons reporting victimization are now asked for information about the attributes of the offender(s) involved. At the present time, nothing is known of the validity of these data, nor can one learn whether the same offender was involved in more than one reported event.

3. The coding of where a reported incident took place (NCS-2, Question 4) lumps together a number of places that clearly should be distinguished and does not appear to be based on any clear theoretical or practical rationale (see Appendix A, Exhibit 3).

4. Published NCS data do not at present permit any comparison of nonvictims, one-time victims, and multiple victims, though this kind of comparison could well be important for an understanding of different kinds of victimization.

5. Finally, data on the nature of certain types of victimization covered by the NCS may be badly affected by response bias: In particular, there is reason to believe that black respondents are underreporting minor and attempted assaults in comparison with white respondents. The effects of this underreporting on other data relating to victimization—e.g., on the time and place of occurrence, the race or age of offender, and the relationship of offenders to victims—cannot, at present, even be estimated, but it may well be substantial.[5]

---

[5]Similar evidence of differential reporting to interviewers of incidents in the category of "assault" has been found in several victimization surveys done elsewhere: see Preben

IDENTIFICATION OF HIGH-RISK SUBGROUPS AND MULTIPLE VICTIMS

It has been expected that victim surveys, and more specifically the NCS, can "be used to identify high-risk subgroups in the population" (Skogan, p. 3; Dodge and Turner, p. 111); to estimate the rate of multiple victimization and develop probability-of-risk models (Turner and Dodge, pp. 4–5); and, more generally, "to provide a measure of victim risk" (Work, p. 2).

There can be no doubt about the importance of this objective for the understanding of crime as a social problem. Data from several sources—including the NCS and other victim surveys done here and in other countries—make it clear that, while being the victim of an NCS crime is for most people a relatively rare event, at least in the short run, for an unfortunate minority of persons, households, and commercial establishments, repeated and frequent criminal victimization is virtually a way of life. There are good reasons, *a priori,* for believing that the explanation of multiple victimization is very different from the explanation of what may be called one-time victimization—just as there are differences between the person who commits the odd crime on this or that isolated occasion and the persistent or "career" criminal. As with the details of incidents, police statistics such as the UCR now provide almost no information on this subject.

The NCS in its present form is not especially informative, for several reasons in addition to the problems of sampling and response bias already mentioned.

1. At present, published data from the NCS take the form of *victimization rates,* i.e., the number of victimizations per hundred or per thousand of the appropriate population group. The numerator used to calculate these rates lumps together all victimizations reported by the population in question and thus counts a person who reports *n* victimizations *n* times. This procedure leads to possible

---

Wolf and Ragnar Hauge, "Criminal Violence in Three Scandinavian Countries," *5 Scandinavian Studies in Criminology* (London: Tavistock, 1975); R. F. Sparks, H. G. Genn, and D. J. Dodd, *Surveying Victims* (London: John Wiley & Sons Ltd., 1976), Chapter 4. In these studies the differentials were associated with social class and not with race. Social class response variation has been pointed out as a problem needing attention in victimization surveys since at least 1965 in this country. See especially, Albert D. Biderman's discussion of selectivity in underreporting in "Surveys of Population Samples for Estimating Crime Incidence," *The Annals of the American Academy of Political and Social Science* 374(November 1967):25–27.

distortion of the characteristics of victims as a group. More importantly, it makes it impossible to distinguish multiple victims from the majority who are victimized only once, or not at all. At a minimum, what is needed for this purpose is the distribution of persons victimized 0, 1, 2, . . . n times. Such a distribution—though possibly recoverable from the public-use data tapes—is nowhere to be found in the published NCS data to date.

2. An equally important problem here is the distribution over time of multiple victimization. To what extent are those reporting victimization in one survey reference period also victims in subsequent time periods? This question might in theory be approached through the NCS, through analysis of its six-wave survey data, but there appears to be no way to insure that exactly the same person has been interviewed over more than one survey reference period. Those who move, after having been interviewed once or twice, are not now followed to their new addresses and are not reinterviewed.[6]

INTER-AREA COMPARISONS OF VICTIMIZATION RATES

It has been said that the NCS would publish data "to display . . . the geographical distribution of crimes and victims—that is, national and regional data, and data from some of the very large cities and states" (Dodge and Turner, p. 1); it has also been suggested that it might be possible to "undertake a comparative study of intercity differences/similarities in the vulnerability to certain types of victimization by specific population subgroups" [Appendix A, Exhibit 12, A(2)].

This objective has been only imperfectly attained by the NCS to date. No data whatsoever have been published from the NCS showing variations in victimization rates among regions. It appears unlikely that state-level data can be disaggregated with any detail, because of sampling errors and because of restrictions relating to confidentiality requirements.[7] At the present time, city-level survey data have been

---

[6]It might be feasible to try to trace out-migrants to their new addresses, though it would clearly be expensive. A question on geographical mobility ("How long have you lived at this address?") is now asked on the NCS-6 Attitude Questionnaire, but data from this question have not yet been analyzed.

[7]These are separate but related restrictions, both of which are due to the fact that certain sorts of victimization are very rare. On the one hand, Census policies now prohibit publication of data relating to areas of less than 250,000 population, since this might lead to identification of individual victims; on the other hand, the small numbers of victimizations reported in small towns or rural areas would lead to unreliable estimates because of sampling errors.

published for 26 cities (some of which have now been surveyed a second time). Observed differences in survey-estimated rates among these cities may be due in part to variations in methods used (e.g., interviewer selection and training, coding) or to response biases or other artifacts. Until the issue of artifacts is explored, little confidence can be put in intercity comparisons. Indeed, unless one hypothesizes such methodological artifacts, it is very difficult to understand some of the findings of the city-level surveys, e.g., the finding that Newark, New Jersey, had lower survey-estimated rates of assault and burglary than Portland, Oregon, or that the survey-estimated rate of personal crime in Miami, Florida, is less than one-third that of Minneapolis, Minnesota.

CALLING THE POLICE

It has been pointed out that victimization surveys "can be used to examine local patterns of non-reporting to the police" (Skogan, p. 2) and that the NCS specifically was expected to "serve as an index of changes in reporting behavior in the population" (Work, p. 3; Turner and Dodge, p. 4).

The NCS at present can reveal little or nothing about local patterns of nonreporting, and it includes almost no measures that might help to account for different levels of reporting or changes in reporting behavior.

As the Census analysts have pointed out (see Appendix A, Exhibit 1), this last point is almost entirely a matter of questionnaire design: Question 20 of the present NCS-2 incident form asks, "Were the police informed of this incident in any way?"—but does *not* ask if *the respondent himself* informed the police. Nor does the present coding frame distinguish the respondent himself from other household members. Question 20b of NCS-2 asks, "What was the reason this incident was not reported to the police?"—but here, too, the question appears, according to the Census analysts, to be "not yielding much in the way of insights into reasons for the failure to report crimes." In fact, the first two field-coded response categories—"Nothing could be done" and "Did not think it important enough"—are now accounting for 60–70 percent of all responses.

Clearly, the questionnaire needs further development to illuminate the extent to which nonreporting is "incident-specific" in the sense of being due to the triviality of the crime or a belief that the police could not solve that particular incident, as opposed to being "generic," i.e., relating to a belief that the police are generally incompetent or would

not bother to deal with the incident. It might also be useful to ask
(when the respondent says he did notify the police) why he did so and
how the crime was reported to the police. This last question could
help to insure validity of responses; it might also permit a follow-
forward of allegedly reported incidents, to throw light on the ways in
which they were dealt with by the police at the successive stages of
investigation and recording.

This problem illustrates a general point about the NCS questionnaires now in use, a point that will be discussed in greater detail
below. This is that very little information is now obtained from
respondents to help in explaining such things as nonreporting, as
distinct from merely describing it. Thus the present Attitude Questionnaire (NCS-6) asks only one main question (plus some follow-ups)
about the police: "Would you say, in general, that your local police
are doing a good job, an average job or a poor job?" Apart from the
superficiality of this question, nothing is asked about the frequency of
respondents' contacts with the police. Nothing is asked about types of
contact that respondents may have had, nor is anything asked about
respondents' satisfaction or dissatisfaction with what the police did on
the occasion of their last (or any other) contact, whether that was in
connection with a crime or with something else. Any attempt to
account for public attitudes to, and demands on, the police must
surely take these factors into account. The NCS survey provides an
unparalleled opportunity to study these and other related issues and
to help law enforcement officials and the general public to understand
the relationships between contacts with the police, attitudes toward
the police, and the reporting of crime. Yet, at present, none of the
relevant questions is being asked, and the one question about the
police is not included in any published analysis. Thus, the NCS is not
now fulfilling this important objective.

EVALUATION AND STRATEGY DEVELOPMENT

The next two objectives relate to the use of victim surveys in
connection with evaluation and operational criminal justice planning:
They can thus be grouped together. They are:

1. Victimization surveys can "establish benchmarks for evaluating
the effectiveness of criminal justice programs" (Skogan, p. 4).
2. Victim surveys can "provide the kinds of data recognized as
needed to develop strategies for crime reduction and overall criminal
justice planning" (Hall, p. 106).

It is open to question how far the present NCS victim surveys can contribute to the accomplishment of either objective, even if the measurement problems already discussed can be overcome. In the case of evaluation, this is in part because measurement of the dependent variable—which a victim survey might accomplish—is only one aspect of the problem. In most cases even greater difficulties are met when trying to measure the independent variable(s)—e.g., new patrolling strategies or crime-prevention campaigns—and in fulfilling the other conditions required for experimental or quasi-experimental design. In addition, many or most crime-prevention or crime-reduction programs cover only a part of a city or operate for only limited time periods. For reasons already given, the NCS is ill-suited to making accurate before-and-after measurements under those conditions.

The evaluation of LEAA's "high-impact" cities programs may be taken to illustrate the difficulties in coordinating the NCS with actual and specific crime reduction programs. Each of these eight cities was surveyed in the late summer and early fall of 1972 (using a reference period covering the preceding 12 months). Each was surveyed again in 1975. In between the two surveys, each city was funded to carry out a variety of crime-reduction programs, covering different areas of the cities and different periods of time. It will be virtually impossible to relate the "impact" programs to any observed differences in crime rates from the two sets of surveys, even assuming that statistically significant and apparently valid differences emerge.

We do not, moreover, know how survey responses are affected by crime-prevention campaigns or new modes of policing. It is easy to imagine, for example, that a campaign aimed at making the public conscious of burglary could lead to greater reporting of attempted burglaries (sc., "suspicious persons") to survey interviewers, and even easier to suppose that widespread publicity given to family crisis-intervention programs could lead to relatively more reporting to interviewers of nonstranger assaults than was found in the Census pretests.[8]

So far as other local law enforcement and criminal justice planning activities are concerned, the obvious drawback of the national and city-level NCS surveys as designed is the difficulty of producing survey-estimated crime rates for those specific areas over which police and planning agencies have jurisdictions, such as precincts.

A further point is that most policing, at least in relation to the kinds of crimes covered by the NCS, is "reactive" in the sense that the police discover the offense and investigate it only if they have been

---

[8]See Chapter 3.

called. "Proactive" policing, e.g., intensive patrolling, leads in most jurisdictions to only a minority of arrests for serious crime. It thus might be that a properly conducted local-area victim survey could provide police with more accurate data on the "ecology" of some types of crime than they now have from their own calls for service.

It is possible that data on the types of crimes surveyed in the NCS and on victims' reporting of these incidents to the police could help law enforcement agencies by giving another standard against which to compare their own patterns. It might also be useful to learn more detail about the *types* of incidents allegedly reported to the police. For example, if the great majority of nonreported crimes are, and are seen by respondents to be, relatively trivial, there might be less need for law enforcement officials to worry about devising strategies to prevent them. But these things are admittedly conjectural, and—in particular, the present series of published reports—yield very little information on which local law enforcement and/or criminal justice planning agencies could draw inferences on patterns of reporting to police.[9]

ESTIMATION OF DIRECT AND INDIRECT COSTS OF CRIME

Two further objectives originally suggested for the NCS are:

1. The NCS will provide a measure of "the direct costs of crime . . . money and property lost through theft, the cost of medical attention, time lost from work and replacement services for persons injured" (Hall, p. 106).
2. The NCS "will provide the means of estimating indirect crime costs such as the flight of citizens from the cities" (Hall, p. 106).

Leaving aside philosophical disputes about, for example, whether the aggregate value of individuals' property loss through theft represents a social cost as distinct from a transfer of wealth, we agree that monetary losses are not adequately measured by the NCS in its present form.

---

[9]Useful information may however come from analyses of victimization rates in relation to community or neighborhood characteristics. See Chapter 9.

1. Little is known about the validity of data on value of stolen property. But the findings of the Baltimore and San Jose pretests suggest that survey-reported losses may not agree with the losses recorded by the police after their investigations (assuming that they were notified of it). In both studies, survey estimates of loss were generally higher than police estimates. In San Jose, for example, the median dollar loss reported in the survey was about 40 percent higher than the police determination of loss for grand larceny and burglary and about 80 percent higher for robbery (*San Jose Methods Test* report, p. 10, and Tables 6–8, pp. 16–17).

2. Question 15b on the NCS-2 questionnaire provides several different bases by which the value of stolen property may be determined (i.e., original costs, replacement cost, insurance report estimate, and so forth). The relations between estimates made in these different ways are unknown, and no published analysis to date has attempted to relate amount of loss sustained to income or to wealth. Except for motor vehicles, no data are at present obtained on the amount of stealable property owned by respondents.

3. As Hall's mention of "replacement services for persons injured" indicates, the cost of medical treatment, even if measured accurately, is not by any means the only social or individual cost of violent victimization, but these other costs are not now investigated in the NCS. Loss of time from work, housework, or school come to mind as possible candidates for inclusion.

4. As the Census analysts have pointed out (Appendix A, Exhibit 2), Question 8b on NCS-2 appears to yield a very poor measure of the extent of injury through violent victimization.

5. Question 8c on the NCS-2 does not ask about all medical treatment that the respondent may have received, but only about treatment at a hospital. It thus excludes medical treatment by a general practitioner, at a factory infirmary, at school, or in many other places besides hospitals.

The question of indirect costs (e.g., flight from cities or psychological injury) is also unexplored in the present NCS. Apart from a few somewhat suggestive questions on the NCS-6 Attitude Questionnaire, nothing whatever is now asked about respondents' behavior as a result of victimization, nor about fear and/or concern about crime. Nothing is asked, for example, about whether household respondents have installed new locks or taken other security precautions as a result of burglary, let alone whether they have moved as a result of victimization.

PERIPHERAL OBJECTIVES

Finally, there are at least three suggested uses of the NCS that can be grouped together on the ground that none of them strictly speaking requires a victimization survey. Each of these uses involves an important issue, yet each is relevant to the NCS only insofar as that issue might in some way be affected by the experience of victimization. These are:

1. "By utilizing the latest socio-metric techniques adapted to mass surveys, we would be able to provide insights into the source of . . . public reaction (to crime)" (Hall, p. 106).
2. The NCS "will also provide more direct input to criminal justice agencies by determining the attitudes of various segments of the population toward those agencies. . . . This will provide justice agencies with the information needed to improve their effectiveness and their image" (Hall, p. 106; cf. Turner and Dodge, p. 29).
3. "One of the activities related to the panel will be a general population survey to assess public attitudes concerning the relative seriousness of actual events. The project will also examine the circumstances surrounding the event to be able to quantify those situations which the public considers extenuating circumstances" (Hall, p. 107).

None of these things would appear to require a victimization survey for its investigation.

A general social survey that did not elicit information about victimization could provide valuable information about societal reaction to crime, attitudes toward criminal justice agencies, and the seriousness of different types of offenses. It would, of course, be valuable to be able to relate survey data on these and other subjects to the respondents' experience of victimization. It is thus unfortunate that none of these issues is now receiving any attention in the NCS (unless we count the question, "Would you say, in general, that your local police are doing a good job, an average job or a poor job?"—Question 14 on NCS-6—as an indicator of "attitudes toward criminal justice agencies").

The questionnaires now in use do not use any sociometric or psychometric methods, though they could do so. They ask nothing about public perceptions of the seriousness of crime, nor do they contain any questions that would seem to make it possible to "quantify what the public considers extenuating circumstances.'' Even if such data were now being collected, the present plan of analysis—which does not include comparisons between victims and nonvictims—would make it impossible to assess the relation of NCS-victim experiences on the structure of these attitudes and opinions.

9

The Utility
of the
National Crime Surveys

INTRODUCTION

The panel has found much to commend, and much to criticize, in the design and execution of the NCS to date. We have argued that a very great amount of methodological and developmental research must be done, and many changes in existing procedures must be made, if certain of the specific initial objectives of the surveys are to be accomplished. The panel also maintains, however, that those objectives themselves need further scrutiny and that a subtle but fundamental change in the official concept of victimization surveying is necessary if the potential value of this relatively new research method is to be fully realized. In what follows we will try to describe that conceptual shift and the implications that it would have for the NCS.

ORIGINS OF THE PRESENT NCS OBJECTIVES

The original impetus for the NCS came from the President's Commission on Law Enforcement and Administration of Justice, which in 1966 commissioned the first victimization surveys ever carried out. The commission was aware that official statistics of crime in the United States were unsatisfactory, in part because of offenses that were never reported to the police and in part because of wide variations in the recording by police of offenses that were reported to them or known by

152

them. Reviewing the findings of its own surveys, the commission expressed its belief that "the [victimization] survey technique has a great untapped potential as a method for providing additional information about the nature and extent of our crime problem. . . ."[1] The commission also pointed out that:

What is needed to answer questions about the volume and trend of crime satisfactorily are a number of different crime indicators showing trends over a period of time to supplement the improved reporting by police agencies. The commission experimented with the development of public surveys of victims of crime and feels this can become a useful supplementary yardstick.[2]

Agreement with this statement, coupled with the commission's criticism of the UCR, appears to have established a primary general goal for the NCS: namely, the provision of a "supplementary yardstick," that would merely "calibrate" the UCR. By implication, it seems to have been generally assumed that such calibration would make it possible to use police statistics (in particular, the UCR) as a basis for inferences about some "true" volume of crime. For example, if it could be shown that only 10 percent of all thefts reported to interviewers were recorded in the UCR, then the true level of theft could be obtained simply by multiplying the UCR figure by a factor of 10.

The panel believes that this emphasis on correcting police statistics has been extreme and that it has seriously restricted the possible uses of the victimization survey as a method of studying crime and societal reaction to it.

It can be argued that official statistics on crime, whether compiled by the police, the courts, or any other administrative agency, can never provide a definitive measure of crime. For one thing, such statistics necessarily exclude a great many types of crime. Many of the defects of the UCR to which the President's Commission pointed refer to the limited scope of those statistics: for example, to the fact that the UCR does not include the great bulk of so-called organized crime (for example, gambling, drug trafficking) nor "white-collar" crime such as price-fixing, tax evasion, consumer fraud, and political corruption. (As

[1]President's Commission on Law Enforcement and Administration of Justice, *The Challenge of Crime in a Free Society* (Washington, D.C.: U.S. Government Printing Office, 1967), p. 22.
[2]*Ibid.*, p. 31. After noting the need for further methodological research, the commission added that victimization surveys "should be supplemented by new types of surveys and censuses which would provide better information about crime in areas where good information is lacking, such as crimes by or against business and other organizations."

we pointed out in Chapter 8,[3] victimization surveys have many of the same limitations.)

Even with respect to those types of crime that they include, however, official statistics are necessarily an imperfect measure. This is so because they are the outcome of a complex series of social and organizational processes, varying over time and place, each one of which almost certainly introduces substantial systematic biases into the statistics. Thus, in order to be recorded in the UCR, a crime must (at a minimum) be perceived by the victim or by someone else, it must be defined as a crime by the victim or observer; and, it must in some way become known to the police, it must be defined by the police as a crime, and it must be recorded by the police. At each step in this process, some crimes are excluded (and, perhaps, some noncrimes are included); and it is clear that those crimes that are finally included among administrative statistics are very unlikely to be representative of, or easily related to, the total number of events that might carry legal sanctions within or across jurisdictional boundaries.

This is not, of course, an argument against the compilation, by the police or indeed any other agency, of statistics relating to crime as defined by that agency. Many more statistics are collected now by the police than are published, and these statistics have many operational and administrative uses, even if they are not perfect indicators of the volume of crime in the United States. Nor is it to say that victimization surveys like the NCS have no role to play in complementing or supplementing police or other official agency statistics. It is to say that for most types of offenses, police statistics never can be expected to provide valid measures of the "true" levels of crime in the United States, no matter how much they might be supplemented (or calibrated) by victimization surveys. It follows that such supplementation should not necessarily be the primary objective of the NCS in the future.

DESCRIPTION AND EXPLANATION

One way to characterize the objects and utility of a survey like the NCS—and thus to improve its design—would be to consider the possible users of the data produced by the survey. In this instance, this would mean distinguishing between routine or special publications by the Census Bureau and LEAA, on the one hand, and public-use data tapes, on the other; or, one might distinguish among the possible needs

---

[3]See Chapter 8, pp. 134–35.

of legislators, law enforcement and criminal justice planning personnel, the general public, and academic or institutional researchers.[4]

A different, and perhaps more fundamental, distinction can be made: This is the distinction, drawn by some students of research methodology, between (a) surveys that are intended merely to *measure* or *describe* certain phenomena and (b) surveys that are intended to *explain* or *analyze* those phenomena.[5] Briefly, the main aim of surveys in the first of these two categories is simply to provide information on particular attributes of a population: to discover, for example, how many people were unemployed last week, how much people spend on food or entertainment, or how many people intend to vote for Candidate X. If, as is usual, such a survey is based on a sample, the main inferences made in analyzing the data involve the estimation of population parameters (for the attributes under investigation). A survey that aims at analysis or explanation, on the other hand, is intended to discover and make understandable relationships among factors such as employment, expenditure, and voting behavior, or between those factors and others that may influence them. Analysis of the sample data in the latter case typically involves computation of functions relating two or more variables and not simply the production of univariate population estimates. Moreover, the sample may be chosen so as to depart from uniform sampling probabilities, in accordance with an experimental design or with analytic goals that require more than the simple proportional representation of subgroups within the population of interest.

These two sets of survey objectives—the descriptive and the analytic—are not, of course, mutually exclusive. Even the simplest of "fact-finding" surveys will usually collect some other information about respondents—for instance, demographic data such as the age and sex of respondents. These data can be regarded as independent variables and can be analyzed in relation to data on, for example, unemployment or education: Such an analysis, by accounting for some

---

[4]The needs of these different groups do not necessarily conflict. It may well be that legislators, or administrators of the criminal justice system, start from premises different from those of the academic criminologist; both, however, will have an interest in the basic factual information that a series like the NCS may provide, and the administrator may benefit from the kind of understanding that the criminologist seeks to provide. The line between "academic" and "practical," between "theoretical" and "applied," is not sharp.

[5]For a discussion of this distinction, which is often clouded by terminological differences, see C. A. Moser and G. Kalton, eds., *Survey Methods in Social Investigation* (New York: Basic Books, 1972), Chapter 1; Earl R. Babbie, *The Practice of Social Research* (Belmont, Calif.: Wadsworth Publishing Co., 1975), Chapter 2.

of the observed population variance in the latter measures, can have some explanatory force. Perhaps it would be more accurate to consider description and analysis as the endpoints on a continuum, with most actual surveys falling in between the two. But the two goals, nonetheless, may have radically different implications, not only for sample design and methods of data tabulation, but also for the choice of variables to be investigated and for the ways in which those variables are measured.

Where, on this continuum, should the NCS in its present form be placed? Even though few, if any, of the statements of objectives quoted in the previous chapter address this issue in explicit terms, there can be no doubt that the NCS, as it is at present being conducted, is primarily descriptive rather than analytic in character. An earlier document produced by the forerunner to NCJISS, for example, states that the primary purpose of a national victimization survey would be "to measure the annual change in crime incidence for a limited set of major crimes and to characterize some of the socio-economic aspects of both the reported events and their victims."[6] The same document referred to providing "a reliable statistical series on the amount of dangerous crime in the United States and the rate of victim experience. . . ." In a similar vein, Turner and Dodge quote the President's (1967) Crime Commission as claiming that, "Statistical indicators as comprehensive as the ones reported by the federal government in labor and agricultural statistics could be achieved with victimization survey findings used in combinations with data from the Uniform Crime Reports."[7]

Many things follow from this. Consider, for example, the current NCS design for the production of quarterly data: an emphasis that appears to have dictated the choice of a 6-month reference for the NCS, though empirical evidence on recall and telescoping does not clearly justify the cost of that choice. The production of quarterly data is understandable if the aim of the survey is merely to measure criminal victimization, but is difficult to understand from an explanatory or analytic point of view except, perhaps, in connection with questions concerning seasonal variation. Similarly, the sampling design of the NCS may be reasonable if the objective of the survey is solely to measure the general population's victimization experience; but, for the purpose of accounting for variation in experiences with phenomena as rare as the crimes sur-

[6]See Appendix G.
[7]Anthony G. Turner and Richard W. Dodge, "Surveys of Personal and Organizational Victimization" (Paper presented at the Symposium on Studies of Public Experience, Knowledge and Opinion of Crime and Justice, March 16–18, 1972, Washington, D.C.), p. 3.

veyed in the NCS, a very different sample design—possibly with differential sampling among strata determined by variables known or believed to be related to victimization—might be more efficient. Again, the choice of victimization rates per thousand persons as the main statistic may be defended perhaps from a purely descriptive point of view; although, as argued earlier, it is in fact severely narrow even for that aim. By itself, the rate makes little sense if what is sought is an explanation of the distribution of criminal victimization.

At a more basic level, the objectives of a survey, and the relative emphasis on measurement or description versus analysis or explanation, will determine the questions to be asked of survey respondents. A descriptive orientation can be clearly seen in the extremely limited number of independent or explanatory variables on which the NCS now collects information. If we reflect on the major sociological theories offered as explanations of crime over the past half-century—from "ecological" and culture-conflict theories, through differential association, anomie and subcultural theory to the most recent adaptations of economic theory to criminal behavior—it is clear that there are few, if any, variables now incorporated in the NCS questionnaires that bear on those theories, except through crude and extremely uncertain *post hoc* "operational" definition.[8] To be sure, most of those theories have paid

---

[8]For examples of exploration of ecological theories, see Clifford R. Shaw *et al.*, *Delinquency Areas* (Chicago: University of Chicago Press, 1942); for a general review, see Judith A. Wilks, "Ecological Correlates of Crime and Delinquency," Appendix A in *Crime and Its Impact—An Assessment* (Task Force Report of the President's Commission on Law Enforcement and Administration of Justice) (Washington, D.C.: U.S. Government Printing Office, 1967); for culture conflict discussion, see Thorsten Sellin, *Culture Conflict and Crime* (New York: Social Science Research Council, 1938); reviews of differential association theories are contained in Edwin H. Sutherland and Donald R. Cressey, *Principles of Criminology*, 7th ed. (Philadelphia: J. B. Lippincott Co., 1966), and Donald R. Cressey, *Delinquency, Crime and Differential Association* (The Hague: Martinus Nijhoff, 1960); the application of the concept of anomie in criminological models is illustrated by Robert K. Merton, "Social Structure and Anomie," *American Sociological Review* 3(1938):672–82, reprinted in Robert K. Merton, *Social Theory and Social Structure* (New York: Free Press, 1957), Chapter 4; the role of subculture is discussed in Albert K. Cohen, *Delinquent Boys: The Culture of the Gang* (New York: Free Press, 1955); Richard A. Cloward and Lloyd Ohlin, *Delinquency and Opportunity* (New York: Free Press, 1960); Walter B. Miller, "Lower-Class Culture as a Generating Milieu of Gang Delinquency," (1958), 14, *Journal of Social Issues* 14(1958):5–19; the convergence of economic and criminological theories can be seen in the works of Gary S. Becker, "Crime and Punishment: An Economic Approach," *Journal of Political Economics* 76(1968):78; Isaac Ehrlich, "Participation in Illegitimate Activities: An Economic Analysis," in *Essays in the Economics of Crime and Punishment*, by Gary S. Becker and William M. Landes (New York: National Bureau of Economic Research, 1974), pp. 68–134.

scant attention to the possible roles of victims or potential victims in the causation of crime; in any case, it is unlikely that an elaborate program of surveys like the NCS could ever be justified solely on the basis of testing abstract and sometimes recondite academic theories.

There are a number of important factors of general explanatory value, however, on which the NCS could easily obtain valuable information that is not now available elsewhere. Most of these factors can be subsumed under the related concepts of vulnerability and risk, discussed in Chapter 6. Some examples can be found in Reppetto's recent study of residential burglary.[9] In addition to obtaining, from Boston police records, residential robbery and burglary rates, Reppetto collected data on two sets of factors that were intended to explain those rates. The first, which he called "environmental factors," included attributes of neighborhoods, such as geographic location in relation to the town center, median income, predominant housing type, racial composition, size of youth population, and burglary rates in surrounding areas. In addition, he obtained data on attributes of particular households and dwellings within neighborhoods, such as daytime occupancy of the house, type of structure, security practices, and ease of access to the building. Some of the first group of factors may be studied in the NCS when data files containing the Census neighborhood characteristics are available, though even then it appears that such things as the income level and victimization rates of surrounding areas may be unavailable. Most of the items in Reppetto's second category are not collected by the NCS at present, although they could be.

Analogous factors relating to vulnerability and risk can easily be thought of for other crimes, such as robbery and assault. We acknowledged earlier that it might be difficult to obtain information about certain prior associations between victims and offenders. Nonetheless, the social location of many incidents surely could be determined with more precision than is now the case. Did a robbery or assault occur in a place of public resort, such as a bar, restaurant, or theater? Did it occur in a private locale, such as the victim's own home or the home of a friend? Did it occur on a public thoroughfare, or on public transportation, such as a bus or subway? Did it occur at the victim's place of employment?[10] None of these questions can now be answered by the

---

[9]Thomas A. Reppetto, *Residential Crime* (Cambridge, Mass.: Ballinger Publishing Co., 1974).

[10]For attempts to construct situational classifications of robbery and assault, using data contained in police records, see F. H. McClintock, *Crimes of Violence* (London: MacMillan & Co., 1963), Chapter 4; F. H. McClintock and E. Gibson, *Robbery in London* (London: MacMillan & Co., 1961), Chapter 2; these classifications make some use of victim–offender relationships as well.

NCS. Yet distinctions of this kind could do much to clarify the degrees of risk attaching to locales characterized by different degrees of privacy or protection, and—together with data on different groups' access to such locales[11]—could do much to explain variations in victimization in the general population.

We believe that an assessment of risk should be a primary objective of the national victimization survey, and we offer in historical support the following statement from the President's 1966 Commission:

The Commission believes that there is a clear public responsibility to keep citizens fully informed of the facts about (violent) crime so they will have facts to go on when they decide what the risks are and what kinds and amounts of precautionary measures they should take.[12]

Victimization surveys are concerned not only with crime, but also with societal reaction to it. Here too there are many important issues awaiting explanatory research. Why do some people report (some) crimes, whereas others do not? To what extent is a victim's decision to call the police "incident-specific," rather than being a consequence of his general attitudes towards the police and other agencies of social control? What are the factors that lead some social groups to define certain sorts of behavior as criminal (or at least as deviant), while other groups regard those same forms of behavior as permissible or even mandatory? To what extent are people's attitudes towards the police, the courts, and the rest of the criminal justice system a consequence of their contacts with that system as victims of crime?

Finally, there is a wide range of issues that could be explored by a survey like the NCS, concerning the impact of crime on the community. Why, for example, does there appear to be little, if any, relationship between expressed concern about crime and direct experience of victimization?[13] To what extent is fear of crime a consequence of physical and/or social vulnerability (e.g., old age, forced reliance on public transportation) and to what extent does it flow from the images of crime presented by the media of mass communication?

[11]For a discussion of the importance of the distribution between public and private places, and access to the latter, in relation to crime, see Arthur Stinchcombe, "Institutions of Privacy in the Determination of Police Administrative Practice," *American Journal of Sociology*, 69(1963):150–60.

[12]President's Commission on Law Enforcement and Administration of Justice. *The Challenge of Crime in A Free Society, op cit.*, p. 52.

[13]Cf. the discussion by Jennie McIntyre, "Public Attitudes Toward Crime and Law Enforcement," *The Annals of the American Academy of Political and Social Science*, 34(1967):34–46.

THE NEED FOR A CONTINUING SERIES OF VICTIMIZATION SURVEYS

We turn now to the importance of having a continuing series of national victimization surveys. Three distinct, but related, perspectives will be considered: (a) that of a social indicator, (b) that of the executive and legislative branches of government, and (c) that of the scientist interested in advancing the state of knowledge of crime and its impact on American society.

THE VICTIMIZATION SURVEY AS A SOCIAL INDICATOR

In the decade since the first victimization surveys were carried out for the President's Commission, substantial progress has been made, in the United States and in other countries, toward the goal of providing a wide range of social indicators—that is, quantitative time-series data analogous to economic indicators, reflecting social change, the accomplishment of specific social goals, and the magnitude of social problems or concerns.[14] A continuing series of victimization surveys could provide a range of social indicators.

In suggesting the use of victimization surveys to provide social indicators, we do not envisage mere counts of crimes or victimizations, nor just aggregate rates of victimizations. Instead, the ideal series also should monitor the impact of crime in both personal and social terms. For example, how many persons are injured, in various degrees, as a result of violent crime—and what are the individual and social costs of such injuries? What are the risks of this kind of injury for different sectors of American society, and how are those risks related to other risks of injury? What is the direct personal cost of theft, in any given year—and how does it compare with the cost in other years and to other forms of loss? What is the distribution of criminal victimization of various kinds in the social structure, and how are changes in that distribution related to other social changes?

A continuing national victimization survey would at first probably provide only indicators of the objective effects of crime on the community. But in time, the surveys should produce data on subjective effects as well. A growing body of surveys has, in recent years, attempted to measure perceptions, expectations, beliefs, attitudes, and values, on

---

[14]For a thorough discussion of this problem and of efforts to construct social indicators in the years up to 1966, see Raymond A. Bauer, ed., *Social Indicators* (Cambridge: MIT Press, 1966).

the assumption that the quality of life is in the eye of the beholder.[15] A fairly consistent finding of these researchers, anticipated to some extent by earlier survey data on the fear of crime, has been that people's subjective perceptions of their own welfare—in this case, their feeling of freedom from crime and/or satisfaction with the workings of the criminal justice system—are not related in any simple or straightforward way to the objective facts of their experience nor to the real risks of crime that they confront. A continuing national victimization survey could thus provide, in a very literal sense, a measure of "domestic tranquility" and could help to relate that sense of tranquility, or its absence, to the relevant facts of social life.

The production of social indicators relating to crime need not involve any particular value premise; in particular, it is not, *per se*, to imply that an increase in crime, of the kinds measured by victim surveys, necessarily means society has changed for the worse. Analysis may show the change is attributable to a change in the population composition, to increases in wealth, and/or to a shift from activities of equal or greater harmfulness to those types of activities registered as crimes of victimization.

A continuing series of victimization surveys, carefully designed and validated in the ways described elsewhere in this report, could help to fill in the details of American life. It could help to illuminate our society's concepts of crime and the moral order, and it could help to provide a factual foundation for a reassessment of that moral order.

EXECUTIVE AND LEGISLATIVE USES OF VICTIMIZATION SURVEYS

For most of the past dozen years, crime has been seen as a serious social problem in the United States and, as such, has been an important political issue. Many of the types of crime or disturbances that caused the most concern in that period—urban and campus riots, assassinations, violent political protest, the Pandora's box known as "Watergate"—did not, of course, require a victimization survey for their investigation. But in addition to those dramatic incidents, there

---

[15]See, for example, Norman M. Bradburn and David Caplovitz, *Reports on Happiness: A Pilot Study of Behavior Related to Mental Health* (Chicago: Aldine Publishing Co., 1965); Norman M. Bradburn, *The Structure of Psychological Well-Being*, NORC Monographs in Social Research, No. 15 (Chicago: Aldine Publishing Co., 1969); Angus Campbell and Philip E. Converse, eds., *The Human Meaning of Social Change* (New York: Russell Sage Foundation, 1972); Mark Abrams, "Social Indicators and Social Equity," *New Society*, November 23, 1972, p. 454.

was a general concern about more traditional forms of lawbreaking—in particular, "street crime" and other violence committed by strangers. This concern is reflected in the legislative origins of the NCS.

It can be forcefully argued that this concern is unrealistic. Evidence from a variety of sources, including the NCS and other victimization surveys, suggests that for the majority of Americans, crime of the type surveyed in the NCS is not, in fact, an important personal problem— compared with issues such as inflation, unemployment, educational costs, or race and sex discrimination. What cannot be denied is that public concern about crime is real. Crime is thus likely to remain an important fact of political life.

As to the utility of a continuing series of national victimization surveys for the executive and legislature, it is conceivable that it would reside largely in showing what could not be done about the crime problem, as well as showing, of course, more clearly what that problem is.[16] The existence of such a series would mean that political decision-makers no longer had to rely solely on the UCR or on other administrative statistics for information on the level of crime. In addition, the victimization series would provide a wealth of information about the distribution and social consequences of crime, which could never be obtained from police statistics. Such a series could thus provide a much more rational basis for expenditures on the criminal justice system than has ever been available. It also could provide data relevant to a wide range of more specific issues, such as gun control and compensation for victims of crime. And, by exploring public attitudes concerning crime and the criminal justice system, as well as the relationship of those attitudes to the experience of victimization, the surveys could help to dispel the ignorance, misunderstanding, and irrational fear that now so often characterize public debate and discussion of crime.

THE SCIENTIFIC UTILITY OF VICTIMIZATION SURVEYS

For the social analyst, a continuing series of victimization surveys at a national level could provide a rich resource of data. Each survey in such a series could be used as a cross-sectional testing ground for criminological theories (if victimization data were to be supplemented with other behavioral and attitudinal data). In addition, if the survey were a continuing one providing annual data over a period of years, it

[16]More precisely, what part of that problem is. Even a series of victimization surveys would give no information about organized or white-collar crime or political corruption, for example. (See also Chapter 8.)

could be used along with other time-series data in longitudinal studies. Finally, if the series used a panel design, it would be possible to use it to study the consequences of criminal victimization. A continuing series of victimization surveys could yield data for testing theories about societal reaction to crime. It would probably have little to say about the microsociology of interpersonal violence and nothing whatever to say about victimless crime. But the NCS has already pointed to the existence of some criminological phenomena—such as series victimization—for which new theoretical approaches may be needed.

More importantly, the victimization survey makes possible for the first time an adequate test of a whole range of social theories, which have attempted to relate crime to the social structure, to culture, to class and class conflict, to economic conditions, or to deterrence. Until now, the only possible test of many of these theories has been official statistics such as the UCR. But, leaving aside their other characteristics, such statistics are a function not only of crime, but also of the working of the system of social control: They thus confound the relationships that theorists have wished to isolate for study. Victimization surveys, which can provide separate measures of crime and of societal response to it, can overcome this limitation. A continuing national survey would thus open the way to an extensive program of retesting of discarded theories and a reexamination of many received truths.

Materials Provided
by the
Crime Statistics
Analysis Group

At the August 1975 meeting of the evaluation panel, members of CSAG of the Bureau of the Census were invited to present analytic issues they had identified in the course of preparing NCS reports. This appendix is a set of supporting materials distributed by CSAG members at the meeting. It is complete except for Exhibit 11, a copy of a computer printout that is not reproducible.

FOURTH MEETING

PANEL FOR THE EVALUATION OF CRIME SURVEYS

COMMITTEE ON NATIONAL STATISTICS

August 14, 1975

Presentation on Analytical Issues
by Members of the
Crime Statistics Analysis Staff
Bureau of the Census

Bob Parkinson, Chief
Al Páez, Supervisory Social Science Analyst
Dick Dodge, Supervisory Survey Statistician
Dick Dickerson, Social Science Analyst
Norm Howard, Social Science Analyst
Harold Lentzner, Social Science Analyst
Fred Shenk, Social Science Analyst

REPORTING OF VICTIMIZATIONS TO THE POLICE:
ISSUES CONCERNING THE DATA

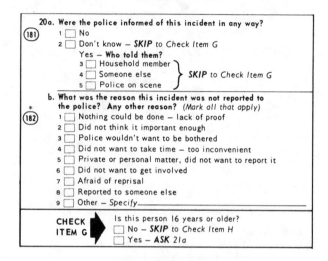

20a. Were the police informed of this incident in any way?
(181) 1 ☐ No
       2 ☐ Don't know — *SKIP* to *Check Item G*
       Yes — **Who told them?**
       3 ☐ Household member ⎫
       4 ☐ Someone else   ⎬ *SKIP* to *Check Item G*
       5 ☐ Police on scene   ⎭

b. **What was the reason this incident was not reported to
   the police? Any other reason?** *(Mark all that apply)*
(182) 1 ☐ Nothing could be done — lack of proof
       2 ☐ Did not think it important enough
       3 ☐ Police wouldn't want to be bothered
       4 ☐ Did not want to take time — too inconvenient
       5 ☐ Private or personal matter, did not want to report it
       6 ☐ Did not want to get involved
       7 ☐ Afraid of reprisal
       8 ☐ Reported to someone else
       9 ☐ Other — *Specify*_____

CHECK   Is this person 16 years or older?
ITEM G   ☐ No — *SKIP* to *Check Item H*
         ☐ Yes — *ASK 21a*

THE PROBLEMS:

(1) Use of the word "informed" in Question 20a is potentially suggestive. That is, it may be ruling out the possibility that the police were on (or happened upon) the scene, or that they were summoned to the scene without the respondent's knowledge.

(2) As now constituted, response categories 3-5 of Question 20a are inappropriate for gathering information on persons who actually reported crimes to the police. Notably, we have no capability for measuring the extent to which victims themselves notified the police, a variable that would appear to be particularly important in relation to personal crimes of violence.

(3) The response categories under Question 20b are not yielding much in the way of insights into reasons for the failure to report crimes.

(4) A capability is absent for ranking Question 20b responses in order of importance.

CONSTRAINTS ON ANALYSIS:

(1) Because of the phraseology of Question 20a, we have felt obliged to couch references to police knowledge of crimes in terms such as "were notified," "were reported," or "were informed."

(2) To the best of our knowledge, and perhaps because of the marginal

analytical utility of the resulting information, data based on response categories 3-5 of Question 20a have not been tabulated.

(3) The first two response categories of Question 20b are producing some 60-70 percent of total reasons for not reporting, with differences among the residual categories often failing to attain statistical significance.

(4) Since multiple response are permitted for Question 20b, the subject must be treated in terms of a percent distribution based on the aggregate level of responses. This conceivably might introduce some distortion in the rank of importance attached by victims to the reasons cited.

EXHIBIT #2

MEDICAL ATTENTION, HOSPITAL TREATMENT, AND EXPENSES: ISSUES CONCERNING THE DATA

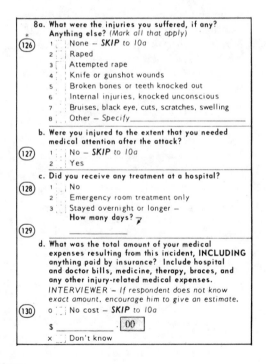

THE PROBLEMS:

(1) In its present form, Question 8b is subject to differing interpretations. According to interviewer training manuals, "need" is determined by actually securing aid from a trained medical professional. However, to a

respondent "need" might be based upon one's conception of the seriousness of the injury, and not on whether medical assistance was obtained. Since the "official" interpretation is not always provided by the interviewer, responses might well be based on differing conceptions of the intent of the question.

(2) Question 8c obtains information on hospital care only. There is no capability for identifying other kinds of medical care, whether professional or nonprofessional, institutional or noninstitutional.

(3) The "Don't know" category in Question 8d is unclear as to meaning.

CONSTRAINTS ON ANALYSIS:

(1) As a result of weaknesses in the structure of Question 8b, we have been unable to analyze the tabulated data.

(2) We have been unable to measure the extent to which injured victims obtained care in places other than hospitals. Perhaps more importantly, we have no mechanism for assessing the number of injured victims who remain untreated.

(3) Because of the ambiguous nature of the "Don't know" category in Question 8d data relating to that question have been excluded. As a result, the analysis of data relating to medical expenses has been fragmentary and weakened by increases in the standard error.

EXHIBIT #3

PLACE OF OCCURRENCE: ISSUES CONCERNING THE DATA

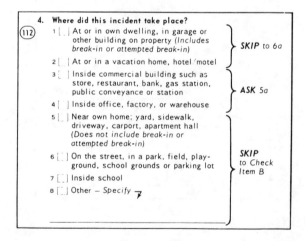

4. Where did this incident take place?

(112)

1 [ ] At or in own dwelling, in garage or other building on property (*Includes break-in or attempted break-in*) ⎫ SKIP *to 6a*

2 [ ] At or in a vacation home, hotel/motel ⎭

3 [ ] Inside commercial building such as store, restaurant, bank, gas station, public conveyance or station ⎫ ASK *5a*

4 [ ] Inside office, factory, or warehouse ⎭

5 [ ] Near own home; yard, sidewalk, driveway, carport, apartment hall (*Does not include break-in or attempted break-in*) ⎫

6 [ ] On the street, in a park, field, playground, school grounds or parking lot ⎬ SKIP *to Check Item B*

7 [ ] Inside school

8 [ ] Other – *Specify*

THE PROBLEM:

For certain (if not most) crimes, the concentration of responses under one or two categories suggests that the categories are not sufficiently discrete.

CONSTRAINTS ON ANALYSIS:

(1) Category #5. Roughly 86% of all household larcenies and 30% of motor vehicle thefts fall into this response. The concept of "near own home" is confusing particularly as it relates to these two crimes. To illustrate, is there essentially any difference among auto thefts from the following kinds of settings: the household garage, the carport, the driveway, the street curb directly in front of the house, the street curb across from the house and the alley in back of the house? If a capability for making these distinctions is desired, then category #5 is not specific enough. If such a capability is undesirable, or unnecessary, then consideration should be given to reconciling category #5 with that part of category #6 now labeled "on the street."

(2) Category #6. About 47% of personal crimes of violence and 64% of motor vehicle thefts fall under this category. For all measured crimes except household burglary and larceny, this response is given at least twice as often as any other one. No capability exists for tallying "street crime incidents," a key variable as it relates to violent offenses.

(3) Category #7. Few sample cases are turning up under this response. Moreover, because play and school grounds are subsumed under category #6, we are unable to measure "school crimes."

(4) Categories Nos. 1, 5, and 6, as they relate to dwellings of different types. Interviewer instructions and the conditions governing the classification of incidents occurring "in home," "near home," "school ground," and "parking lot" are complicated by differences in the architecture and sites of housing structures. Example A: An assault of a victim living in a detached single-family home and occurring on the sidewalk in front of the dwelling would be categorized under #5; but, a comparable assault occurring in the parking lot of the victim's apartment building would be categorized under #6. Consequently, analytical references to the category "near own home" are misleading to persons unfamiliar with the applicable definitions. Example B: An incident occurring to a boarding school student within a dormitory room would be categorized under #1; but, if the incident occurs on grounds outside the dormitory, it would fall under #6.

EXHIBIT #4

MISCELLANEOUS QUESTIONNAIRE ISSUES

Question #2.   About what time did this incident happen?

Comment: Daytime category is very broad and might be subdivided into 6 a.m. to noon, Noon to 6 p.m. classifications in order to effect comparability between daytime and nighttime categories and to enhance utility of the data.

Question #8a.   What were the injuries you suffered, if any?

Comment: Responses 2 ("Raped") and 3 ("Attempted rape") are two of the determinants of physical injury. Yet, attempted rape may involve simply a verbal threat. The inclusion of rapes, especially attempts, would appear to be causing distortions in the data on physical injury.

Question #11b. How old would you say the person was? (With respect to the offender)

Comment: Response 5 "21 or over," a large category, might be subdivided into more specific and meaningful age ranges.

Question #17c. Was any of this loss recovered through insurance?

Comment: A comparable question might be asked regarding recovery of loss through police action. As it now stands, the only methods of recovery elicited through the questionnaire are "insurance" and "other" or a combination of both.

Question #18a. Did any household member lose any time from work because of this incident?

Comment: Clarification is needed on what constitutes "work." Should housewives who lose time from work be included?

EXHIBIT #5

CONCEPTUAL PROBLEM AREAS

1. Larceny: Household larceny and personal larceny without contact are arbitrarily distinguished from one another solely by the incident's place of occurrence, i.e., by the response to Question 4, "Where did this incident take place?" If the response is 1 (At or in own dwelling, etc.) or 5 (Near own home, etc.), the incident is considered a household larceny. All other responses are classified as larcenies away from home—hence, *personal* larcenies without contact. This could lead to the anomaly of an incident involving the theft of an item of general household use, such as a beach umbrella, from a site other than a dwelling being classified as a personal larceny without contact instead of a household larceny. In terms of their rate of incidence, both are very large categories. Yet, each may contain differences, particularly as relates to the types of stolen property, that have not been taken into consideration in classifying the incidents. As it now stands, the analytical utility of the distinction between the two types of larceny is suspect.

2. Organization of reports and treatment of data are complicated by the dichotomy between the two basic units of measure—victimizations and inci-

dents—as well as by the fact that several topical areas do not relate to either of these units as such, but to all possible responses given by victims. These latter topics are: types of weapons used by offenders, self-protective measures used by the victims, and reasons cited by victims for not reporting to the police.

3. The category "no monetary value" used in tabulations of economic loss is not specifically defined. Losses of no monetary value, such as those involving irreplaceable heirlooms or items having intrinsic worth, are not distinguished from loss of trivial, truly valueless items.

4. Attempted robbery with injury is not broken out from its parent category, robbery with injury, in the tabulations. The same is also true of pocket picking, attempts not being categorized.

SERIES VICTIMIZATIONS

Present practice, as exemplified by the advance report on the 1973 data, is to exclude series incidents from the data tables and to discuss them in the statistical appendix to the household survey. The issue is whether this is sufficient or should series incidents be given more prominence or even be incorporated in some fashion with the regular data.

The findings from the 1973 data, which are reproduced here as Exhibit 7, indicate that series victimizations are disproportionately represented in 2 of the crimes being measured: assault and household larceny. Within these two, series crimes fall more heavily in simple assaults and in larcenies under $50 or where the amount was not reported. A set of tabulations are currently produced for the series victimizations which permit some limited comparisons of characteristics of victims of series crimes with those from the regular tabulations. These results have been summarized and presented as Exhibits 8 and 9.[1] The most striking finding is in robberies where 65 percent of series victimizations occur in the 12 to 19 age group, contrasted with 32 percent for regular crimes. Series victimizations are also more likely to involve nonstrangers than is the case with all other victimizations, and whites have greater representation, as well. Differences in household crimes are less striking, although renters are disproportionately victims of burglary and motor vehicle theft; also, the oldest age group is apparently more prone to series burglaries.

If series incidents were to be added to the main body of crime data, several problems emerge. The first is how to assign series incidents to a particular data quarter when the regular estimation procedure is based on the month in which an incident occurred. One way would be to allocate series incidents to one of the six months within each reference period. At present, series incidents are identified as to season of occurrence, which can be as many as 3 for a given series. The next problem would be whether series incidents should be weighted by a factor approximating the number of incidents in the series. At

[1] The series data are for the collection year 1973, while the regular tabulations are based on incidents that occurred entirely within the calendar year.

present, series incidents are weighted as a single incident with no attempt being made to account for the number of incidents, which, by definition, must be at least three. Detailed information is obtained about the most recent incident only. For this reason, it is probably better in the short run to treat series incidents as single units for tabulation purposes until more is known about the nature of these phenomena. Another issue is whether the most recent incident in the series should be used as the one for which details of the series are tabulated—i.e., is it really typical of the entire series?

A short run solution to the handling of series victimizations would be to produce basic tabulations with and without series incidents, counting each incident as one. Month of occurrence would have to be allocated to one of the months in the reference period or to the most recent quarter.

Ultimately, however, a more thorough study of series crimes should be made. It is probable—and this is part of what should be investigated—that there are different kinds of series incidents. Some may be due to interviewer error—in classifying multiple incidents as series crimes—although the number of series incidents fell about 30 percent between 1973 and 1974, indicating progress in this area. Other series incidents might be amenable to more intensive interviewer probing which could result in disentangling the various events so that separate incident reports could be filled and the incidents could then be amalgamated with the regular crimes. However, no matter how fruitful the progress in this area, we would still be left with a residue of legitimate series incidents which could not be separated into discrete episodes. These would presumably be situations in which being a victim was almost a condition of existence, such as by reason of the nature of a person's job or the location of his residence. Thus, the issue would remain of how this "hard core" of series victimizations should be treated.

In the longer run, it would seem to be desirable to find out in more detail the nature of series crimes. Although the requirement to the interviewer in classifying certain incidents as series stresses the similarity of the details of each incident, how similar are they, in fact? Are the times and places of occurrence the same? Are they perpetrated by the same offenders? Over how long a period do they occur—or are they never ending? And a related question, in asking for details of the most recent incident, are we getting a "typical" incident—and what is it that we really want?

A number of approaches might be explored in trying to get at this problem. One would be to produce the standard package of rate tables for series victimizations, once the allocation problem has been resolved. Because these tables have many more victim characteristics than the existing series tables, especially for personal crimes, they might provide more clues as to who the victims of series incidents are. Another step would be to review the summaries that the interviewers make of each incident or series of incidents at the end of the interview. These two steps could be taken in the near future. Beyond this, it would be desirable to design an experiment in the field in which interviewers were trained to probe much more intensively into the circumstances surrounding series incidents. This would provide answers to some of the questions posed earlier and might eventually lead to either revising the basic questionnaire or designing a supplemental document to obtain as many details as possible about series crimes.

[Statement prepared for the Panel for the Evaluation of Crime Surveys, Committee on National Statistics, August 14, 1975.]

EXHIBIT #6

SERIES VICTIMIZATIONS

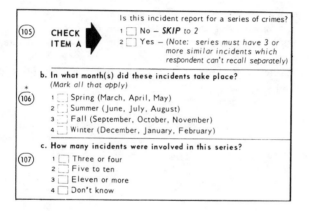

INTERVIEWER INSTRUCTIONS

There are circumstances under which you may report several incidents as a "series" on one Incident Report form. *All of the following conditions must exist before you may do this:*

1. The incidents must be very similar in detail.

2. There must be *at least THREE* incidents in a series, but there will generally be more.

3. *The respondent must not be able to recall dates and other details of the individual incidents* well enough to report them separately.

If a respondent *can* report a series of the same or similar incidents separately, you must fill out one incident report for each incident, regardless of how many incidents are involved.

This device of reporting incidents as a series is *not* to be used for your own convenience but only if necessary, and *as a last resort.* The more serious the crime (for example, a serious attack or an armed robbery), the less likely it will be that it will meet the necessary conditions for a series.

THE PROBLEM:

Should series incidents be given more prominence in analytical reports, possibly to the extent of being incorporated with the regular data?

ISSUES:

(1) Allocation of series incidents to specific months.

(2) Weighting of series incidents as one incident, as is done at present, or by a factor reflecting the number of incidents.

(3) Use of most recent incident to collect details on the incident report.

POSSIBLE APPROACHES:

(1) Produce equivalent of personal and household rate tables for series incidents, once allocation to specific month is resolved.

(2) Review interviewer written descriptions of series incidents.

(3) Design field experiments to probe more intensively into details of serious incidents.

(4) Design new questions to elicit details of series incidents as regular part of NCP interview.

EXHIBIT #7

Number of Series Victimizations and Percent Distribution of Series Victimizations Compared with Victimizations Not in Series, by Type of Crime[a]

Type of Crime	Number of Series Victimizations	Percent Distribution	
		Series 4/73-3/74	Not in Series 1973
Crimes against persons	1,052,800	100.0	100.0[2]
Crimes of violence	487,420	46.3	27.1
Rape	8,120[1]	0.8	0.8
Robbery	51,570	4.9	5.5
Robbery and attempted robbery with injury	7,490[1]	0.7	1.9
Robbery without injury	19,950	1.9	2.1
Attempted robbery without injury	24,130	2.3	1.6
Assault	427,730	40.6	20.8
Aggravated assault	134,560	12.8	8.3
With injury	42,530	4.0	2.7
Attempted assault with weapon	92,030	8.7	5.6
Simple assault	293,170	27.9	12.5
With injury	46,630	4.4	3.1
Attempted assault without weapon	246,540	23.4	9.4
Crimes of theft	565,380	53.7	72.9
Personal larceny with contact	9,350[1]	0.9	2.5
Personal larceny without contact	556,030	52.8	70.4
Crimes against households	760,280	100.0	100.0[2]
Burglary	277,560	36.5	41.9
Forcible entry	70,840	9.3	13.3
Unlawful entry without force	150,230	19.8	19.3
Attempted forcible entry	56,500	7.4	9.3
Household larceny	458,150	60.3	49.4
Under $50	318,640	41.9	31.8
$50 or more	88,820	11.7	12.3
Amount not available	31,090	4.1	1.8
Attempted larceny	19,600	2.6	3.6
Motor vehicle theft	24,570	3.2	8.7
Completed theft	8,620[1]	1.1	5.6
Attempted theft	15,950	2.1	3.0

NOTE: Detail may not add to total shown because of rounding.

[a]Data are for the United States.
[1]Estimate, based on 10 or fewer sample cases, is statistically unreliable.
[2]Percents based on 1973 totals of 20,281,700 victimizations against persons and 15,354,200 directed against households.

EXHIBIT #8

Percent Distribution of Series and Regular Victimizations by Selected Characteristics of Victim and Type of Personal Crime, 1973[a]

Type of Personal Crime	Relationship		Race		Sex		Age				
	Stranger	Nonstranger	White	Black	Male	Female	12-19	20-34	35-49	50-64	65+
Crimes of violence[1]											
Regular	66	34	85	15	65	35	37	39	13	7	3
Series	55	45	90	10	65	35	33	44	13	7	3
Robbery											
Regular	86	14	76	22	72	28	32	33	15	12	9
Series	70	30	80	20	67	33	65	12	17	2	4
Assault											
Regular	60	40	87	13	65	35	39	40	13	6	2
Series	53	47	91	9	66	34	29	48	12	8	3
Aggravated assault											
Regular	62	38	81	18	72	28	39	42	14	5	1
Series	50	50	86	14	66	34	21	54	14	6	5
Simple assault											
Regular	58	42	90	9	61	39	39	39	13	7	2
Series	55	45	94	6	66	34	32	45	12	9	3

NOTE: Detail may not add to 100 percent because of rounding. For the characteristic "Race," the category "Other" was included in the base from which the percentages were calculated.

[a]Data are for the United States.
[1]Includes data on rape, not shown separately.

EXHIBIT #9

Percent Distribution of Series and Regular Victimizations by Selected Characteristics of Household and Type of Household Crime, 1973[a]

Type of Household Crime	Race of Head		Age of Head					Tenure	
	White	Black	12-19	20-34	35-49	50-64	65+	Owned	Rented
Household crime									
Regular	87	12	3	38	30	20	10	57	43
Series	89	10	3	34	31	21	11	57	43
Burglary									
Regular	84	15	4	37	28	20	12	54	46
Series	86	13	4	31	28	20	17	49	51
Larceny									
Regular	89	10	3	38	31	20	9	60	40
Series	91	7	1	35	33	22	8	63	37
Motor vehicle theft									
Regular	85	13	3	42	29	21	5	50	50
Series	84	16	0	40	33	18	8	37	63

NOTE: Detail may not add to 100 percent because of rounding. For the characteristic "Race of Head," the category "Other" was included in the base from which the percentages were calculated.

[a]Data are for the United States.

179

EXHIBIT #10

Washington, D.C.: Victimization Rates for Persons Age 12 and Over, by Selected Characteristics of Victims and Type of Crime (Rate per 1,000 resident population age 12 and over)[a]

	Personal Crimes of Violence								Personal Crimes of Theft		
			Robbery			Assault					
Characteristic[1]	All Personal Crimes of Violence	Rape	All Robberies	Robbery with Injury	Robbery without Injury	All Assaults	Aggravated Assault	Simple Assault	All Personal Crimes of Theft	Personal Larceny with Contact	Personal Larceny without Contact
Total (510,500)	31	1	17	5	13	13	6	7	65	12	53
Sex											
Male (223,400)	41	0	26	7	18	15	8	7	63	4	59
Female (287,200)	23	2	10	2	8	11	4	6	66	18	48
Age											
12-15 (39,100)	32	0	14	4[2]	11	18	6	11	29	4[2]	25
16-19 (44,300)	45	3[2]	27	7	20	15	6	9	67	9	58
20-24 (72,500)	45	4	19	4	15	22	10	11	80	11	69
25-34 (106,600)	39	1[2]	19	5	13	19	8	11	91	11	81
35-49 (100,600)	25	1[2]	15	4	11	9	5	4	64	11	53
50-64 (88,600)	21	0	16	4	12	5	2[2]	2[2]	48	13	35
65 and over (58,800)	14	0	10	3[2]	7	3[2]	3[2]	Z[2]	44	21	23
Race											
White (151,200)	43	1[2]	21	6	15	21	6	15	106	16	90
Black (352,000)	26	1	16	4	12	9	6	3	47	10	37
Annual family income											
Less than $3,000 (47,100)	56	2[2]	27	10	17	27	12	15	67	21	46
$3,000-$7,499 (119,700)	36	3	19	4	15	14	7	7	53	15	39
$7,500-$9,999 (68,800)	26	Z[2]	15	6	9	11	5	6	58	14	44
$10,000-$14,999 (106,700)	23	Z[2]	13	3	9	10	5	5	63	8	54
$15,000-$24,999 (85,300)	23	1[2]	15	4	10	8	3	5	70	8	62
$25,000 or more (52,300)	32	0	17	3[2]	14	15	5	9	98	9	89
Not available (30,700)	32	1[2]	23	5[2]	19	7[2]	5[2]	2[2]	55	10	45

NOTE: Detail may not add to total shown because of rounding.

Z Less than 0.5 per 1,000.

[a] Data refer to a 12-month period ending during first quarter 1974.

[1] Numbers in parentheses refer to population in the group.

[2] Estimate, based on about 10 or fewer sample cases, is statistically unreliable.

EXHIBIT #12

SUGGESTIONS CONCERNING FURTHER ANALYTICAL USES OF NATIONAL CRIME PANEL DATA

In recognition of the fact that the functional subjects and topical areas of possible analysis are quite extensive, the listing that follows below is far from exhaustive. Part of any in-depth analysis of a specific subject matter area, close scrutiny should be made of the questionnaires, variables, and tabulations presently in use to ensure that pertinent information being collected is being processed in usable form. For example, it may be desirable to know in more detail the elements that constitute the crime of "Personal larceny without contact," the single most prevalent type of offense, or more about weapons other than firearms and knives. It is possible that existing variables are not sufficiently detailed or that new variables need to be created, either by expanding the list of categories or by aggregating those already in use. And lastly, consideration should be given as to whether the present tabulations make maximum use of the relevant variables for a particular subject matter area. If not, new tabulations would be required.

A. Drawing on survey results for some or all of the cities sampled to date, it would be possible to isolate any crime grouping, such as "Crimes of violence," or any single crime such as "personal robbery," to conduct the following types of analysis:

(1) Explore general patterns of victimization, as reflected by NCP rates, for the population at large. E.g., "Patterns of Household Burglary in Selected Large Cities."

(2) Undertake a comparative study of intercity differences/similarities in the vulnerability to certain types of victimization by specific population subgroups. E.g., "Patterns of Assault among Black Residents of Selected Large Cities." Such analysis might focus on any possible correspondence between size of the subgroup in question and susceptibility to victimization.

(3) Develop characteristics (time and place of occurrence, number of offenders, weapons use, and extent of losses/damages) common to specific types of crime. E.g., "Characteristics of Personal Robbery in Selected Large Cities."

B. LEAA's special interest in stranger-to-stranger violent crime and burglary suggests several possible areas of analysis, using either city or national survey results.

(1) Comparative study of stranger vs. nonstranger crime in an attempt to identify population subgroups that are more vulnerable to each of the two types of victimization.

(2) A comparative analysis of the characteristics of stranger vs. nonstranger crime to identify salient differences as to their time and place of occurrence, etc.

(3) Exploration of ways in which NCP data on burglary (household

and/or commercial) might complement the findings of other LEAA-supported research on that crime.

C. In the absence of other empirical data, police statistics have served as bases for many current hypotheses concerning victimization. Also, other concepts relating to victimization are the result of highly localized observations by criminologists and law enforcement specialists. After compiling an inventory of selected contemporary hypotheses on victimization from relevant literature, the concepts might be scrutinized in the light of NCP findings.

D. Intercity comparative studies of victimization (or of narrow subject matter areas) among cities sharing common characteristics, be they of a demographic, geographical, or other nature. Such work might well draw upon Census data or on results of household surveys, namely the CPS.

E. Application of correlation analysis techniques in the development of victim profiles or of "typical crime characteristics."

F. Brief reports on narrow, highly specialized topics, either on a city by city basis or for the nation as a whole. E.G., "Firearms Use in the Commission of Personal Robbery." "Motor Vehicle Theft Outside the City of Residence." "Losses and Damages Incurred by the Victims of Household Burglary."

G. Completed vs. attempted crime. Exploration of the elements that seem to govern the outcome of a given type of victimization. This probably would require examination both of the victims involved and of the environmental circumstances in which victimizations occurred.

H. Criminal victimizations among nonstrangers.

(1) If an intercity comparative approach were taken, such an effort might highlight variations in the level of violence among nonstrangers as well as shed some new light on the problem of family/community disharmony.

(2) Comparison of aggregate data for several cities, such as the five largest, with those of the national survey as a test of the preconception that family/community disharmony is more widespread in large urban areas than elsewhere.

I. A comparison of NCP findings with those of the NORC and other surveys of victimization conducted during the mid-1960's. In addition to national results, some analytical comparisons could be done for Boston, Chicago, and Washington.

J. Characteristics of offenders. We have not yet analyzed survey results concerning the demographic characteristics of offenders, as perceived by victims. Thus, we have little or no feel as to the extent to which offenders victimize across race, sex, or age lines. Perhaps more importantly, no groundwork has been prepared to serve as a potential base for studies drawing on independent research into relevant subject matters, of the extent to which victim preconceptions (or prejudices) influence the perception of offender identity or of the degree to which the stress of victimization blurs victim perception.

[Drafted for Mr. Levine 12/5/74]

Cities Originally Selected
but Not Now Planned
To Be Surveyed in 1976

February 19, 1975

Dr. Charles R. Kindermann
Acting Director, Statistics Division
Law Enforcement Assistance Administration
U.S. Department of Justice
Washington, D.C. 20530

Dear Charlie,

We are beginning the planning activities for the 1976 group of cities in the
National Crime Panel. Previous communications (see memorandum of June
16, 1972, to Mr. Shapiro from Mr. Turner) between LEAA and Census have
listed the following cities to be included in this group:

St. Paul	Kansas City
Seattle	*Anaheim, Santa Ana, Garden Grove
Phoenix	*Paterson, Clifton, Passaic
Columbus	*San Bernardino, Riverside, Ontario
Indianapolis	*Tampa, St. Petersburg
San Jose	

We would like verification of this list as the group to be surveyed next
year. If additional cities are to be included (we have been doing 13 cities
each year) they should be identified.

For your consideration in reviewing cities to be included, the following information may be useful. The groups of cities marked with an asterisk may be sampled to provide data for the group or to provide data for each city within the group. If individual city statistics are desired with about the same reliability as other Cities Sample areas, the total sample size for the group will be larger. On the other hand, if the group of cities are to be combined for tabulation, the normal sample size will be used for the area and they will be sampled as a group.

In addition, the total population of Paterson, Clifton, Passaic is under 250,000. Thus a data tape would not be released for this group in order to maintain confidentiality.

In order to meet an early 1976 interview start date, we must begin work on sample selection early in March. If this list of cities is to be surveyed, or a revised list is contemplated, please let us know as soon as possible so that planning and scheduling of work can proceed.

Sincerely,

(*signed*) Earle J. Gerson

EARLE J. GERSON
Chief, Demographic Surveys Division
Bureau of the Census

cc:

C. Kindermann (LEAA)	M. Boisen (SMD)
D. Nelson	E. Gerson/M. Thompson (DSD)
B. Eidson (NRC)	B. Cohen
W. Simmons	B. Sharp
D. Levine (DIRS)	R. Goodson
S. Kallek	G. Gray
M. Hendry (BUS)	K. Daniels
R. Burt (FLD)	L. Murphy
R. Parkinson (ODA)	

DSD:LMurphy:bjs 2/14/75

Confidentiality Restrictions on Geographical Identification

December 6, 1974

Dr. Charles Kindermann
Law Enforcement Assistance Administration
U.S. Department of Justice
416 5th Street, N.W.
Washington, D.C. 20530

Dear Charlie,

As a result of recent discussions with you, Tony Turner of SRD, and Paul Bettin of SMD regarding identifying items that need to be deleted from the NCS National Sample data tape to preserve confidentiality, we propose the following regarding geographic identification for the tape.

We propose deleting State, County, and Universal Area codes as well as place description codes. We suggest adding a code identifying the 10 OMB regions and a code to identify central city of SMSA, in SMSA but not in central city, and not SMSA. Because we propose to delete State codes, we would like to retain as many place size codes as possible, within confidentiality requirement limits. However, as it may take some time to determine the maximum number of place size codes allowable, we propose to collapse the codes as indicated below for the initial tapes, perhaps through Data Quarter 2, 1974, and expand the range of codes for subsequent tapes. The recommended collapsed place size codes are:

13 = 250,000 to 499,999
14 = 500,000 to 999,999
15 = 1,000,000 or more
16 = remainder, including non-place sample areas

If this proposal is acceptable, please let us know so that we may proceed with preparation of the National Sample data tapes.

Sincerely,

(*Signed*) Marvin M. Thompson

MARVIN M. THOMPSON
Assistant Division Chief for Special Surveys
Bureau of the Census

cc:

B. Eidson	G. Shapiro	B. Sharp
W. Simmons	D. Bateman	R. Goodson
D. Nelson	P. Bettin	G. Gray
R. Parkinson	E. Gerson/M. Thompson	L. Murphy
M. Boisen	B. Cohen	

DSD:LMurphy:bjs 12/6/74

NCS Household Interview Schedule and Classification Scheme

The interview schedules (Forms NCS 1 and 2) and the description of the NCS classification scheme contained in this appendix are taken from *National Crime Survey Documentation*, U.S. Bureau of the Census.

PART A: NCS HOUSEHOLD INTERVIEW SCHEDULE

FORM NCS-500 (10-19-78) U.S. DEPARTMENT OF COMMERCE — BUREAU OF THE CENSUS

CONTROL CARD
NATIONAL CRIME SURVEY
NATIONAL SAMPLE

NOTICE – Your report to the Census Bureau is confidential by law (U.S. Code 42, Section 3761). All identifiable information will be used only by persons engaged in and for the purposes of the survey, and may not be disclosed or released to others for any purpose.

Form approved O.M.B. No. 41-R2661

1. LETTER SENT (Circle Y or N)	2. HOUSE-HOLD NO.	3. SEGMENT TYPE	4. SAMPLE	5. CONTROL NUMBER	Serial
		☐ Area ☐ Permit ☐ Address	J O	PSU Segment Ck.	

6a. ADDRESS (Sheet_____ Line_____) What is your exact address?
(Include House No., St., Apt. No., or other identification)

Place, State, and ZIP code

6b. Is this is also your mailing address? If same mark box. → ☐
(If different, specify below — include ZIP code.)

6c. Special Place name — Type code — Sample No.

ASK AREA SEGMENTS ONLY

6d. YEAR BUILT
- ☐ Ask 1st — Ask
- ☐ Do NOT Ask

7. ASK: Ask during 1st and 4th enumeration periods

a. Are there any other occupied or vacant living quarters besides your own in this building?

b. Are there any occupied or vacant living quarters besides your own on this floor?

c. Is there any other building on this property for people to live in — either occupied or vacant?

☐ 4. NONE

ASK 1st, 4th, 5th, and 7th ENUMERATION PERIODS — Circle Y or N

8. TENURE
- Are your living quarters —
- Owned or being bought by you or someone in your household?
- Rented for cash?
- Occupied without payment of cash rent?

9.–11. LAND USE

9a. ☐ URBAN (A) – SKIP to 10a   ☐ RURAL
- Reg. units, and So. Pl. units — coded 85–88 in 6c: Go to 9b
- So. Pl. units not coded 85–88 : Skip to 10a

9b. You told me your living quarters are — (Read entry in Control Card (Item 8))
Does the place you (own/own) have 10 acres or more? — Circle Y or N
Y – Ask 10   N – Ask 11

10. During the past 12 months, did sales of crops, livestock and other farm products from this place amount to $50 or more?

11. During the past 12 months did sales of crops, livestock and other farm products from this place amount to $250 or more?

NOTE: TRANSCRIBE FINAL CODE (A, B, C, D, E) TO NCS-1.

12. NAME (Last name first)

What is the name of the head of this household?

What are the names of all others persons who are living or staying here?

List all persons staying/living here and all persons who usually live here who are absent. Be sure to INCLUDE infants under 1 year of age.

13a. RELATIONSHIP TO HOUSEHOLD HEAD
Example: Head, wife, son, daughter-in-law, partner, lodger, lodger's wife, etc.

13b. HOUSEHOLD MEMBER — Circle Y – Yes or N – No

14. Ask each line the household (in interviewed, (if "Yes," enter name in Item 13a above)):
- I have listed (Read names in Item 13a)
- Have I missed:
  - Any babies or small children?
  - Any lodgers, boarders, or persons in your employ who live here?
  - Anyone who usually lives here but is away at present traveling or in the hospital?
  - Anyone else staying here?

15. LIVING QUARTERS
- ☐ House, apartment, flat
- ☐ HU in rooming house
- ☐ HU in nontransient hotel, motel, etc.
- ☐ HU-permanent in transient hotel, motel, etc.

15a. HOUSING UNIT (Indicate type, access and kitchen facilities)
- ☐ HU in rooming house
- ☐ Mobile home or trailer
- ☐ HU not specified above (Describe in notes)

15b. ACCESS
- ☐ Direct
- ☐ Through another unit

15c. COMPLETE KITCHEN FACILITIES
- ☐ For this unit only
- ☐ Also used by another household
- ☐ None

15d. OTHER UNIT (Indicate type)
- ☐ Quarters not HU in rooming house or boarding house
- ☐ Unit not permanent in transient hotel, motel, etc.
- ☐ Not specified above (Describe in notes)

16. AGE LAST BIRTHDAY
What is ___'s date of birth?
If under 1 year of age, enter "0". Enter in numerals.
Month / Day / Year

GO TO 17 if MEMBER

17. Enter in numerals

18. MARITAL STATUS — Is ___ now married, widowed, divorced, separated, or has ___ never been married? (Circle No.)

19a. RACE — W-White, N-Negro, or Amer. Indian, Japanese, Chinese, etc. (Circle No.)

19b. Origin or descent — code from above

20. SEX — Circle M-Male or F-Female / Armed Forces?

21. MALES 18+ — Circle Y-Yes or N-No / Is ___ now in the Armed Forces?

22. Did ___ attend school? What is the highest grade (or year) of regular school ___ has ever attended?
- Never attended or Kindergarten — 00
- Elementary — 1–8
- High School — 9–12
- College — 1–4, 5+

23. Did ___ complete that grade (year)? — Circle Y – Yes or N – No

NOTE: ASK FOR PERSONS WITH "YES" IN ITEM 13c

24. CHANGES IN HOUSEHOLD COMPOSITION — Continue in note 24 if necessary

25. USE OF TELEPHONE (Circle or mark (X))
a. Is there a telephone in this house/apartment? Y – Yes   N – No – Skip to e
b. Is there a telephone elsewhere on which people in this household can be called? Y – Yes   N – No – Skip to e
c. What is the telephone number?
d. Is a telephone interview acceptable? Y   N
 - Area code.
 - Refused number – Skip to e
e. What is the best time to call or visit?

26. UNITS IN STRUCTURE How many housing units are in this structure? (If not sure, ask.)
1 / 2 / 3 / 4 / 5–9 / 10+ / Mobile home or trailer / Only OTHER units

27. TOTAL FAMILY INCOME IN PAST 12 MONTHS — Ask for all household members 12 or older; then for each household in past 12 months? This includes wages and salaries, net income from business or farm, pensions, interest, rent, and any other money income received by the members of this family. (Show flashcard.) (Mark "X" appropriate column)
- Under $1,000
- $1,000 to 1,999
- 2,000 to 2,999
- 3,000 to 3,999
- 4,000 to 4,999
- 5,000 to 5,999
- $7,500 to 9,999
- 10,000 to 11,999
- 12,000 to 14,999
- 15,000 to 19,999
- 20,000 to 24,999
- 25,000 to 49,999
- 50,000 and over

15c. If NONE, and unit is vacant, did last occupants have complete kitchen facilities?

28a. CONTROL NUMBER — ORIGINAL SAMPLE UNIT

28b. In area segments, enter HU as FIRST listed on property. Listing sheet. Sheet___ Line___
- ☐ Vacant tent site or trailer site
- ☐ Unit not permanent in transient hotel, motel, etc.
- ☐ Not specified above (Describe in notes)

Codes for Item 19b
41 – German
42 – Italian
43 – Irish
44 – French
45 – Polish
46 – Russian
47 – English
48 – Scottish
49 – Welsh
50 – Mexican-American
51 – Chicano
52 – Mexican
53 – Mexicano
54 – Puerto Rican
55 – Cuban
56 – Central or South American
57 – Other Spanish
58 – Negro
59 – Another group NOT listed

188

29. RECORD OF VISITS AND TELEPHONE CALLS

Month and year (e.g. 1/76) a.	Tally of personal visits b.			Tally of phone calls c.		Notes (on callbacks, etc.) d.
	Before 5 p.m.	5 p.m. and after	Before 5 p.m.	5 p.m. and after		
1						
2						
3						
4						
5						
6						
7						
Notes						

30. SUPERVISOR'S USE
R – Reinterview
O – Observed

31. RECORD OF INCIDENTS (Bounding information)

Date of incident (season of series) a.	Description of incident b.	Person involved c.

TABLE X – LIVING QUARTERS DETERMINATIONS AT LISTED ADDRESS

Line No. (1)	LOCATION OF UNIT (2) Where are these quarters located? Enter exact description or location, e.g., basement; 2nd floor, rear. After entering description or location: • In Area Segment, go to (3). • In other type of Segments. – If living quarters are not within the same specific sample address (and structure, if Permit Segment) – STOP TABLE X. – Otherwise, go to (3)	If listed, enter line number and STOP • If unlisted, – And Area Segment, go to (4). – And another type of segment, go to (5). (3)	If outside AREA SEGMENT boundary, mark loss below, STOP and – • Go to next line of Table X, if additional quarters determined, or • Continue with interview for original unit (4)	Are these (Specify location) quarters for more than one group of people? If Yes, fill one line for each group (5)		OCCUPIED Do the occupants of these (specify location) quarters live and eat with any other group of people? (6)	Direct access free the outside or through a common hall? (7)	Complete kitchen facilities for this unit only? (8)	CLASSIFICATION N – Not a separate unit, add occupants to this Control Card; HU/OT Separate unit – Interview on a separate Control Card (9)	
				Yes	No					
1		5 ____ L ____	☐ Outside segment boundary	Yes	No	Yes – Go to (9) and circle N ___ No	Yes ___ No	Yes ___ No	N HU	OT
2		5 ____ L ____	☐ Outside segment boundary	Yes	No	Yes – Go to (9) and circle N ___ No	Yes ___ No	Yes ___ No	N HU	OT
3		5 ____ L ____	☐ Outside segment boundary	Yes	No	Yes – Go to (9) and circle N ___ No	Yes ___ No	Yes ___ No	N HU	OT

USE OR CHARACTERISTICS — ALL QUARTERS

NOTE: BE SURE TO CONTINUE INTERVIEW FOR ORIGINAL UNIT AFTER COMPLETING TABLE X FOR ALL LINES.

FORM HC-5400 (10-15-75)

☆USGPO: 1975 — 659-965/34 Region 5-II

189

O.M.B. No. 41-R2661; Approval Expires June 30, 1977

FORM **NCS-1** AND **NCS-2**
(8-15-75)

U.S. DEPARTMENT OF COMMERCE
BUREAU OF THE CENSUS
ACTING AS COLLECTING AGENT FOR THE
LAW ENFORCEMENT ASSISTANCE ADMINISTRATION
U.S. DEPARTMENT OF JUSTICE

NATIONAL CRIME SURVEY
NATIONAL SAMPLE

NCS-1 – BASIC SCREEN QUESTIONNAIRE
NCS-2 – CRIME INCIDENT REPORT

NOTICE – Your report to the Census Bureau is confidential by law (U.S. Code 42, Section 3761). All identifiable information will be used only by persons engaged in and for the purposes of the survey, and may not be disclosed or released to others for any purpose.

Sample (cc 4)	Control number (cc 5)			
	PSU	Segment	Ck	Serial
JO _____				

Household number (cc 2) | Land use (cc 9–11)

N C S 1 and 2

INTERVIEWER: *Fill Sample and Control numbers, and items 1, 2, 4, and 9 at time of interview.*

1. Interviewer identification
(010) Code | Name

2. Record of interview
(011) Line number of household respondent (cc 12) | Date completed

3. TYPE Z NONINTERVIEW
Interview not obtained for ↗
Line number
(016) _____ NOTE: *Fill NCS-7 Noninterview Record, for Types A, B, and C noninterviews.*
(017) _____
(018) _____
(019) _____
Complete 14–21 for each line number listed.

4. Household status
(020)
1 [ ] Same household as last enumeration
2 [ ] Replacement household since last enumeration
3 [ ] Previous noninterview or not in sample before

5. Special place type code (cc 6c)
(021) _____

6. Tenure (cc 8)
(022)
1 [ ] Owned or being bought
2 [ ] Rented for cash
3 [ ] No cash rent

7. Type of living quarters (cc 15)
Housing unit
(023)
1 [ ] House, apartment, flat
2 [ ] HU in nontransient hotel, motel, etc.
3 [ ] HU – Permanent in transient hotel, motel, etc.
4 [ ] HU in rooming house
5 [ ] Mobile home or trailer
6 [ ] HU not specified above – Describe ↗

OTHER Unit
7 [ ] Quarters not HU in rooming or boarding house
8 [ ] Unit not permanent in transient hotel, motel, etc.
9 [ ] Vacant tent site or trailer site
10 [ ] Not specified above – Describe ↗
_____

8. Number of housing units in structure (cc 26)
(024)
1 [ ] 1   5 [ ] 5–9
2 [ ] 2   6 [ ] 10 or more
3 [ ] 3   7 [ ] Mobile home or trailer
4 [ ] 4   8 [ ] Only OTHER units

ASK IN EACH HOUSEHOLD:

9. (Other than the . . . business) does anyone in this household operate a business from this address?
(025)
1 [ ] No
2 [ ] Yes – What kind of business is that? ↗

INTERVIEWER: *Enter unrecognizable businesses only*

CENSUS USE ONLY

(026) **10. Family income (cc 27)**
1 [ ] Under $1,000
2 [ ] $1,000 to 1,999
3 [ ] 2,000 to 2,999
4 [ ] 3,000 to 3,999
5 [ ] 4,000 to 4,999
6 [ ] 5,000 to 5,999
7 [ ] 6,000 to 7,499
8 [ ] 7,500 to 9,999
9 [ ] 10,000 to 11,999
10 [ ] 12,000 to 14,999
11 [ ] 15,000 to 19,999
12 [ ] 20,000 to 24,999
13 [ ] 25,000 to 49,999
14 [ ] 50,000 and over

11a. Household members 12 years of age and OVER ↗
(027) _____ Total number

b. Household members UNDER 12 years of age ↗
(028) _____ Total number
0 [ ] None

12. Crime Incident Reports filled ↗
(029) _____ Total number – Fill item 31
on Control Card
0 [ ] None

13a. Use of telephone (cc 25)
[ ] Phone in unit (Yes in cc 25a)
Phone interview acceptable? (cc 25c or 25d)
(030)
1 [ ] Yes . . . . } SKIP to next
2 [ ] No – Refused number } applicable item
[ ] Phone elsewhere (Yes in cc 25b)
Phone interview acceptable? (cc 25c or 25d)
3 [ ] Yes . . . . } SKIP to next
4 [ ] No – Refused number } applicable item
5 [ ] No phone (No in cc 25a and 25b)

13b. Proxy information – Fill for all proxy interviews
(1) Proxy interview obtained for line number _____
Proxy respondent name | Line number
_____
Reason for proxy interview
_____

(2) Proxy interview obtained for line number _____
Proxy respondent name | Line number
_____
Reason for proxy interview
_____

If more than 2 Proxy Interviews, continue in notes.

(031) | (032) | (033)

PERSONAL CHARACTERISTICS

14. NAME (of household respondent) KEYER – BEGIN NEW RECORD	15. TYPE OF INTERVIEW	16. LINE NO. (cc 12)	17. RELATIONSHIP TO HOUSEHOLD HEAD (cc 13b)	18. AGE LAST BIRTH-DAY (cc 17)	19. MARITAL STATUS (cc 18)	20a. RACE (cc 19a)	20b. ORIGIN (cc 19b)	21. SEX (cc 20)	22. ARMED FORCES MEMBER (cc 21)	23. Education– highest grade (cc 22)	24. Education– complete that year? (cc 23)
Last	(034) 1 ⌐ ¬ Per – Self-respondent 2 ⌐ ¬ Tel. – Self-respondent 3 ⌐ ¬ Per. – Proxy *Fill 13b on* 4 ⌐ ¬ Tel. – Proxy } *cover page* 5 ⌐ ¬ NI – *Fill 16-21*	(035) Line No.	(036) 1 ⌐ ¬ Head 2 ⌐ ¬ Wife of head 3 ⌐ ¬ Own child 4 ⌐ ¬ Other relative 5 ⌐ ¬ Non-relative	(037) Age	(038) 1 ⌐ ¬ M. 2 ⌐ ¬ Wd. 3 ⌐ ¬ D. 4 ⌐ ¬ Sep. 5 ⌐ ¬ NM	(039) 1 ⌐ ¬ W. 2 ⌐ ¬ Neg. 3 ⌐ ¬ Ot. Origin		(040) 1 ⌐ ¬ M 2 ⌐ ¬ F	(041) 1 ⌐ ¬ Yes 2 ⌐ ¬ No	(042) Grade	(043) 1 ⌐ ¬ Yes 2 ⌐ ¬ No
First											

CHECK ITEM A ➤ Look at item 4 on cover page. Is this the same household as last enumeration? (Box *1* marked)
☐ Yes – **SKIP** to Check Item B ☐ No

25a. Did you live in this house on April 1, 1970?
(044) 1 ☐ Yes – **SKIP** to Check Item B 2 ☐ No

b. Where did you live on April 1, 1970? (State, foreign country, U.S. possession, etc.)
State, etc. _____ County _____

c. Did you live inside the limits of a city, town, village, etc.?
(045) 1 ☐ No 2 ☐ Yes – Name of city, town, village, etc. ⌐
(046) ☐☐☐☐

(Ask males 18+ only)
d. Were you in the Armed Forces on April 1, 1970?
(047) 1 ☐ Yes 2 ☐ No

CHECK ITEM B ➤ Is this person 16 years old or older?
☐ No – **SKIP** to 29 ☐ Yes

26a. What were you doing most of LAST WEEK – (working, keeping house, going to school) or something else?
(048)
1 ☐ Working – **SKIP** to 28a 6 ☐ Unable to work – **SKIP** to 26d
2 ☐ With a job but not at work 7 ☐ Retired
3 ☐ Looking for work 8 ☐ Other – Specify ⌐
4 ☐ Keeping house _____
5 ☐ Going to school *(If Armed Forces, SKIP to 28a)*

b. Did you do any work at all LAST WEEK, not counting work around the house? (Note *If farm or business operator in HH, ask about unpaid work.)*
(049) 0 ☐ No Yes – How many hours? _____ – **SKIP** to 28a

c. Did you have a job or business from which you were temporarily absent or on layoff LAST WEEK?
(050) 1 ☐ No 2 ☐ Yes – Absent – **SKIP** to 28a
3 ☐ Yes – Layoff – **SKIP** to 27

26d. Have you been looking for work during the past 4 weeks?
(051) 1 ☐ Yes No – When did you last work?
2 ☐ Less than 5 years ago – **SKIP** to 28a
3 ☐ 5 or more years ago } **SKIP** to 29
4 ☐ Never worked

27. Is there any reason why you could not take a job LAST WEEK?
(052) 1 ☐ No Yes – 2 ☐ Already had a job
3 ☐ Temporary illness
4 ☐ Going to school
5 ☐ Other – Specify ⌐

28a. For whom did you (last) work? (Name of company, business, organization or other employer)
(053) x ☐ Never worked – **SKIP** to 29

b. What kind of business or industry is this? (E.g.: TV and radio mfg., retail shoe store, State Labor Department, farm)
(054)

c. Were you –
(055)
1 ☐ An employee of a PRIVATE company, business or individual for wages, salary or commissions?
2 ☐ A GOVERNMENT employee (Federal, State, county, or local)?
3 ☐ SELF-EMPLOYED in OWN business, professional practice or farm?
4 ☐ Working WITHOUT PAY in family business or farm?

d. What kind of work were you doing? (E.g.: electrical engineer, stock clerk, typist, farmer, Armed Forces)
(056)

e. What were your most important activities or duties? (E.g.: typing, keeping account books, selling cars, Armed Forces)

Notes

FORM NCS-1 (8-15-75)

HOUSEHOLD SCREEN QUESTIONS

29. Now I'd like to ask some questions about crime. They refer only to the last 6 months —

between _____ 1, 197___ and _____, 197___.
During the last 6 months, did anyone break into or somehow illegally get into your (apartment/home), garage, or another building on your property?

☐ Yes – How many times?
☐ No

30. (Other than the incident(s) just mentioned) Did you find a door jimmied, a lock forced, or any other signs of an ATTEMPTED break in?

☐ Yes – How many times?
☐ No

31. Was anything at all stolen that is kept outside your home, or happened to be left out, such as a bicycle, a garden hose, or lawn furniture? (other than any incidents already mentioned)

☐ Yes – How many times?
☐ No

32. Did anyone take something belonging to you or to any member of this household, from a place where you or they were temporarily staying, such as a friend's or relative's home, a hotel or motel, or a vacation home?

☐ Yes – How many times?
☐ No

33. What was the total number of motor vehicles (cars, trucks, etc.) owned by you or any other member of this household during the last 6 months?

(057)
0 ☐ None – SKIP to 36
1 ☐ 1
2 ☐ 2
3 ☐ 3
4 ☐ 4 or more

34. Did anyone steal, TRY to steal, or use (it/any of them) without permission?

☐ Yes – How many times?
☐ No

35. Did anyone steal or TRY to steal parts attached to (it/any of them), such as a battery, hubcaps, tape-deck, etc.?

☐ Yes – How many times?
☐ No

INDIVIDUAL SCREEN QUESTIONS

36. The following questions refer only to things that happened to YOU during the last 6 months —

between _____ 1, 197___ and _____, 197___.
Did you have your (pocket picked/purse snatched)?

☐ Yes – How many times?
☐ No

37. Did anyone take something (else) directly from you by using force, such as by a stickup, mugging or threat?

☐ Yes – How many times?
☐ No

38. Did anyone TRY to rob you by using force or threatening to harm you? (other than any incidents already mentioned)

☐ Yes – How many times?
☐ No

39. Did anyone beat you up, attack you or hit you with something, such as a rock or bottle? (other than any incidents already mentioned)

☐ Yes – How many times?
☐ No

40. Were you knifed, shot at, or attacked with some other weapon by anyone at all? (other than any incidents already mentioned)

☐ Yes – How many times?
☐ No

41. Did anyone THREATEN to beat you up or THREATEN you with a knife, gun, or some other weapon, NOT including telephone threats? (other than any incidents already mentioned)

☐ Yes – How many times?
☐ No

42. Did anyone TRY to attack you in some other way? (other than any incidents already mentioned)

☐ Yes – How many times?
☐ No

43. During the last 6 months, did anyone steal things that belonged to you from inside ANY car or truck, such as packages or clothing?

☐ Yes – How many times?
☐ No

44. Was anything stolen from you while you were away from home, for instance at work, in a theater or restaurant, or while traveling?

☐ Yes – How many times?
☐ No

45. (Other than any incidents you've already mentioned) was anything (else) at all stolen from you during the last 6 months?

☐ Yes – How many times?
☐ No

46. Did you find any evidence that someone ATTEMPTED to steal something that belonged to you? (other than any incidents already mentioned)

☐ Yes – How many times?
☐ No

47. Did you call the police during the last 6 months to report something that happened to YOU which you thought was a crime? (Do not count any calls made to the police concerning the incidents you have just told me about.)

☐ No – SKIP to 48
☐ Yes – What happened?

_____

_____

(058) ☐☐
      ☐☐
      ☐☐

CHECK ITEM C ▶ Look at 47. Was HH member 12+ attacked or threatened, or was something stolen or an attempt made to steal something that belonged to him?

☐ Yes – How many times?
☐ No

48. Did anything happen to YOU during the last 6 months which you thought was a crime, but did NOT report to the police? (other than any incidents already mentioned)

☐ No – SKIP to Check Item E
☐ Yes – What happened?

_____

_____

(059) ☐☐
      ☐☐
      ☐☐

CHECK ITEM D ▶ Look at 48. Was HH member 12+ attacked or threatened, or was something stolen or an attempt made to steal something that belonged to him?

☐ Yes – How many times?
☐ No

CHECK ITEM E ▶ Do any of the screen questions contain any entries for "How many times?"
☐ No – *Interview next HH member. End interview if last respondent, and fill item 12 on cover page.*
☐ Yes – *Fill Crime Incident Reports.*

FORM NCS-1 (8-15-75)

PERSONAL CHARACTERISTICS

14. NAME KEYER – BEGIN NEW RECORD	15. TYPE OF INTERVIEW	16. LINE NO. (cc 12)	17. RELATIONSHIP TO HOUSEHOLD HEAD (cc 13b)	18. AGE LAST BIRTH-DAY (cc 17)	19. MARITAL STATUS (cc 18)	20a. RACE (cc 19a)	20b. ORIGIN (cc 19b)	21. SEX (cc 20)	22. ARMED FORCES MEMBER (cc 21)	23. Education– highest grade (cc 22)	24. Education– complete that year? (cc 23)
Last	(034) 1 Per – Self respondent 2 Tel. – Self respondent 3 Per. – Proxy } Fill 13b on 4 Tel. – Proxy } cover page 5 NI – Fill 16–21	(035)	(036) 1 Head 2 Wife of head 3 Own child 4 Other relative 5 Non-relative	(037)	(038) 1 M. 2 Wd. 3 D. 4 Sep. 5 NM	(039) 1 W. 2 Neg. 3 Ot.	Origin	(040) 1 M 2 F	(041) 1 Yes 2 No	(042) Grade	(043) 1 Yes 2 No
First		Line No.		Age							

CHECK ITEM A ▶ Look at item 4 on cover page. Is this the same household as last enumeration? (Box 1 marked)
☐ Yes – *SKIP* to Check Item B   ☐ No

25a. Did you live in this house on April 1, 1970?
(044) 1 ☐ Yes – *SKIP* to Check Item B   2 ☐ No

b. Where did you live on April 1, 1970? (State, foreign country, U.S. possession, etc.)
State, etc. _____ County _____

c. Did you live inside the limits of a city, town, village, etc.?
(045) 1 ☐ No   2 ☐ Yes – *Name of city, town, village, etc.* ⤵
(046) ☐☐☐☐

(Ask males 18+ only)
d. Were you in the Armed Forces on April 1, 1970?
(047) 1 ☐ Yes   2 ☐ No

CHECK ITEM B Is this person 16 years old or older?
☐ No – *SKIP* to 36   ☐ Yes

26a. What were you doing most of LAST WEEK – (working, keeping house, going to school) or something else?
(048) 1 ☐ Working – *SKIP* to 28a   6 ☐ Unable to work – *SKIP* to 26d
2 ☐ With a job but not at work   7 ☐ Retired
3 ☐ Looking for work   8 ☐ Other – Specify ⤵
4 ☐ Keeping house
5 ☐ Going to school   (If Armed Forces, *SKIP* to 28a)

b. Did you do any work at all LAST WEEK, not counting work around the house? (Note: If farm or business operator in HH, ask about unpaid work.)
(049) 0 ☐ No   Yes – How many hours? ____ – *SKIP* to 28a

c. Did you have a job or business from which you were temporarily absent or on layoff LAST WEEK?
(050) 1 ☐ No   2 ☐ Yes – Absent – *SKIP* to 28a
3 ☐ Yes – Layoff – *SKIP* to 27

26d. Have you been looking for work during the past 4 weeks?
(051) 1 ☐ Yes   No – When did you last work?
2 ☐ Less than 5 years ago – *SKIP* to 28a
3 ☐ 5 or more years ago }
4 ☐ Never worked } *SKIP* to 36

27. Is there any reason why you could not take a job LAST WEEK?
(052) 1 ☐ No   Yes – 2 ☐ Already had a job
3 ☐ Temporary illness
4 ☐ Going to school
5 ☐ Other – Specify ⤵

28a. For whom did you (last) work? (Name of company, business, organization or other employer)
(053) x ☐ Never worked – *SKIP* to 36

b. What kind of business or industry is this? (E.g. TV and radio mfg., retail shoe store, State Labor Department, farm)
(054) ☐☐☐☐

c. Were you –
(055) 1 ☐ An employee of a PRIVATE company, business or individual for wages, salary or commissions?
2 ☐ A GOVERNMENT employee (Federal, State, county, or local)?
3 ☐ SELF-EMPLOYED in OWN business, professional practice or farm?
4 ☐ Working WITHOUT PAY in family business or farm?

d. What kind of work were you doing? (E.g. electrical engineer, stock clerk, typist, farmer, Armed Forces)
(056) ☐☐☐☐

e. What were your most important activities or duties? (E.g. typing, keeping account books, selling cars, Armed Forces)

INDIVIDUAL SCREEN QUESTIONS

	Yes – How many times?	No
36. The following questions refer only to things that happened to YOU during the last 6 months – between ___ 1, 197___ and ___, 197___. Did you have your (pocket picked/purse snatched)?	Yes – How many times?	No
37. Did anyone take something (else) directly from you by using force, such as by a stickup, mugging or threat?	Yes – How many times?	No
38. Did anyone TRY to rob you by using force or threatening to harm you? (other than any incidents already mentioned)	Yes – How many times?	No
39. Did anyone beat you up, attack you or hit you with something, such as a rock or bottle? (other than any incidents already mentioned)	Yes – How many times?	No
40. Were you knifed, shot at, or attacked with some other weapon by anyone at all? (other than any incidents already mentioned)	Yes – How many times?	No
41. Did anyone THREATEN to beat you up or THREATEN you with a knife, gun, or some other weapon, NOT including telephone threats? (other than any incidents already mentioned)	Yes – How many times?	No
42. Did anyone TRY to attack you in some other way? (other than any incidents already mentioned)	Yes – How many times?	No
43. During the last 6 months, did anyone steal things that belonged to you from inside ANY car or truck, such as packages or clothing?	Yes – How many times?	No
44. Was anything stolen from you while you were away from home, for instance at work, in a theater or restaurant, or while traveling?	Yes – How many times?	No
45. (Other than any incidents you've already mentioned) Was anything (else) at all stolen from you during the last 6 months?	Yes – How many times?	No

46. Did you find any evidence that someone ATTEMPTED to steal something that belonged to you? (other than any incidents already mentioned) — Yes – How many times? / No

47. Did you call the police during the last 6 months to report something that happened to YOU which you thought was a crime? (Do not count any calls made to the police concerning the incidents you have just told me about.)
(058) ☐ No – *SKIP* to 48
☐ Yes – What happened? _____

CHECK ITEM C ▶ Look at 47 – Was HH member 12+ attacked or threatened, or was something stolen or an attempt made to steal something that belonged to him? — Yes – How many times? / No

48. Did anything happen to YOU during the last 6 months which you thought was a crime, but did NOT report to the police? (other than any incidents already mentioned)
(059) ☐ No – *SKIP* to Check Item E
☐ Yes – What happened? _____

CHECK ITEM D ▶ Look at 48 – Was HH member 12+ attacked or threatened, or was something stolen or an attempt made to steal something that belonged to him? — Yes – How many times? / No

CHECK ITEM E ▶ Do any of the screen questions contain any entries for "How many times?"
☐ No – Interview next HH member. End interview if last respondent, and fill item 12 on cover page.
☐ Yes – Fill Crime Incident Reports.

FORM NCS-1 8-15-75

PERSONAL CHARACTERISTICS

14. NAME KEYER – BEGIN NEW RECORD	15. TYPE OF INTERVIEW	16. LINE NO.	17. RELATIONSHIP TO HOUSEHOLD HEAD	18. AGE LAST BIRTH-DAY	19. MARITAL STATUS	20a. RACE	20b. ORIGIN	21. SEX	22. ARMED FORCES MEMBER	23. Education – highest grade	24. Education – complete that year?
		(cc 12)	(cc 13b)	(cc 17)	(cc 18)	(cc 19a)	(cc 19b)	(cc 20)	(cc 21)	(cc 22)	(cc 23)
Last	(034) 1 ☐ Per. – Self-respondent 2 ☐ Tel. – Self-respondent 3 ☐ Per. – Proxy ⎫ Fill 13b or 4 ☐ Tel. – Proxy ⎭ cover page 5 ☐ NI – Fill 16–21	(035) Line No.	(036) 1 ☐ Head 2 ☐ Wife of head 3 ☐ Own child 4 ☐ Other relative 5 ☐ Non-relative	(037) Age	(038) 1 ☐ M. 2 ☐ Wd. 3 ☐ D. 4 ☐ Sep. 5 ☐ NM	(039) 1 ☐ W. 2 ☐ Neg. 3 ☐ Ot. Origin		(040) 1 ☐ M 2 ☐ F	(041) 1 ☐ Yes 2 ☐ No Grade	(042)	(043) 1 ☐ Yes 2 ☐ No
First											

CHECK ITEM A ➤ Look at item 4 on cover page. Is this the same household as last enumeration? (Box 1 marked)
☐ Yes – *SKIP to Check Item B* ☐ No

(044) **25a.** Did you live in this house on April 1, 1970?
1 ☐ Yes – *SKIP to Check Item B* 2 ☐ No

b. Where did you live on April 1, 1970? (State, foreign country, U.S. possession, etc.)

State, etc._____ County _____

(045) (046) **c.** Did you live inside the limits of a city, town, village, etc.?
1 ☐ No 2 ☐ Yes – Name of city, town, village, etc. ⬎

☐☐☐☐

(Ask males 18+ only)
(047) **d.** Were you in the Armed Forces on April 1, 1970?
1 ☐ Yes 2 ☐ No

CHECK ITEM B ➤ Is this person 16 years old or older?
☐ No – *SKIP to 36* ☐ Yes

(048) **26a.** What were you doing most of LAST WEEK – (working, keeping house, going to school) or something else?
1 ☐ Working – *SKIP to 28a* 6 ☐ Unable to work – *SKIP to 26d*
2 ☐ With a job but not at work 7 ☐ Retired
3 ☐ Looking for work 8 ☐ Other – Specify ⬎
4 ☐ Keeping house
5 ☐ Going to school *(If Armed Forces, SKIP to 28a)*

(049) **b.** Did you do any work at all LAST WEEK, not counting work around the house? (Note: If farm or business operator in HH, ask about unpaid work.)
0 ☐ No Yes – How many hours?_____ – *SKIP to 28a*

(050) **c.** Did you have a job or business from which you were temporarily absent or on layoff LAST WEEK?
1 ☐ No 2 ☐ Yes – Absent – *SKIP to 28a*
3 ☐ Yes – Layoff – *SKIP to 27*

(051) **26d.** Have you been looking for work during the past 4 weeks?
1 ☐ Yes No – When did you last work?
2 ☐ Less than 5 years ago – *SKIP to 28a*
3 ☐ 5 or more years ago ⎫ *SKIP to 36*
4 ☐ Never worked ⎭

(052) **27.** Is there any reason why you could not take a job LAST WEEK?
1 ☐ No Yes – 2 ☐ Already had a job
3 ☐ Temporary illness
4 ☐ Going to school
5 ☐ Other – Specify ⬎

28a. For whom did you (last) work? (Name of company, business, organization or other employer)

(053) x ☐ Never worked – *SKIP to 36*

(054) **b.** What kind of business or industry is this? (E.g.: TV and radio mfg., retail shoe store, State Labor Department, farm)

(055) **c.** Were you –
1 ☐ An employee of a PRIVATE company, business or individual for wages, salary or commissions?
2 ☐ A GOVERNMENT employee (Federal, State, county, or local)?
3 ☐ SELF-EMPLOYED in OWN business, professional practice or farm?
4 ☐ Working WITHOUT PAY in family business or farm?

(056) **d.** What kind of work were you doing? (E.g.: electrical engineer, stock clerk, typist, farmer, Armed Forces)

e. What were your most important activities or duties? (E.g.: typing, keeping account books, selling cars, Armed Forces)

INDIVIDUAL SCREEN QUESTIONS

36. The following questions refer only to things that happened to YOU during the last 6 months – between ____ 1, 197__ and ____, 197__. Did you have your (pocket picked/purse snatched)?
☐ Yes – How many times: _____ ☐ No

37. Did anyone take something (else) directly from you by using force, such as by a stickup, mugging or threat?
☐ Yes – How many times: _____ ☐ No

38. Did anyone TRY to rob you by using force or threatening to harm you? (other than any incidents already mentioned)
☐ Yes – How many times: _____ ☐ No

39. Did anyone beat you up, attack you or hit you with something, such as a rock or bottle? (other than any incidents already mentioned)
☐ Yes – How many times: _____ ☐ No

40. Were you knifed, shot at, or attacked with some other weapon by anyone at all? (other than any incidents already mentioned)
☐ Yes – How many times: _____ ☐ No

41. Did anyone THREATEN to beat you up or THREATEN you with a knife, gun, or some other weapon, NOT including telephone threats? (other than any incidents already mentioned)
☐ Yes – How many times: _____ ☐ No

42. Did anyone TRY to attack you in some other way? (other than any incidents already mentioned)
☐ Yes – How many times: _____ ☐ No

43. During the last 6 months, did anyone steal things that belonged to you from inside ANY car or truck, such as packages or clothing?
☐ Yes – How many times: _____ ☐ No

44. Was anything stolen from you while you were away from home, for instance at work, in a theater or restaurant, or while traveling?
☐ Yes – How many times: _____ ☐ No

45. (Other than any incidents you've already mentioned) Was anything (else) at all stolen from you during the last 6 months?
☐ Yes – How many times: _____ ☐ No

46. Did you find any evidence that someone ATTEMPTED to steal something that belonged to you? (other than any incidents already mentioned)
☐ Yes – How many times: _____ ☐ No

(058) **47.** Did you call the police during the last 6 months to report something that happened to YOU which you thought was a crime? (Do not count any calls made to the police concerning the incidents you have just told me about.)
☐ No – *SKIP to 48*
☐ Yes – What happened?_____

CHECK ITEM C ➤ Look at 47 – Was HH member 12+ attacked or threatened, or was something stolen or an attempt made to steal something that belonged to him?
☐ Yes – How many times: _____ ☐ No

(059) **48.** Did anything happen to YOU during the last 6 months which you thought was a crime, but did NOT report to the police? (other than any incidents already mentioned)
☐ No – *SKIP to Check Item E*
☐ Yes – What happened?_____

CHECK ITEM D ➤ Look at 48 – Was HH member 12+ attacked or threatened, or was something stolen or an attempt made to steal something that belonged to him?
☐ Yes – How many times: _____ ☐ No

CHECK ITEM E ➤ Do any of the screen questions contain any entries for "How many times?"
☐ No – Interview next HH member. End interview if last respondent, and fill item 12 on cover page.
☐ Yes – Fill Crime Incident Reports.

FORM NCS-1 (8-15-75)

PERSONAL CHARACTERISTICS

14. NAME	15. TYPE OF INTERVIEW	16. LINE NO.	17. RELATIONSHIP TO HOUSEHOLD HEAD	18. AGE LAST BIRTH-DAY	19. MARITAL STATUS	20a. RACE	20b. ORIGIN	21. SEX	22. ARMED FORCES MEMBER	23. Education – highest grade	24. Education – complete that year?
KEYER – BEGIN NEW RECORD		(cc 12)	(oc 13b)		(cc 18)	(cc 19a)	(cc 19b)	(cc 20)	(cc 21)	(cc 22)	(cc 23)
Last	(034)	(035)	(036)	(037)	(038)	(039)		(040)	(041)	(042)	(043)
	1 ☐ Per – Self-respondent		1 ☐ Head		1 ☐ M.	1 ☐ W.		1 ☐ M	1 ☐ Yes		1 ☐ Yes
First	2 ☐ Tel. – Self-respondent		2 ☐ Wife of head		2 ☐ Wd.	2 ☐ Neg.		2 ☐ F	2 ☐ No		2 ☐ No
	3 ☐ Per. – Proxy } Fill 13b on	Line	3 ☐ Own child	Age	3 ☐ D.	3 ☐ Ot.					
	4 ☐ Tel. – Proxy } cover page	No.	4 ☐ Other relative		4 ☐ Sep.	Origin			Grade		
	5 ☐ NI – Fill 16–21		5 ☐ Non-relative		5 ☐ NM						

CHECK ITEM A ► Look at item 4 on cover page. Is this the same household as last enumeration? (Box 1 marked?)
☐ Yes – *SKIP* to Check Item B ☐ No

25a. Did you live in this house on April 1, 1970?
(044) 1 ☐ Yes – *SKIP* to Check Item B 2 ☐ No

b. Where did you live on April 1, 1970? (State, foreign country, U.S. possession, etc.)

State, etc. _____ County _____

c. Did you live inside the limits of a city, town, village, etc.?
(045) 1 ☐ No 2 ☐ Yes – Name of city, town, village, etc. �ググ
(046)

(Ask males 18+ only)
d. Were you in the Armed Forces on April 1, 1970?
(047) 1 ☐ Yes 2 ☐ No

CHECK ITEM B ► Is this person 16 years old or older?
☐ No – *SKIP* to 36 ☐ Yes

26a. What were you doing most of LAST WEEK – (working, keeping house, going to school) or something else?
(048)
1 ☐ Working – *SKIP* to 28a 6 ☐ Unable to work – *SKIP* to 26d
2 ☐ With a job but not at work 7 ☐ Retired
3 ☐ Looking for work 8 ☐ Other – Specify ➜
4 ☐ Keeping house
5 ☐ Going to school (If Armed Forces, *SKIP* to 28a)

b. Did you do any work at all LAST WEEK, not counting work around the house? (Note: If farm or business operator in HH, ask about unpaid work.)
(049) 0 ☐ No Yes – How many hours?____ – *SKIP* to 28a

c. Did you have a job or business from which you were temporarily absent or on layoff LAST WEEK?
(050)
1 ☐ No 2 ☐ Yes – Absent – *SKIP* to 28a
3 ☐ Yes – Layoff – *SKIP* to 27

26d. Have you been looking for work during the past 4 weeks?
(051) 1 ☐ Yes No – When did you last work?
2 ☐ Less than 5 years ago – *SKIP* to 28a
3 ☐ 5 or more years ago
4 ☐ Never worked } *SKIP* to 36

27. Is there any reason why you could not take a job LAST WEEK?
(052) 1 ☐ No Yes – 2 ☐ Already had a job
3 ☐ Temporary illness
4 ☐ Going to school
5 ☐ Other – Specify ➜

28a. For whom did you (last) work? (Name of company, business, organization or other employer)

(053) x ☐ Never worked – *SKIP* to 36

b. What kind of business or industry is this? (E.g.: TV and radio mfg., retail shoe store, State Labor Department, farm)
(054)

c. Were you –
(055)
1 ☐ An employee of a PRIVATE company, business or individual for wages, salary or commissions?
2 ☐ A GOVERNMENT employee (Federal, State, county, or local)?
3 ☐ SELF-EMPLOYED in OWN business, professional practice or farm?
4 ☐ Working WITHOUT PAY in family business or farm?

d. What kind of work were you doing? (E.g.: electrical engineer, stock clerk, typist, farmer, Armed Forces)
(056)

e. What were your most important activities or duties? (E.g.: typing, keeping account books, selling cars, Armed Forces)

INDIVIDUAL SCREEN QUESTIONS

36. The following questions refer only to things that happened to YOU during the last 6 months – between ____ 1, 197__ and ____, 197__. Did you have your (pocket picked/purse snatched)?
☐ Yes – How many times? ____
☐ No

37. Did anyone take something (else) directly from you by using force, such as by a stickup, mugging or threat?
☐ Yes – How many times? ____
☐ No

38. Did anyone TRY to rob you by using force or threatening to harm you? (other than any incidents already mentioned)
☐ Yes – How many times? ____
☐ No

39. Did anyone beat you up, attack you or hit you with something, such as a rock or bottle? (other than any incidents already mentioned)
☐ Yes – How many times? ____
☐ No

40. Were you knifed, shot at, or attacked with some other weapon by anyone at all? (other than any incidents already mentioned)
☐ Yes – How many times? ____
☐ No

41. Did anyone THREATEN to beat you up or THREATEN you with a knife, gun, or some other weapon, NOT including telephone threats? (other than any incidents already mentioned)
☐ Yes – How many times? ____
☐ No

42. Did anyone TRY to attack you in some other way? (other than any incidents already mentioned)
☐ Yes – How many times? ____
☐ No

43. During the last 6 months, did anyone steal things that belonged to you from inside ANY car or truck, such as packages or clothing?
☐ Yes – How many times? ____
☐ No

44. Was anything stolen from you while you were away from home, for instance at work, in a theater or restaurant, or while traveling?
☐ Yes – How many times? ____
☐ No

45. (Other than any incidents you've already mentioned) Was anything (else) at all stolen from you during the last 6 months?
☐ Yes – How many times? ____
☐ No

46. Did you find any evidence that someone ATTEMPTED to steal something that belonged to you? (other than any incidents already mentioned)
☐ Yes – How many times? ____
☐ No

47. Did you call the police during the last 6 months to report something that happened to YOU which you thought was a crime? (Do not count any calls made to the police concerning the incidents you have just told me about.)
(058)
☐ No – *SKIP* to 48
☐ Yes – What happened? _____

CHECK ITEM C ► Look at 47 – Was HH member 12+ attacked or threatened, or was something stolen or an attempt made to steal something that belonged to him?
☐ Yes – How many times? ____
☐ No

48. Did anything happen to YOU during the last 6 months which you thought was a crime, but did NOT report to the police? (other than any incidents already mentioned)
(059)
☐ No – *SKIP* to Check Item E
☐ Yes – What happened? _____

CHECK ITEM D ► Look at 48 – Was HH member 12+ attacked or threatened, or was something stolen or an attempt made to steal something that belonged to him?
☐ Yes – How many times? ____
☐ No

CHECK ITEM E ► Do any of the screen questions contain any entries for "How many times?"
☐ No – Interview next HH member. End interview if last respondent, and fill item 12 on cover page.
☐ Yes – Fill Crime Incident Reports.

FORM NCS-1 (8-15-75)

PERSONAL CHARACTERISTICS

14. NAME	15. TYPE OF INTERVIEW	16. LINE NO.	17. RELATIONSHIP TO HOUSEHOLD HEAD	18. AGE LAST BIRTH-DAY	19. MARITAL STATUS	20a. RACE	20b. ORIGIN	21. SEX	22. ARMED FORCES MEMBER	23. Education – highest grade	24. Education – complete that year?
KEYER – BEGIN NEW RECORD		(cc 12)	(cc 13b)	(cc 17)	(cc 18)	(cc 19a)	(cc 19b)	(cc 20)	(cc 21)	(cc 22)	(cc 23)
Last	(034)	(035)	(036)	(037)	(038)	(039)		(040)	(041)	(042)	(043)
	1 ☐ Per. – Self-respondent		1 ☐ Head		1 ☐ M.	1 ☐ W.		1 ☐ M	1 ☐ Yes		1 ☐ Yes
	2 ☐ Tel. – Self-respondent		2 ☐ Wife of head		2 ☐ Wd.	2 ☐ Neg.		2 ☐ F	2 ☐ No		2 ☐ No
First	3 ☐ Per. – Proxy ⎫ Fill 13b on	Line No.	3 ☐ Own child	Age	3 ☐ D.	3 ☐ Ot.	Origin			Grade	
	4 ☐ Tel. – Proxy ⎰ cover page		4 ☐ Other relative		4 ☐ Sep.						
	5 ☐ NI – Fill 16–21		5 ☐ Non-relative		5 ☐ NM						

CHECK ITEM A ▶ Look at item 4 on cover page. Is this the same household as last enumeration? *(Box I marked)*
☐ Yes – *SKIP to Check Item B*   ☐ No

25a. Did you live in this house on April 1, 1970?
(044)   1 ☐ Yes – *SKIP to Check Item B*   2 ☐ No

b. Where did you live on April 1, 1970? (State, foreign country, U.S. possession, etc.)

State, etc. _____ County _____

c. Did you live inside the limits of a city, town, village, etc.?
(045) 1 ☐ No   2 ☐ Yes – Name of city, town, village, etc.
(046) ☐☐☐
(Ask males 18+ only)

d. Were you in the Armed Forces on April 1, 1970?
(047)   1 ☐ Yes   2 ☐ No

CHECK ITEM B ▶ Is this person 16 years old or older?
☐ No – *SKIP to 36*   ☐ Yes

26a. What were you doing most of LAST WEEK – (working, keeping house, going to school or something else?
(048)
1 ☐ Working – *SKIP to 28a*   6 ☐ Unable to work – *SKIP to 26d*
2 ☐ With a job but not at work   7 ☐ Retired
3 ☐ Looking for work   8 ☐ Other – Specify
4 ☐ Keeping house
5 ☐ Going to school   (If Armed Forces, *SKIP to 28a*)

b. Did you do any work at all LAST WEEK, not counting work around the house? (Note: If farm or business operator in HH, ask about unpaid work.)
(049) 0 ☐ No   Yes – How many hours? ___ – *SKIP to 28a*

c. Did you have a job or business from which you were temporarily absent or on layoff LAST WEEK?
(050) 1 ☐ No   2 ☐ Yes – Absent – *SKIP to 28a*
   3 ☐ Yes – Layoff – *SKIP to 27*

26d. Have you been looking for work during the past 4 weeks?
(051) 1 ☐ Yes   No – When did you last work?
   2 ☐ Less than 5 years ago – *SKIP to 28a*
   3 ☐ 5 or more years ago ⎫ *SKIP to 36*
   4 ☐ Never worked ⎰

27. Is there any reason why you could not take a job LAST WEEK?
(052) 1 ☐ No   Yes – 2 ☐ Already had a job
   3 ☐ Temporary illness
   4 ☐ Going to school
   5 ☐ Other – Specify

28a. For whom did you (last) work? (Name of company, business, organization or other employer)

(053) x ☐ Never worked – *SKIP to 36*

b. What kind of business or industry is this? (E.g.: TV and radio mfg., retail shoe store, State Labor Department, farm)
(054)

c. Were you –
(055)
1 ☐ An employee of a PRIVATE company, business or individual for wages, salary or commissions?
2 ☐ A GOVERNMENT employee (Federal, State, county, or local)?
3 ☐ SELF-EMPLOYED in OWN business, professional practice or farm?
4 ☐ Working WITHOUT PAY in family business or farm?

d. What kind of work were you doing? (E.g.: electrical engineer, stock clerk, typist, farmer, Armed Forces)
(056) ☐☐☐

e. What were your most important activities or duties? (E.g.: typing, keeping account books, selling cars, Armed Forces)

INDIVIDUAL SCREEN QUESTIONS

36. The following questions refer only to things that happened to YOU during the last 6 months – between ___ 1, 197__ and ___, 197__.
Did you have your (pocket picked/purse snatched)?
☐ Yes – How many times? ___   ☐ No

37. Did anyone take something (else) directly from you by using force, such as by a stickup, mugging or threat?
☐ Yes – How many times? ___   ☐ No

38. Did anyone TRY to rob you by using force or threatening to harm you? (other than any incidents already mentioned)
☐ Yes – How many times? ___   ☐ No

39. Did anyone beat you up, attack you or hit you with something, such as a rock or bottle? (other than any incidents already mentioned)
☐ Yes – How many times? ___   ☐ No

40. Were you knifed, shot at, or attacked with some other weapon by anyone at all? (other than any incidents already mentioned)
☐ Yes – How many times? ___   ☐ No

41. Did anyone THREATEN to beat you up or THREATEN you with a knife, gun, or some other weapon, NOT including telephone threats? (other than any incidents already mentioned)
☐ Yes – How many times? ___   ☐ No

42. Did anyone TRY to attack you in some other way? (other than any incidents already mentioned)
☐ Yes – How many times? ___   ☐ No

43. During the last 6 months, did anyone steal things that belonged to you from inside ANY car or truck, such as packages or clothing?
☐ Yes – How many times? ___   ☐ No

44. Was anything stolen from you while you were away from home, for instance at work, in a theater or restaurant, or while traveling?
☐ Yes – How many times? ___   ☐ No

45. (Other than any incidents you've already mentioned) Was anything (else) at all stolen from you during the last 6 months?
☐ Yes – How many times? ___   ☐ No

46. Did you find any evidence that someone ATTEMPTED to steal something that belonged to you? (other than any incidents already mentioned)
☐ Yes – How many times? ___   ☐ No

47. Did you call the police during the last 6 months to report something that happened to YOU which you thought was a crime? (Do not count any calls made to the police concerning the incidents you have just told me about.)
(058)
☐ No – *SKIP to 48*
☐ Yes – What happened? ___

CHECK ITEM C ▶ Look at 47 – Was HH member 12+ attacked or threatened, or was something stolen or an attempt made to steal something that belonged to him?
☐ Yes – How many times? ___   ☐ No

48. Did anything happen to YOU during the last 6 months which you thought was a crime, but did NOT report to the police? (other than any incidents already mentioned)
(059)
☐ No – *SKIP to Check Item E*
☐ Yes – What happened? ___

CHECK ITEM D ▶ Look at 48 – Was HH member 12+ attacked or threatened, or was something stolen or an attempt made to steal something that belonged to him?
☐ Yes – How many times? ___   ☐ No

CHECK ITEM E ▶ Do any of the screen questions contain any entries for "How many times?"
☐ No – *Interview next HH member. End interview if last respondent, and fill item 12 on cover page.*
☐ Yes – *Fill Crime Incident Reports.*

FORM NCS-1 (8-15-76)

PERSONAL CHARACTERISTICS

14. NAME KEYER – BEGIN NEW RECORD	15. TYPE OF INTERVIEW (cc 12)	16. LINE NO. (cc 13b)	17. RELATIONSHIP TO HOUSEHOLD HEAD	18. AGE LAST BIRTH-DAY (cc 17)	19. MARITAL STATUS (cc 18)	20a. RACE (cc 19a)	20b. ORIGIN (cc 19b)	21. SEX (cc 20)	22. ARMED FORCES MEMBER (cc 21)	23. Education – highest grade (cc 22)	24. Education – complete that year? (cc 23)
Last	(034)	(035)	(036)	(037)	(038)	(039)		(040)	(041)	(042)	(043)
	1 ☐ Per. – Self-respondent		1 ☐ Head		1 ☐ M.	1 ☐ W.		1 ☐ M	1 ☐ Yes		1 ☐ Yes
First	2 ☐ Tel. – Self-respondent		2 ☐ Wife of head		2 ☐ Wd.	2 ☐ Neg.		2 ☐ F	2 ☐ No		2 ☐ No
	3 ☐ Per. – Proxy ⎫ Fill 13b on	Line No.	3 ☐ Own child	Age	3 ☐ D.	3 ☐ Ot.				Grade	
	4 ☐ Tel. – Proxy ⎰ cover page		4 ☐ Other relative		4 ☐ Sep.	Origin					
	5 ☐ NI – Fill 16—21		5 ☐ Non-relative		5 ☐ NM						

CHECK ITEM A ➤ Look at item 4 on cover page. Is this the same household as last enumeration? (Box 1 marked)
☐ Yes – *SKIP* to Check Item B ☐ No

(044) **25a.** Did you live in this house on April 1, 1970?
1 ☐ Yes – *SKIP* to Check Item B 2 ☐ No

b. Where did you live on April 1, 1970? (State, foreign country, U.S. possession, etc.)
State, etc. _____ County _____

(045)
(046) **c.** Did you live inside the limits of a city, town, village, etc.?
1 ☐ No 2 ☐ Yes – Name of city, town, village, etc. ➚

(Ask males 18+ only)
(047) **d.** Were you in the Armed Forces on April 1, 1970?
1 ☐ Yes 2 ☐ No

CHECK ITEM B ➤ Is this person 16 years old or older?
☐ No – *SKIP* to 36 ☐ Yes

(048) **26a.** What were you doing most of LAST WEEK – (working, keeping house, going to school) or something else?
1 ☐ Working – *SKIP* to 28a 6 ☐ Unable to work – *SKIP* to 26d
2 ☐ With a job but not at work 7 ☐ Retired
3 ☐ Looking for work 8 ☐ Other – Specify ➚
4 ☐ Keeping house
5 ☐ Going to school *(If Armed Forces, SKIP to 28a)*

b. Did you do any work at all LAST WEEK, not counting work around the house? *(Note: If farm or business operator in HH, ask about unpaid work.)*
(049) 0 ☐ No Yes – How many hours? _____ – *SKIP* to 28a

(050) **c.** Did you have a job or business from which you were temporarily absent or on layoff LAST WEEK?
1 ☐ No 2 ☐ Yes – Absent – *SKIP* to 28a
3 ☐ Yes – Layoff – *SKIP* to 27

(051) **26d.** Have you been looking for work during the past 4 weeks?
1 ☐ Yes No – When did you last work?
2 ☐ Less than 5 years ago – *SKIP* to 28a
3 ☐ 5 or more years ago ⎱ *SKIP* to 36
4 ☐ Never worked ⎰

(052) **27.** Is there any reason why you could not take a job LAST WEEK?
1 ☐ No Yes – 2 ☐ Already had a job
3 ☐ Temporary illness
4 ☐ Going to school
5 ☐ Other – Specify ➚

(053) **28a.** For whom did you (last) work? (Name of company, business, organization or other employer)
x ☐ Never worked – *SKIP* to 36

(054) **b.** What kind of business or industry is this? (E.g.: TV and radio mfg., retail shoe store, State Labor Department, farm)

(055) **c.** Were you –
1 ☐ An employee of a PRIVATE company, business or individual for wages, salary or commissions?
2 ☐ A GOVERNMENT employee (Federal, State, county, or local)?
3 ☐ SELF-EMPLOYED in OWN business, professional practice or farm?
4 ☐ Working WITHOUT PAY in family business or farm?

(056) **d.** What kind of work were you doing? (E.g.: electrical engineer, stock clerk, typist, farmer, Armed Forces)

e. What were your most important activities or duties? (E.g.: typing, keeping account books, selling cars, Armed Forces)

INDIVIDUAL SCREEN QUESTIONS

36. The following questions refer only to things that happened to YOU during the last 6 months – between ____ 1, 197__ and ____, 197__. Did you have your (pocket picked/purse snatched)?	☐ Yes – How many times? _____ ☐ No
37. Did anyone take something (else) directly from you by using force, such as by a stickup, mugging or threat?	☐ Yes – How many times? _____ ☐ No
38. Did anyone TRY to rob you by using force or threatening to harm you? (other than any incidents already mentioned)	☐ Yes – How many times? _____ ☐ No
39. Did anyone beat you up, attack you or hit you with something, such as a rock or bottle? (other than any incidents already mentioned)	☐ Yes – How many times? _____ ☐ No
40. Were you knifed, shot at, or attacked with some other weapon by anyone at all? (other than any incidents already mentioned)	☐ Yes – How many times? _____ ☐ No
41. Did anyone THREATEN to beat you up or THREATEN you with a knife, gun, or some other weapon, NOT including telephone threats? (other than any incidents already mentioned)	☐ Yes – How many times? _____ ☐ No
42. Did anyone TRY to attack you in some other way? (other than any incidents already mentioned)	☐ Yes – How many times? _____ ☐ No
43. During the last 6 months, did anyone steal things that belonged to you from inside ANY car or truck, such as packages or clothing?	☐ Yes – How many times? _____ ☐ No
44. Was anything stolen from you while you were away from home, for instance at work, in a theater or restaurant, or while traveling?	☐ Yes – How many times? _____ ☐ No
45. (Other than any incidents you've already mentioned) Was anything (else) at all stolen from you during the last 6 months?	☐ Yes – How many times? _____ ☐ No

46. Did you find any evidence that someone ATTEMPTED to steal something that belonged to you? (other than any incidents already mentioned)
☐ Yes – How many times? _____ ☐ No

(058) 47. Did you call the police during the last 6 months to report something that happened to YOU which you thought was a crime? (Do not count any calls made to the police concerning the incidents you have just told me about.)
☐ No – *SKIP* to 48
☐ Yes – What happened? _____

CHECK ITEM C ➤ Look at 47 – Was HH member 12+ attacked or threatened, or was something stolen or an attempt made to steal something that belonged to him?
☐ Yes – How many times? _____ ☐ No

(059) 48. Did anything happen to YOU during the last 6 months which you thought was a crime, but did NOT report to the police? (other than any incidents already mentioned)
☐ No – *SKIP* to Check Item E
☐ Yes – What happened? _____

CHECK ITEM D ➤ Look at 48 – Was HH member 12+ attacked or threatened, or was something stolen or an attempt made to steal something that belonged to him?
☐ Yes – How many times? _____ ☐ No

CHECK ITEM E ➤ Do any of the screen questions contain any entries for "How many times?"
☐ No – Interview next HH member. End interview if last respondent, and fill item 12 on cover page.
☐ Yes – Fill Crime Incident Reports.

FORM NCS-1 (8-15-75)

O.M.B. No. 41-R2661; Approval Expires June 30, 1977

KEYER – BEGIN NEW RECORD	Notes

Line number

(101)

Screen question number

(102)

Incident number

(103)

NOTICE – Your report to the Census Bureau is confidential by law (U.S. Code 42, Section 3761). All identifiable information will be used only by persons engaged in and for the purposes of the survey, and may not be disclosed or released to others for any purpose.

FORM **NCS-2**
(8-15-75)

U.S. DEPARTMENT OF COMMERCE
BUREAU OF THE CENSUS
ACTING AS COLLECTING AGENT FOR THE
LAW ENFORCEMENT ASSISTANCE ADMINISTRATION
U.S. DEPARTMENT OF JUSTICE

CRIME INCIDENT REPORT

NATIONAL CRIME SURVEY – NATIONAL SAMPLE

NCS 2 INCIDENT REPORT

1a. You said that during the last 6 months – *(Refer to appropriate screen question for description of crime)*

In what month **(did this did the first)** incident happen? *(Show flashcard if necessary. Encourage respondent to give exact month.)*

(104) _____ Month (01–12)   Year 197____

(105) **CHECK ITEM A** ➤ Is this incident report for a series of crimes?
1 ☐ No – **SKIP** to 2
2 ☐ Yes – (Note: series must have 3 or more similar incidents which respondent can't recall separately)

b. In what month(s) did these incidents take place? *(Mark all that apply)*

(106)
1 ☐ Spring (March, April, May)
2 ☐ Summer (June, July, August)
3 ☐ Fall (September, October, November)
4 ☐ Winter (December, January, February)

c. How many incidents were involved in this series?

(107)
1 ☐ Three or four
2 ☐ Five to ten
3 ☐ Eleven or more
4 ☐ Don't know

INTERVIEWER: If this report is for a series, read the following statement.
(The following questions refer only to the most recent incident.)

2. About what time did (this the most recent) incident happen?

(108)
1 ☐ Don't know
2 ☐ During the day (6 a.m. to 6 p.m.)
   At night (6 p.m. to 6 a.m.)
3 ☐ 6 p.m. to midnight
4 ☐ Midnight to 6 a.m.
5 ☐ Don't know

3a. In what State and county did this incident occur?

☐ Outside U.S. – *END INCIDENT REPORT*

State _____ County _____

b. Did it happen **INSIDE THE LIMITS** of a city, town, village, etc.?

(110)
1 ☐ No
2 ☐ Yes – Enter name of city, town, etc. ⌐

(111) ☐☐☐☐☐

4. Where did this incident take place?

(112)
1 ☐ At or in own dwelling, in garage or other building on property (Includes break-in or attempted break-in)   **SKIP** to 6a
2 ☐ At or in a vacation home, hotel, motel
3 ☐ Inside commercial building such as store, restaurant, bank, gas station, public conveyance or station   **ASK** 5a
4 ☐ Inside office, factory, or warehouse
5 ☐ Near own home, yard, sidewalk, driveway, carport, apartment hall (Does not include break-in or attempted break-in)
6 ☐ On the street, in a park, field, playground, school grounds or parking lot   **SKIP** to Check Item B
7 ☐ Inside school
8 ☐ Other – Specify ⌐

5a. Were you a customer, employee, or owner?

(113)
1 ☐ Customer
2 ☐ Employee
3 ☐ Owner
4 ☐ Other – Specify _____

b. Did the person(s) steal or **TRY** to steal anything belonging to the store, restaurant, office, factory, etc.?

(114)
1 ☐ Yes
2 ☐ No   **SKIP** to Check Item B
3 ☐ Don't know

6a. Did the offender(s) live there or have a right to be there, such as a guest or a workman?

(115)
1 ☐ Yes – **SKIP** to Check Item B
2 ☐ No
3 ☐ Don't know

b. Did the offender(s) actually get in or just **TRY** to get in the building?

(116)
1 ☐ Actually got in
2 ☐ Just tried to get in
3 ☐ Don't know

c. Was there any evidence, such as a broken lock or broken window, that the offender(s) (forced his way in **TRIED** to force his way in) the building?

(117)
1 ☐ No
   Yes – What was the evidence? Anything else? *(Mark all that apply)*
2 ☐ Broken lock or window
3 ☐ Forced door or window
4 ☐ Slashed screen   **SKIP** to Check Item B
5 ☐ Other – Specify ⌐

d. How did the offender(s) (get in try to get in)?

(118)
1 ☐ Through unlocked door or window
2 ☐ Had key
3 ☐ Don't know
4 ☐ Other – Specify _____

(119) **CHECK ITEM B** ➤ Was respondent or any other member of this household present when this incident occurred? *(If not sure, ASK)*
1 ☐ No – **SKIP** to 13a
2 ☐ Yes

7a. Did the person(s) have a weapon such as a gun or knife, or something he was using as a weapon, such as a bottle, or wrench?

(120)
1 ☐ No
2 ☐ Don't know
   Yes – What was the weapon? Anything else? *(Mark all that apply)*
3 ☐ Gun
4 ☐ Knife
5 ☐ Other – Specify _____

b. Did the person(s) hit you, knock you down, or actually attack you in any way?

(121)
1 ☐ Yes – **SKIP** to 7f
2 ☐ No

c. Did the person(s) threaten you with harm in any way?

(122)
1 ☐ No – **SKIP** to 7e
2 ☐ Yes

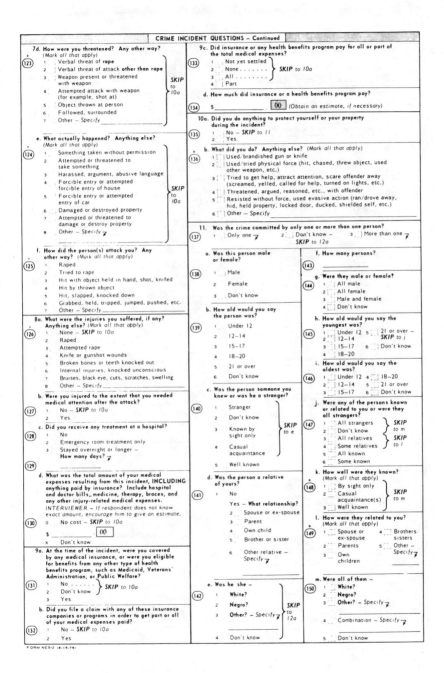

CRIME INCIDENT QUESTIONS – Continued

7d. How were you threatened? Any other way?
(Mark all that apply)
(123)
1 Verbal threat of rape
2 Verbal threat of attack **other than** rape
3 Weapon present or threatened with weapon
4 Attempted attack with weapon (for example, shot at)
5 Object thrown at person
6 Followed, surrounded
7 Other – Specify ____
SKIP to 10a

e. What actually happened? Anything else?
(Mark all that apply)
(124)
1 Something taken without permission
2 Attempted or threatened to take something
3 Harassed, argument, abusive language
4 Forcible entry or attempted forcible entry of house
5 Forcible entry or attempted entry of car
6 Damaged or destroyed property
7 Attempted or threatened to damage or destroy property
8 Other – Specify ____
SKIP to 10a

f. How did the person(s) attack you? Any other way? *(Mark all that apply)*
(125)
1 Raped
2 Tried to rape
3 Hit with object held in hand, shot, knifed
4 Hit by thrown object
5 Hit, slapped, knocked down
6 Grabbed, held, tripped, jumped, pushed, etc.
7 Other – Specify ____

8a. What were the injuries you suffered, if any? Anything else? *(Mark all that apply)*
(126)
1 None – **SKIP to 10a**
2 Raped
3 Attempted rape
4 Knife or gunshot wounds
5 Broken bones or teeth knocked out
6 Internal injuries, knocked unconscious
7 Bruises, black eye, cuts, scratches, swelling
8 Other – Specify ____

b. Were you injured to the extent that you needed medical attention after the attack?
(127)
1 No – **SKIP to 10a**
2 Yes

c. Did you receive any treatment at a hospital?
(128)
1 No
2 Emergency room treatment only
3 Stayed overnight or longer – How many days? ____
(129)

d. What was the total amount of your medical expenses resulting from this incident, INCLUDING anything paid by insurance? Include hospital and doctor bills, medicine, therapy, braces, and any other injury-related medical expenses.
INTERVIEWER – If respondent does not know exact amount, encourage him to give an estimate.
(130)
0 No cost – **SKIP to 10a**
$ ____ | 00 |
x Don't know

9a. At the time of the incident, were you covered by any medical insurance, or were you eligible for benefits from any other type of health benefits program, such as Medicaid, Veterans' Administration, or Public Welfare?
(131)
1 No
2 Don't know
3 Yes
SKIP to 10a

b. Did you file a claim with any of these insurance companies or programs in order to get part or all of your medical expenses paid?
(132)
1 No – **SKIP to 10a**
2 Yes

9c. Did insurance or any health benefits program pay for all or part of the total medical expenses?
(133)
1 Not yet settled
2 None
3 All
4 Part
SKIP to 10a

d. How much did insurance or a health benefits program pay?
(134)
$ ____ | 00 | *(Obtain an estimate, if necessary)*

10a. Did you do anything to protect yourself or your property during the incident?
(135)
1 No – **SKIP to 11**
2 Yes

b. What did you do? Anything else? *(Mark all that apply)*
(136)
1 Used/brandished gun or knife
2 Used/tried physical force (hit, chased, threw object, used other weapon, etc.)
3 Tried to get help, attract attention, scare offender away (screamed, yelled, called for help, turned on lights, etc.)
4 Threatened, argued, reasoned, etc., with offender
5 Resisted without force, used evasive action (ran/drove away, hid, held property, locked door, ducked, shielded self, etc.)
6 Other – Specify

11. Was the crime committed by only one or more than one person?
(137)
1 Only one ⌐   2 Don't know –   3 More than one ⌐
SKIP to 12a

a. Was this person male or female?
(138)
1 Male
2 Female
3 Don't know

b. How old would you say the person was?
(139)
1 Under 12
2 12–14
3 15–17
4 18–20
5 21 or over
6 Don't know

c. Was the person someone you knew or was he a stranger?
(140)
1 Stranger
2 Don't know
3 Known by sight only
4 Casual acquaintance
5 Well known
SKIP to e

d. Was the person a relative of yours?
(141)
1 No
Yes – What relationship?
2 Spouse or ex-spouse
3 Parent
4 Own child
5 Brother or sister
6 Other relative – Specify ⌐

e. Was he she –
(142)
1 White?
2 Negro?
3 Other? – Specify ⌐
4 Don't know
SKIP to 12a

f. How many persons?
(143) ____

g. Were they male or female?
(144)
1 All male
2 All female
3 Male and female
4 Don't know

h. How old would you say the youngest was?
(145)
1 Under 12   5 21 or over –
2 12–14   **SKIP to j**
3 15–17   6 Don't know
4 18–20

i. How old would you say the oldest was?
(146)
1 Under 12   4 18–20
2 12–14   5 21 or over
3 15–17   6 Don't know

j. Were any of the persons known or related to you or were they all strangers?
(147)
1 All strangers
2 Don't know
3 All relatives
4 Some relatives
5 All known
6 Some known
SKIP to m / **SKIP to l**

k. How well were they known?
(Mark all that apply)
(148)
1 By sight only
2 Casual acquaintance(s)
3 Well known
SKIP to m

l. How were they related to you? *(Mark all that apply)*
(149)
1 Spouse or ex-spouse
2 Parents
3 Own children
4 Brothers/sisters
5 Other – Specify ⌐

m. Were all of them –
(150)
1 White?
2 Negro?
3 Other? – Specify ⌐
4 Combination – Specify ⌐
5 Don't know

CRIME INCIDENT QUESTIONS – Continued

12a. Were you the only person there besides the offender(s)?

(151) 1 ☐ Yes – *SKIP to 13a*
2 ☐ No

b. How many of these persons, not counting yourself, were robbed, harmed, or threatened? Do not include persons under 12 years of age.

(152) 0 ☐ None – *SKIP to 13a*

_____ Number of persons

c. Are any of these persons members of your household now? Do not include household members under 12 years of age.

(153) 0 ☐ No
☐ Yes – How many, not counting yourself?

(ALSO MARK "YES" IN CHECK ITEM I ON PAGE 12)

13a. Was something stolen or taken without permission that belonged to you or others in the household?
INTERVIEWER – Include anything stolen from unrecognizable business in respondent's home. Do not include anything stolen from a recognizable business in respondent's home or another business, such as merchandise or cash from a register.

(154) 1 ☐ Yes – *SKIP to 13f*
2 ☐ No

b. Did the person(s) ATTEMPT to take something that belonged to you or others in the household?

(155) 1 ☐ No – *SKIP to 13e*
2 ☐ Yes

c. What did they try to take? Anything else?
(Mark all that apply)

(156) 1 ☐ Purse
2 ☐ Wallet or money
3 ☐ Car
4 ☐ Other motor vehicle
5 ☐ Part of car (hubcap, tape-deck, etc.)
6 ☐ Don't know
7 ☐ Other – Specify _____

CHECK ITEM C ➤ Did they try to take a purse, wallet, or money? (Box 1 or 2 marked in 13c)
☐ No – *SKIP to 18a*
☐ Yes

d. Was the (purse/wallet/money) on your person, for instance in a pocket or being held?

(157) 1 ☐ Yes ⎫
2 ☐ No ⎬ *SKIP to 18a*

e. What did happen? Anything else? *(Mark all that apply)*

(158) 1 ☐ Attacked
2 ☐ Threatened with harm
3 ☐ Attempted to break into house or garage
4 ☐ Attempted to break into car
5 ☐ Harassed, argument, abusive language
6 ☐ Damaged or destroyed property
7 ☐ Attempted or threatened to damage or destroy property
8 ☐ Other – Specify _____

SKIP to 18a

f. What was taken that belonged to you or others in the household? Anything else?

(159) Cash: $ _____ . ☐☐
and/or
Property: *(Mark all that apply)*

(160) 0 ☐ Only cash taken – *SKIP to 14c*
1 ☐ Purse
2 ☐ Wallet
3 ☐ Car
4 ☐ Other motor vehicle
5 ☐ Part of car (hubcap, tape-deck, etc.)
6 ☐ Other – Specify _____

CHECK ITEM D ➤ Was a car or other motor vehicle taken? (Box 3 or 4 marked in 13f)
☐ No – *SKIP to Check Item E*
☐ Yes

14a. Had permission to use the (car/motor vehicle) ever been given to the person who took it?

(161) 1 ☐ No . . . . . ⎫
2 ☐ Don't know ⎬ *SKIP to Check Item E*
3 ☐ Yes

b. Did the person return the (car/motor vehicle)?

(162) 1 ☐ Yes
2 ☐ No

CHECK ITEM E ➤ Is Box 1 or 2 marked in 13f?
☐ No – *SKIP to 15a*
☐ Yes

c. Was the (purse/wallet/money) on your person, for instance, in a pocket or being held by you when it was taken?

(163) 1 ☐ Yes
2 ☐ No

CHECK ITEM F ➤ Was only cash taken? (Box 0 marked in 13f)
☐ Yes – *SKIP to 16a*
☐ No

15a. Altogether, what was the value of the PROPERTY that was taken?
INTERVIEWER – Exclude stolen cash, and enter $0 for stolen checks and credit cards, even if they were used.

(164) $ _____ ☐☐

b. How did you decide the value of the property that was stolen? Any other way? *(Mark all that apply)*

(165) 1 ☐ Original cost
2 ☐ Replacement cost
3 ☐ Personal estimate of current value
4 ☐ Insurance report estimate
5 ☐ Police estimate
6 ☐ Don't know
7 ☐ Other – Specify _____

16a. Was all or part of the stolen money or property recovered, not counting anything received from insurance?

(166) 1 ☐ None ⎫
2 ☐ All ⎬ *SKIP to 17a*
3 ☐ Part

b. What was recovered? Anything else?

(167) Cash: $ _____ . ☐☐
and/or
Property: *(Mark all that apply)*

(168) 0 ☐ Cash only recovered – *SKIP to 17a*
1 ☐ Purse
2 ☐ Wallet
3 ☐ Car
4 ☐ Other motor vehicle
5 ☐ Part of car (hubcap, tape-deck, etc.)
6 ☐ Other – Specify _____

c. What was the value of the property recovered (excluding recovered cash)?

(169) $ _____ ☐☐

FORM NCS-2 (8-15-75)

CRIME INCIDENT QUESTIONS – Continued	

17a. Was there any insurance against theft?

(170)
1 ☐ No . . . . . ⎫
2 ☐ Don't know ⎬ **SKIP** to 18a
3 ☐ Yes ⎭

b. Was this loss reported to an insurance company?

(171)
1 ☐ No . . . . . ⎫
2 ☐ Don't know ⎬ **SKIP** to 18a
3 ☐ Yes ⎭

c. Was any of this loss recovered through insurance?

(172)
1 ☐ Not yet settled ⎫
2 ☐ No . . . . ⎬ **SKIP** to 18a
3 ☐ Yes ⎭

d. How much was recovered?

INTERVIEWER – If property replaced by insurance company instead of cash settlement, ask for estimate of value of the property replaced.

(173) $_____ . ☐☐ 00

18a. Did any household member lose any time from work because of this incident?

(174)
0 ☐ No – **SKIP** to 19a

Yes – How many members? ⌐

b. How much time was lost altogether?

(175)
1 ☐ Less than 1 day
2 ☐ 1–5 days
3 ☐ 6–10 days
4 ☐ Over 10 days
5 ☐ Don't know

19a. Was anything that belonged to you or other members of the household damaged but not taken in this incident? For example, was a lock or window broken, clothing damaged, or damage done to a car, etc.?

(176)
1 ☐ No – **SKIP** to 20a
2 ☐ Yes

b. (Was/were) the damaged item(s) repaired or replaced?

(177)
1 ☐ Yes – **SKIP** to 19d
2 ☐ No

c. How much would it cost to repair or replace the damaged item(s)?

(178)
$_____ . ☐☐ 00 ⎫ **SKIP** to 20a
x ☐ Don't know ⎭

d. How much was the repair or replacement cost?

(179)
x ☐ No cost or don't know – **SKIP** to 20a

$_____ . ☐☐ 00

e. Who paid or will pay for the repairs or replacement? Anyone else? *(Mark all that apply)*

(180)
1 ☐ Household member
2 ☐ Landlord
3 ☐ Insurance
4 ☐ Other – Specify _____

FORM NCS-2 (8-15-75)

20a. Were the police informed of this incident in any way?

(181)
1 ☐ No
2 ☐ Don't know – **SKIP** to Check Item G
Yes – Who told them?
3 ☐ Household member ⎫
4 ☐ Someone else ⎬ **SKIP** to Check Item G
5 ☐ Police on scene ⎭

b. What was the reason this incident was not reported to the police? Any other reason? *(Mark all that apply)*

(182)
1 ☐ Nothing could be done – lack of proof
2 ☐ Did not think it important enough
3 ☐ Police wouldn't want to be bothered
4 ☐ Did not want to take time – too inconvenient
5 ☐ Private or personal matter, did not want to report it
6 ☐ Did not want to get involved
7 ☐ Afraid of reprisal
8 ☐ Reported to someone else
9 ☐ Other – Specify _____

CHECK ITEM G ▶ Is this person 16 years or older?
☐ No – **SKIP** to Check Item H
☐ Yes – **ASK** 21a

21a. Did you have a job at the time this incident happened?

(183)
1 ☐ No – **SKIP** to Check Item H
2 ☐ Yes

b. What was the job?

(186)
1 ☐ Same as described in NCS-1 items 28a–e – **SKIP** to Check Item H
2 ☐ Different than described in NCS-1 items 28a–e

c. For whom did you work? *(Name of company, business, organization or other employer)*

d. What kind of business or industry is this? *(For example: TV and radio mfg., retail shoe store, State Labor Dept., farm)*

(187) ☐☐☐☐

e. Were you –

(188)
1 ☐ An employee of a **PRIVATE** company, business or individual for wages, salary or commissions?
2 ☐ A **GOVERNMENT** employee (Federal, State, county or local)?
3 ☐ **SELF-EMPLOYED** in **OWN** business, professional practice or farm?
4 ☐ Working **WITHOUT PAY** in family business or farm?

f. What kind of work were you doing? *(For example: electrical engineer, stock clerk, typist, farmer)*

(189) ☐☐☐

g. What were your most important activities or duties? *(For example: typing, keeping account books, selling cars, finishing concrete, etc.)*

CHECK ITEM H ▶ Summarize this incident or series of incidents.
_____
_____
_____
_____
_____
_____

CHECK ITEM I ▶ Look at 12c on Incident Report. Is there an entry for "How many?"
☐ No
☐ Yes – Be sure you have an Incident Report for each HH member 12 years of age or over who was robbed, harmed, or threatened in this incident.

CHECK ITEM J ▶ Is this the last Incident Report to be filled for this person?
☐ No – Go to next Incident Report.
☐ Yes – Is this the last HH member to be interviewed?
☐ No – Interview next HH member.
☐ Yes – END INTERVIEW. Enter total number of Crime Incident Reports filled for this household in Item 12 on the cover of NCS-1.

PART B: NCS CLASSIFICATION SCHEME

The kinds of criminal victimizations being measured in the National Crime Panel (NCP) are various forms of common theft and interpersonal assaultive behavior. The descriptions of these types of crimes differ from those utilized by the Federal Bureau of Investigation in conjunction with its *Uniform Crime Reporting System* (UCR), not only in the labels used, but also in the method of classification.

In the NCP surveys, a complete description of a criminal victimization reported during the interview is recorded by the interviewer. The description is computer-coded and hence, classified into the NCP crime categories, based upon the presence or absence of certain elements in the incident. Since this description, identifies various aspects of the crime, the NCP classification scheme is able to utilize this information to show combination events; e.g., when a person is assaulted and robbed at the same time. On the other hand, the UCR classification scheme depends on a hierarchy of seriousness to select only one aspect of a combination event for classification; e.g., an assault and robbery is classified as a robbery only.

In the NCP classification scheme for crimes against individuals and households (Attachment I), there are six main types of crime categories (assaultive violence with theft, assaultive violence without theft, personal theft without assault, burglary, larceny, and auto theft), each of which is comprised of several subcategories. The conditions which must be present for a main category must also be present for each of its subcategories even though the conditions are not repeated each time in the outline. For example, rape as a subcategory of assaultive violence with theft must include a theft or attempted theft or commercial theft in addition to the rape attack/injury.

It should be noted, however, that the *individual* elements which make up a given NCP definition are fully consistent with the UCR definitions. It is, therefore, possible to re-combine NCP crime categorizations to achieve the appropriate UCR counterpart (See Attachment II). LEAA publications use crime categories that are comparable with the UCR definitions.

It should also be noted that some types of crimes may be classified as such by meeting only one set of two or more possible sets of conditions. When this is the case, the italicized word *or* is used to separate the different sets of conditions which may be met. The word *and* is italicized when there are no alternative sets of conditions and, instead, all of the conditions stated must be present in the incident description for that classification.

The column labeled "source code entries" denotes the location on the questionnaire incident report form (NCS-2) of the conditions which must be met for that classification. The source code refers to the circled number to the left of a question on the incident report form and the entry numbers for each source code correspond to the question's pre-coded response categories. Thus, the source code entries are used as a basis for classifying the description of an incident into a technical definition.

ATTACHMENT I, APPENDIX D

Type of Crime	Conditions	Source Code Entries
PERSONAL CRIMES		
Assaultive Violence		
With Theft	Theft or Attempted Theft or Commercial Theft[1]	$154 = 1$ or $155 = 2$ or $114 = 1$
Rape	Rape—method of attack or type of injury	$125 = 1$ or $126 = 2$
Attempted rape	Verbal threat of rape or attempted rape as method of attack or attempted rape injuries	$123 = 1$ or $125 = 2$ or $126 = 3$
Serious assault with weapon	Weapon present and any injury	$120 = x$, 3-5 and $126 = 4$-8
no weapon	No weapon[2] and serious injury[3] or	$120 = 1$ or 2 and $126 = 4$-6 or
	No weapon,[3] other injury[4] and hospitalized for 2 or more days	$120 = 1$ or 2, $126 = 8$ and $129 = 2$ or more days
Minor assault	No weapon,[2] attacked, and minor injury[5] or	$120 = 1$ or 2, $121 = 1$, $126 = 7$ or
	No weapon,[2] attacked, other injury[4] and not hospitalized 2 or more days	$120 = 1$ or 2, $121 = 1$, $126 = 8$, and $129 \neq 2$ or more days
Without Theft	No theft and no attempted theft and no commercial theft[1]	$154 = 2$, $155 = 1$ and $114 \neq 1$
Rape	Rape—method of attack or type of injury	$125 = 1$ or $126 = 2$
Attempted rape	Verbal threat of rape or attempted rape as method of attack or injury	$123 = 1$ or $125 = 2$ or $126 = 3$
Serious assault with weapon	Weapon present and any injury	$120 = x$, 3-5, and $126 = 4$-8
no weapon	No weapon[2] and serious injury[3] or	$120 = 1$ or 2 and $126 = 4$-6 or
	No weapon,[2] other injury[4] and hospitalized 2 or more days	$120 = 1$ or 2, $126 = 8$ and $129 = 2$ or more days
Att. assault, w/weapon	Weapon present and threatened or	$120 = x$, 3-5, and $122 = 2$ or
	Weapon present, attacked, and no injury	$120 = x$, 3-5, $121 = 1$ and $126 = 1$
Minor assault	No weapon,[2] attacked, and minor injury[5] or	$120 = 1$ or 2, $121 = 1$, and $126 = 7$ or
	No weapon,[2] attacked, other injury[4] and not hospitalized 2 or more days	$120 = 1$ or 2, $121 = 1$, $126 = 8$, and $129 \neq 2$ or more days

203

Attachment I (continued)

Type of Crime	Conditions	Source Code Entries
Att. assault, no weapon	No weapon[2] and threatened or	$120 = 1$ or 2 and $122 = 2$ or
	No weapon,[2] attacked and no injury	$120 = 1$ or $2, 121 = 1$, and $126 = 1$
Personal Theft w/o assault	Theft or attempted theft[6]	
Robbery	Theft	$154 = 1$
with weapon	Weapon present	$120 = x, 3\text{-}5$
no weapon	No weapon[2] and threatened or	$120 = 1$ or 2 and $122 = 2$ or
	No weapon,[2] attacked and no injury	$120 = 1$ or $2, 121 = 1$ and $126 = 1$
Attempted robbery	Attempted theft	$155 = 2$
with weapon	Weapon present	$120 = x, 3\text{-}5$
no weapon	No weapon[2] and threatened or	$120 = 1$ or 2 and $122 = 2$ or
	No weapon,[2] attacked and no injury	$120 = 1$ or $2, 121 = 1$ and $126 = 1$
Purse snatch, no force	No weapon,[2] not attacked, not threatened, purse taken, and property on person	$120 = 1$ or $2, 121 = 2, 122 = 1, 160 = 1$ and $163 = 1$
Attempted purse snatch, no force	No weapon,[2] not attacked, not threatened, att. take purse, and property on person	$120 = 1$ or $2, 121 = 2, 122 = 1, 156 = 1$ and $157 = 1$
Pocket picking	No weapon,[2] not attacked, not threatened, property on person, and cash or wallet taken	$120 = 1$ or $2, 121 = 2, 122 = 1, 163 = 1$ and $160 = 0$ or 2 or $159 = \$1\text{-}9999$
PROPERTY CRIMES		
Burglary	No right to be in home, etc.	$115 = 2$ or 3
Forcible entry	Got in and evidence of force	$116 = 1$ and $117 = x$ or $2\text{-}5$
Nothing taken	No theft	$154 = 2$
Property damage	Something damaged	$176 = 2$
No property damage	Nothing damaged	$176 = 1$
Something taken	Theft	$154 = 1$
Unlawful entry w/o force	Got in and no evidence of force[7]	$116 = 1$ and $117 = 1$ or N.A.
Attempted forcible entry	Tried to get in and evidence of force	$116 = 2$ or 3 and $117 = x, 2\text{-}5$

204

Category	Definition	Code
Larceny	Theft except motor vehicle *or* attempted theft except motor vehicle	160 = 0, 1, 2, 5, 6 and ≠ 3 or 4 *or* 156 = 1, 2, 5, 6, 7 and ≠ 3 or 4
Under $50	Sum of stolen cash and property value = $0-49	159 + 164 = $0-49
Under $10	Sum of stolen cash and property value = $0-9	159 + 164 = $0-9
$10-24	Sum of stolen cash and property value = $10-24	159 + 164 = $10-24
$25-49	Sum of stolen cash and property value = $25-49	159 + 164 = $25-49
$50 or more	Sum of stolen cash and property value = $50-19,998	159 + 164 = $50-19,998
$50-99	Sum of stolen cash and property value = $50-99	159 + 164 = $50-99
$100-249	Sum of stolen cash and property value = $100-249	159 + 164 = $100-249
$250 or more	Sum of stolen cash and property value = $250-19,998	159 + 164 = $250-19,998
NA amount	Amount of stolen cash NA *or* value of stolen property NA	159 or 164 = NA
Attempted larceny	Attempted theft except motor vehicle	156 = 1, 2, 5, 6, 7 and ≠ 3 or 4
Auto Theft		
Theft of car	Theft of car *and* no permission or permission, not returned	160 = 3 and 161 = 1, 2 or 161 = 3 and 162 = 2
Theft of other vehicle	Theft of other motor vehicle *and* no permission or permission, not returned	160 = 4 *and* 161 = 1, 2 or 161 = 3 and 162 = 2
Att. theft of car	Attempted theft of car	156 = 3
Att. theft of other vehicle	Attempted theft of other motor vehicle	156 = 4

[1] Includes attempted commercial theft.
[2] Includes "Don't Know" if weapon—victim must be present.
[3] Includes knife or gunshot wounds, broken bones, teeth knocked out, internal injuries or knocked unconscious.
[4] "Other" injury—can't tell if minor or serious.
[5] Includes bruises, black eye, cuts, scratches, swelling.
[6] Excludes commercial theft and attempted commercial theft. Victim must be present.
[7] Includes "NA" for evidence of force.

205

ATTACHMENT II, APPENDIX D

Comparison of Classification Schemes between UCR and NCP for Crimes Against Persons

UCR	National Crime Panel
Rape	Rape with theft
	Attempted rape with theft
	Rape without theft
	Attempted rape without theft
Aggravated Assault	Serious assault without theft
	Attempted assault with weapon without theft
Armed Robbery	Serious assault with theft with weapon
	Robbery, no assault, with weapon
	Attempted robbery, no assault, with weapon
Unarmed Robbery	Serious assault, no weapon with theft
	Minor† assault with theft
	Robbery, no assault, no weapon
	Attempted robbery, no assault, no weapon
Simple Assault	Minor† assault without theft
	Attempted assault, no weapon, without theft
(Larceny)*	Purse snatch without force
	Attempted purse snatch without force
	Pocket picking

*UCR definition of larceny includes many more types of offenses than the personal confrontation crimes.

†Minor is defined to exclude weapons; presence of weapon automatically classifies assault as serious by NCP rules.

Victimization Survey Grants Sponsored by the National Criminal Justice Information and Statistics Service

This appendix contains information on victimization survey grants let by the NCJISS's Statistics Division in the following form: First, there is a letter to Miss Dawn Nelson of the LEAA from Conrad Taeuber, chairman of the panel, requesting details on the grant program discussed in Chapter 7. This is followed by Miss Nelson's response, including a set of attachments describing individual grants.

November 10, 1975

Miss Dawn Nelson
NCJISS-Statistics Division
Law Enforcement Assistance Administration
U.S. Department of Justice
Washington, D.C. 20350

Dear Miss Nelson:

The Academy's Panel for the Evaluation of Crime Surveys is aware that NCJISS is sponsoring victimization survey research at institutions outside the federal government, but the Panel lacks "official" documentation on the scope of this activity. Because knowledge of analysis and dissemination of this statistical series is important to our evaluation, I am requesting that you forward to our staff a description of the Statistics Division's research program that addresses the following items:

Budget: We would like to know simply the *amount* of total funds allo-cated by the Statistics Division to nongovernmental research on any aspects of LEAA-sponsored victimization surveys, by fiscal year, beginning with FY 1974.

Request for Proposals: Has the Statistics Division issued any RFP's so-liciting bids for work related to victimization surveys or associated method-ology? If so, would it be possible to furnish the Panel with a list annotated with a sentence or two describing the topic of each RFP?

Grants and Contracts: It would be beneficial to have a complete list of grants and contracts which were awarded by the Statistics Division after FY 1973 and which focus on some facet of victimization surveys, whether they be substantive analyses of existing data, methodological investigations, data collection efforts, user oriented studies, or dissemination programs. It would be good if details on each grant or contract included a reference to the prin-cipal investigator, institutional base, a descriptive title of project, the date of approval, the beginning and completion dates, the level of funding, publica-tion obligations or rights, and deliverable items.

Relationships with Other LEAA Units: It is the Panel's understanding that organizational units within LEAA other than NCJISS have sponsored re-search on the LEAA victimization survey data. For instance, we know that the National Institute of Law Enforcement and Criminal Justice has sup-ported both data collection and substantive analytic efforts in the victimiza-tion area, but we are not clear as to whether we should take these activities into account as part of our evaluation of the NCJISS victimization program. Hence, the Panel would appreciate your providing a brief statement on any pertinent relationship—whether formal or informal—between or among your group's victimization activities and those of other LEAA units.

If you have any problem in responding to this request, please contact the Panel's staff. I thank you for your cooperation.

Sincerely,

CONRAD TAEUBER
Chairman
Panel for the Evaluation of Crime Surveys

cc: Panel for the Evaluation of Crime Surveys (Members)
      Committee on National Statistics (Staff)
      William H. Kruskal

Copies also to: Walt R. Simmons
                  Richard F. Sparks

November 24, 1975

Mr. Conrad Taeuber
National Research Council
Committee on National Statistics
2101 Constitution Avenue, N.W.
Washington, D.C. 20418

Dear Mr. Taeuber:

I have received your letter of November 10, 1975 requesting information on the National Criminal Justice Information and Statistics Service (NCJISS) sponsored non-governmental victimization survey research.

The following information is provided in response to the specific items outlined in your letter:

Budget: In FY 1974, $423,189 was allocated to non-governmental research related to the National Crime Panel program. In FY 1975, the comparable amount was $1,485,873. In FY 1976, the amount, so far, is $183,226.

Request for Proposals: The Statistics Division of NCJISS has never issued any RFP's soliciting bids for work related to victimization surveys or associated methodology.

Grants and Contracts: Accompanying this letter are descriptions of the nine applicable grants awarded by NCJISS since the beginning of FY 1974. NCJISS has not let any contracts for work related to the National Crime Panel program.

Relationships with Other LEAA Units: As was noted in your letter, other LEAA units have sponsored research on the victimization survey data. NCJISS does not have direct responsibility for these research activities. However, we have and do provide input into these activities in the form of advice, information, and materials, upon request, to the responsible LEAA unit. For the Academy's evaluation, these activities should not be considered as a part of the on-going statistical survey, but some consideration might be given to these activities during your examination of the utility of the results to present and potential users of the victimization data.

I hope this information satisfies your request. If you should require any additional information, please do not hesitate to contact me again.

In closing let me indicate that Mr. Renshaw, who recently arrived as Director of the Statistics Division, has been reviewing the work of the

Academy and will be in touch with you in the next two weeks on the course of this work.

Sincerely,

DAWN D. NELSON
Statistics Division
National Criminal Justice Information and Statistics Service

Enclosure

Xeroxes to: Panel for the Evaluation of Crime Surveys (Mbrs)
                William H. Kruskal
                Margaret E. Martin
                Maurice E. B. Owens
                Bettye K. Penick
                Walt R. Simmons
                Richard F. Sparks

GRANTS AWARDED BY NCJISS SINCE BEGINNING OF FY 1974

1. Grant Number: 74-SS-99-6001
2. Principal investigator: Michael J. Hindelang
3. Institution: Criminal Justice Research Center, Inc., Latham, New York
4. Title: "Analysis of National Crime Survey Data" (1972 Eight Impact Cities)
5. Award date: 9/20/73
6. Performance period: 9/20/73-7/19/74, extended with supplemental funds to 10/5/74
7. $90,715 plus supplemental funds of $13,479 for a total of $104,194
8. Publication obligations or rights: Grant Application Form LEAA-INST. 1 (Ed. 3-24-69) Conditions—SEE ATTACHMENT A.
9. Deliverable items: a) A comprehensive report containing an analysis of the nature and extent of criminal victimizations in the households and businesses in the eight Impact cities; b) Edited final reports prepared by each participating Impact city with a critical evaluation of the quality of the report and its potential for publication; c) A summary report of problems encountered in data analysis and recommendations regarding changes in data collection; d) A package of educational materials and documentation for future data users.

1. Grant Number: 74-SS-99-6002
2. Principal investigator: Bettye Eidson Penick
3. Institution: National Academy of Sciences, Washington, D.C.
4. Title: "Evaluation of National Crime Panel"
5. Award date: 1/23/74

6. Performance period: 1/23/74-1/23/76
7. Funding: $300,000
8. Publication obligations or rights: Grant Application Form LEAA-INST. 1 (Ed. 3/24/69) Conditions—SEE ATTACHMENT A.
9. Deliverable items: A final report summarizing fundings and recommendations based on an evaluation of the National Crime Panel from two points of view: 1) as an on-going statistical survey in terms of its presently accepted objectives on such aspects as completeness, accuracy, reliability, perceptive analysis, and careful dissemination; and 2) the utility of the results assessed in light of the statistical needs of present and potential users.

1. Grant Number: 74-SS-99-6003
2. Principal investigator: Albert D. Biderman
3. Institution: Bureau of Social Science Research, Washington, D.C.
4. Title: "A Social Indicator of Interpersonal Harm"
5. Award date: 12/12/73
6. Performance period: 12/28/73-9/27/74, extended at no-cost to 3/15/75
7. Funding: $18,995
8. Publication obligations or rights: Grant Application Form LEAA 3621/2 (2/72) Conditions—SEE ATTACHMENT B
9. Deliverable items: A final report will discuss the results of a feasibility study undertaken to explore the adaptability of data from interviews on injuries, such as those carried out by the National Health Interview Survey, to criminal victimization statistics development and make a recommendation on whether a large-scale injury oriented questionnaire should be developed for future use.

1. Grant Number: 75-SS-99-6002
2. Principal investigator: Michael J. Hindelang
3. Institution: Criminal Justice Research Center, Inc., Latham, New York
4. Title: "Analysis of NCP Attitude and Victimization Data" (1972 Eight Impact Cities and 1973 Five Largest Cities)
5. Award date: 7/25/74
6. Performance period: 7/1/74-8/1/75, extended at no-cost to 10/31/75 and extended with supplemental funds from 10/31/75 to 1/30/76
7. Funding: $171,234 plus supplemental funds of $29,916 for a total of $201,150
8. Publication obligations or rights: Financial Management for Planning and Action Grants Guideline Manual-M7100.1A—SEE ATTACHMENT C
9. Deliverable items: a) A report on the development of a series of "function-specific" crime classification schemes; b) A report containing an in-depth examination of the National Crime Panel attitude data and its relationship to victimization experiences in the 1972 eight Impact cities and the 1973 five largest cities; c) A report on the development of a series of "victimization specific" classifications of victims; d) A report with recom-

mendations for including additional data elements in future victimization surveys to enhance the use of the data.

1. Grant Number: 75-SS-99-6005
2. Principal investigator: Marilyn W. Andrulis
3. Institution: Mid-Atlantic Research Institute, Bethesda, Maryland
4. Title: "Development of Methodology for Self-Reporting of Crime by Offenders and Victims"
5. Award date: 8/9/74
6. Performance period: 9/1/74-7/31/75, extended at no-cost to 11/30/75
7. Funding: $214,000
8. Publication obligations or rights: Financial Management for Planning and Action Grants Guideline Manual-M7100.1A–SEE ATTACHMENT C
9. Deliverable items: A final report presenting the results of experimentation to develop measurement techniques for: 1) the self-reporting of crimes involving victims, such as vandalism, shoplifting, fraud, etc.; 2) the self-reporting of crimes without victims, such as prostitution, gambling, drug abuse, etc.; and 3) assessing the validity of current methods of reporting offenses and victimizations.

1. Grant Number: 75-SS-99-6013
2. Principal investigator: Albert J. Reiss, Jr.
3. Institution: Institution for Social and Policy Studies-Yale University, New Haven, Connecticut
4. Title: "Analytical Studies of Victimization by Crime Using NCSP"
5. Award date: 10/24/74
6. Performance period: 10/24/74-10/23/76
7. Funding: $295,489
8. Publication obligations or rights: Financial Management for Planning and Action Grants Guideline Manual-M7100.1A–SEE ATTACHMENT C
9. Deliverable items: A report or reports on analytical studies of crime and victimization by crime over time, utilizing the specific panel features of the survey design. Some of the specific analyses to be conducted are: 1) An examination of victim proneness focusing on its nature and distribution; 2) An examination of citizen mobilization of the police and changes in mobilization over time; 3) An examination of attempted versus actual victimizations; and, 4) An examination of the patterns of crime victimization.

1. Grant Number: 75SS-99-6026
2. Principal investigator: Marvin E. Wolfgang
3. Institution: Center for Studies in Criminology and Criminal Law-University of Pennsylvania, Philadelphia, Pennsylvania
4. Title: "National Survey of Crime Severity"
5. Award date: 6/23/75
6. Performance period: 6/30/75-6/29/76
7. Funding: $251,811
8. Publication obligation or rights: Financial Management for Planning and Action Grants Guideline Manual-M7100.1A–SEE ATTACHMENT C

9. Deliverable items: This is the first year of a three year project. After the first year a report will be prepared to present the results of pretests using category and magnitude scaling techniques to measure perceived offense severity. These results will be used in the second year to determine the most effective scale to be administered by the Census Bureau as a part of the National Crime Panel Survey. In the third year, a final report will be prepared containing a set of general offense severity weights, variable specific weights composed of various combinations of personal and environmental variables, and a complete analysis of the components of variation in these offense severity weights.

1. Grant Number: 75SS-99-6029
2. Principal investigator: Michael J. Hindelang
3. Institution: Criminal Justice Research Center, Inc., Latham, New York
4. Title: "Application of Victimization Survey Results"
5. Award date: 6/30/75
6. Performance period: 7/24/75-7/23/77
7. Funding: $523,423
8. Publication obligations or rights: Financial Management for Planning and Action Grants Guideline Manual-M7100.1A—SEE ATTACHMENT C
9. Deliverable items: a) A report on the results of a requirements analysis of state and local needs relative to the victimization data available from the National Crime Panel Survey; b) Eight to ten reports applying victimization data to identified needs to serve as illustrative models of how state and local practitioners can utilize the data; c) Eighteen analytic monographs presenting the findings of in-depth analyses of the cities and national data produced to date. Briefly, these monographs will cover the following topics: intercity variation in victimization, variation of city victimization data over time, the application of function-specific offense classifications to the national data, application of the victim classification results to the national data, spatial and temporal ecological analyses of the national data, multiple victimization, and implications of victimization data for national policy.

1. Grant Number: 76SS-99-6005
2. Principal investigator: David McClintock
3. Institution: Data Use and Access Laboratories (DUALabs), Arlington, Virginia
4. Title: "A Data Use Assistance Program to Facilitate Use of the Victim Survey Data Tape Files."
5. Award date: 10/2/75
6. Performance period: 10/10/75-10/9/76
7. Funding: $183,226
8. Publication obligations or rights: Financial Management for Planning and Action Grants Guideline Manual-M7100.1A—SEE ATTACHMENT C
9. Deliverable items: a) Reformatted National Crime Panel data tape files which were originally prepared by the Census Bureau; b) Technical docu-

mentation for processing the data tape files; c) A series of user seminars to provide assistance in the use of the National Crime Panel tapes and documentation; and, e) A continuing technical consultation service for the data tape users.

ATTACHMENT A

Grant Application Form LEAA-INST. 1 (Ed. 3-24-69): "K. that the grantee may publish the results of grant activity without prior review by the Statistical Research Center with an acknowledgment of the Statistical Research Center support, furnishing 25 copies to the Statistical Research Center. However, each such publication must contain the following statement, or its equivalent: 'The fact that the National Criminal Justice Statistical Research Center furnished financial support to the activity described in this publication does not necessarily indicate the concurrence of the Statistical Research Center in the statements or conclusions contained herein.'

1. that where grant projects produce original books, manuals, films, or other copyrightable material, the grantee may copyright such, but the Department reserves a royalty-free, non-exclusive and irrevocable license to reproduce, publish, translate, or otherwise use, and to authorize others to publish and use such materials. Where such license is exercised, appropriate acknowledgment of the grantee's contribution will be made."

ATTACHMENT B

LEAA Grant Application Form 3621/2 (2/72): "The grantee may publish at his own expense, the results of grant activity without prior review by LEAA provided that any publication (written, visual, or sound) contains an acknowledgment of LEAA grant support. At least 10 copies of any such publication must be furnished to LEAA but only 5 copies of training materials (where used in grant project) need be supplied, except as otherwise requested or approved by LEAA. Publication of documents or reports with grant funds beyond quantities required to meet standard report requirements must be provided for in approved project plans or budgets or otherwise approved by LEAA and, for large quantity publication, manuscripts must be submitted in advance to LEAA."

ATTACHMENT C

LEAA Financial Management for Planning and Action Grants Guideline Manual-M7100.1A, Appendix 9, item 7b: "Where the grant results in a book or other copyrightable material, the author or grantee is free to copyright the work, but the Federal grantor agency reserves a royalty-free, non-exclusive and irrevocable license to reproduce, publish, or otherwise use, and to authorize others to use the work for Government purposes."

Analysis of Security Measures Data

The purpose of this appendix is to present an example of the panel's substantive review of NCS reports. The topic examined here—the analysis of security measures data—has been selected to provide supporting material for Chapter 7.

One of the broad objectives of the NCS is to provide information on the context within which certain victim-events occur. A derivative objective is to identify sets of circumstances that either enhance or mitigate the chances of an entity being victimized. A conceptual model for operationalizing this objective in regard to the NCS household surveys is proposed in Chapter 6 of this report.

The potential of the NCS for providing data on the benefits of security devices was recognized during formative stages of the NCS, and this recognition is reflected in the commercial survey instruments.[1] During the course of commercial survey interviews, each respondent is asked the following question:

What security measures, if any, are present at this location now to protect it against burglary and/or robbery?

(Mark all that apply)[2]

1. Alarm system—outside building
2. Central alarm

---

[1] U.S. Department of Justice, Law Enforcement Assistance Administration, *Criminal Victimization Surveys in the Nations Five Largest Cities* (Final Report) (Washington, D.C.: U.S. Government Printing Office, April 1975), p. 149.
[2] In later versions of the instrument, *mirrors, locks,* and *lights* have been added as separate categories.

3. Reinforcing devices, such as bars on windows
4. Guard, watchman
5. Watch dog
6. Firearms
7. Cameras
8. Other (Specify)
9. None

A measure of the installation date of each checked item also is obtained. For each reported incident, the respondent is asked if any of the devices on the list was installed as a result of the incident. Consequently, time-based data are available on selected security measures for each commercial establishment included in NCS surveys.

These data are analyzed in the section of the *Five Largest Cities* (Final Report) titled "Security Measures."[3] The opening sentence in that section is:

Roughly two-thirds of all commercial establishments were protected against possible victimization by some form of security arrangement.[4]

No definition of "security measures" is given in the text. Nor is the survey instrument cited. A reader must take the initiative to refer to the instrument in an appendix to be informed of the meaning of "security measures." Furthermore, because of the other category in the cited list, the interpretation that should be attached to the quoted sentence is that roughly one-third of establishments have no security arrangements, at least insofar as respondents define and have knowledge of security measures.

The basic finding noted in the second and last paragraph of that section is:

Businesses that had been victimized were less likely to have had security measures before victimization than were those that had not been victimized.[5]

This statement hints at a relationship between security measures and victimizations, but its meaning is not clear.

Assume for the moment that each business establishment is either not victimized or victimized no more than once during the reference year, an assumption that we know is erroneous. Then a literal interpretation of the above statement would be that of those firms victimized the proportion having at least one security measure before the event is less than the fraction of nonvictimized establishments protected by some security measure. That is, roughly speaking, security measures are more common among nonvictims than among victims of burglary or robbery.

It is reasonable to assume that an entrepreneur would install, for instance, bars on windows to deter potential burglars from victimizing his establish-

---

[3] U.S. Department of Justice, LEAA, *Five Largest Cities* (Final Report), *op. cit.*, p. 39.
[4] *Ibid.*
[5] *Ibid.*

ment. Because a security measure is present either to prevent or to make difficult some type of victimization, the measure could be viewed as an independent variable and treated as such in the analysis. A pertinent question then would be, "Among those establishments surveyed, to what degree does the presence of a specific security measure distinguish between victims and non-victims?" No quantitative inference on this question can be made with the data available in the document, and this question is not addressed in the text. Instead, the presence of victimization is treated, in both the text and tables, as the independent variable and the presence or absence of security measures is treated as the dependent variable.[6]

To illustrate, see Table F-1, which is reproduced in part from Table Series 29 of the *Five Largest Cities* (Final Report). The data for wholesale and service establishments are omitted to conserve space; additional categories add nothing to the discussion here.

Although the title indicates that the base of the tabulated percentages is establishments, the numbers of establishments victimized and not victimized by burglary and robbery are not given in the table, nor are these numbers presented anywhere in the document. While victimization rates are available from the document, evidence presented in Chapter 7 of this report shows that the annual rate can be a misleading indicator of the number of commercial establishments victimized by either of the two categories of victimization. Moreover, we have no indication of the standard errors of the percentages in Table Series 29, except the table footnote, which implies that each percentage is based on a number of sample cases greater than "about 10."[7]

The tabulations for victimized establishments are more complex. Recall that each respondent is asked to specify which security measures are employed at the establishment and which, if any, were installed as a result of each incident. This interviewing procedure may provide a partial clue to the meaning of the three mutually exclusive subcategories of installation in the table labeled "after, before, and before and after" victimization, but the precise algorithm for distributing victims over the subclasses is not given.

It is shown elsewhere in this report that among commercial establishments victimized by either burglary or robbery during a period of 1 year, a substantial fraction is victimized more than once. We suspect that this implies one of two things about the data shown in the table. For those establishments victimized more than once, either one victimization is selected in an unspecified manner for analysis or the establishment is counted in the analy-

---

[6]Document tables related to this discussion are found in Appendix I of the *Five Largest Cities* (Final Report), *op. cit.*: Table Series 27—Percent of Commercial Establishments Equipped with Security Measures by Kind of Establishment and City, 1972; Table Series 28 (one table for each city)—Percent of Commercial Establishments by Type of Security Measure and Kind of Establishment, 1972; and Table 29—Percent Distribution of Commercial Establishments, Victimized and Not Victimized, by Presence of Security Measures and Kind of Establishment, 1972.

[7]From its use in this and other NCS publications, it is not clear whether the phrase, "number of sample cases," refers to the numerator or to the denominator in a quotient.

TABLE F-1   Chicago: Percent Distribution of Commercial Establishments, Victimized and Not Victimized, by Presence of Security Measures and Kind of Establishment, 1972[a]

Item	All Establishments	Retail
Victimized		
With security measures	74	79
After victimization	18	12
Before victimization	34	38
Before and after victimization	22	29
Without security measures	24	19
Not available	2	b
Not victimized		
With security measures	61	70
Without security measures	35	27
Not available	4	3

[a]SOURCE: *Five Largest Cities* (Final Report), Table Series 29.
[b]Estimate, based on about 10 or fewer sample cases, is statistically unreliable.

sis as many times as it was victimized. If the latter is the case, the base of the percentages is a victimization, not a victimized establishment, which would be inconsistent with the title.

Another problem with this analysis is that kinds of security measures and kinds of victimizations both are aggregated. Neither tabular material nor the text indicates which specific security measures might be associated with deterrence of robbery or with deterrence of burglary.

We especially are concerned about the treatment of attempted robberies and burglaries in the LEAA publications. Within the context of the NCS, both robbery and burglary by definition include incidents involving attempts as well as those successfully completed, yet the published tabulations make no distinction between completed and attempted victimizations. If a potential burglar is, however, thwarted by an alarm, by extra locks, or by a reinforcing device, then the corresponding security measure was effective. Analysis directed at assessment of risk and its amelioration clearly requires a distinction between completed and attempted criminal acts.

We conclude that the treatment of data on security measures in the *Five Largest Cities* (Final Report) is inappropriate. Victimizations have been aggregated with respect to type, degree of completion, and place of occurrence. Security measures apparently have been collapsed into a global binary attribute. This degree of aggregation conceals any relationships between particular types of victimizations and specific security devices. Furthermore, multiple victimizations have been treated so as to distort true risk across all establishments surveyed. The one question that is explored in the cited document—the degree to which victimizations can be used as predictors of the presence of security measures—seems peripheral to the many important issues that could be examined with the present field design and survey instrument.

LEAA Statement
on NCS Objectives

This appendix is a reproduction of a portion of an internal LEAA document on NCS objectives. It was prepared by Dr. Charles Kindermann, of LEAA, at the request of Mr. Charles R. Work, also of LEAA. It was transmitted to the staff of this panel as part of an April 1, 1975, letter from Dr. Kindermann to Dr. Bettye K. Penick.

Statistics Division
March 7, 1975

I. Objectives of the NCP and of Victimization Surveys

The idea for establishing a national victimization survey has had
a long history within LEAA, nearly as long as LEAA's existence.
As early as September 1969, LEAA formally opened discussion with
the Bureau of the Census on this topic in a memorandum from
Richard Velde to the Director of the Census Bureau. Several
months of informal discussion had preceded this.

Over a year later, in October 1970 after much research and discussion,
the first proposed study plan was developed by the National Criminal
Justice Statistics Center (forerunner to NCJISS). According to this
plan, the primary purpose of a national victimization survey would be
twofold:

> "to measure the annual change in crime incidents for a
> limited set of major crimes and to characterize some
> of the socio-economic aspects of both the reported
> events and their victims."

The survey objectives as outlined in this same document were:

"Survey Objectives

The purpose of the National Victimization Survey is to provide
a reliable statistical series on the amount of dangerous crime
in the United States and the rate of victim experience. In
the beginning, we will measure crime events on an annual basis.
Methodologically, the assessment of crime incidence will be
accomplished by focusing on the victim rather than on police
statistics. The latter data failed on two accounts to provide
a complete estimate of crime incidence - only crimes known to
the police are included and variable police agency practices
in classifying and reporting crimes blur the national (and
statewide) figures.

"Information to be obtained in the household surveys will
include personal and household victimization experience for a
few major crimes; socio-economic data on victims including age,
sex, race, educational attainment, family income, and marital
status; and various details about the crime event, such as
extent of economic loss, time of occurrence, weapon use, whether
reported to the police, and where known, characteristics of
the offender and his relationship to the victim. In addition,
since human behavior is quite often a function of the fear or
perception of crime rather than actual victimization, a series
of attitudinal questions will be administered to the respondents,
both victims and non-victims, to determine public perception
of the crime problem."

It is important to remember that at this point in time, the design
of the National Crime Panel Program focused on satisfying the
primary purpose, viz., to provide <u>national</u> data on victimization
to determine <u>annual</u> victim experience. However, even at this early
stage, it was recognized that local data would be required and plans
were made accordingly. The following section from the October 1970
Proposed Study Plan elaborated on our understanding of the local
needs and how they could be addressed by the NCP program:

"Since law enforcement is local rather than federal, national
crime rates as determined from NCP would be far less useful
to local officials than data about their own areas. We expect,
therefore, to expand the geographic scope of NCP once the
program is established. At this point, we foresee providing
victim data for the central cities of the ten (perhaps 15)
largest SMSA's.... These supplemental samples would permit
a change of 15 percent per city to be measured in the year-
to-year violent crime rate.... We would also like the Bureau
of the Census to explore the requirements in sample expansion
to provide reliable statistics for each of the 15 largest
states."

This entire original planning document was distributed for comments
to a variety of persons, including: L. Bloomberg, D. Barbour, and
J. Gregg of OMB; A. Biderman of BSSR; M. Wolfgang of the University
of Pa.; A. Reiss of Yale University; R. Beattie of the California
Bureau of Criminal Statistics; L. Wilkins of SUNY; and various
division heads and administrative officials within LEAA. Suggestions
made at this point were an important factor in shaping the NCP
program.

This document did not address the uses of the survey data other than
the general purpose of measuring crime. However, other internal
memoranda during this developmental stage did begin to list possible
uses. A number of uses of victimization data were also proposed
during a conference held at the Bureau of the Census. To summarize
briefly, the uses identified at this time were:

1. to provide an independent calibration for the UCR;

2. to provide a measure of victim risk;

3. to enable a shift in concentration in the criminal justice
   system from the offender to the victim;

4. to provide an indicator of the crime problem outside those
   indicators generated by police activities;

5. to serve as an index of changes in reporting behavior in
   the population;

6. to provide an indicator of social "outlook" in the
   population as well as an indicator of society's definitions
   of crime;

7. to measure the effectiveness of new criminal justice
    programs, especially in local areas.

As can be readily seen, most of the immediately apparent uses were
oriented toward adding to a body of knowledge about victims and a
better understanding of the dimensions of the crime problem.

As the research process continued with the necessary methodological
tests prior to establishment of the Crime Panel, the objectives and
uses were continuously modified. The approach remained one of
building gradually with research and developmental work, expanding
the objectives based on the results of previous work, until it could
be determined what survey information could be <u>routinely</u> collected
and published from a continuous national crime survey panel.

Although the uses of the data were not thoroughly documented at this
point, the issue of "user utility" was kept in mind throughout the
planning stages. The following discussion on this subject appeared
in memorandum to Richard Velde from George Hall dated August 2, 1972:

"I. <u>User Utility</u>

For local planners, evaluators, SPA, and others a broad array of
geographic detail will be available from the National Crime Panel,
which will be of considerable value in the assessment and evaluation of local efforts to combat crime. Initially, of course, data
will be published for 16 of the nation's largest cities, where
common crime is heavily concentrated. Later, the coverage of NCP
will be expanded to provide data for the central cities of an
additional 20 SMSAs.

"For individual State statistics, we are exploring the cost and
feasibility of providing the crime data for the largest (perhaps
top 15) States. At this point, data for each of the remaining
35 States on an individual basis could not reasonably be provided
without an enormous increase in sample coverage and hence, cost.

"The data will be tabulated for each of the 10 Federal regions,
which, of course, are the same as the LEAA regions. In addition,
data will be shown for cities in the following size groupings:

        50,000 - 249,999 population
       250,000 - 499,999 population
       500,000 - 999,999 population
     1,000,000 or more population

"Moreover, we will provide tabulations for suburban metropolitan
areas (balance of SMSAs, excluding central cities), as well as small
urban and rural territory, so that trends in the incidence of
violence and common theft can be charted for change in these
important segments of America.

"Regarding the issue of user utility on a more substantive level,
our discussions with local people - including regional personnel,
SPAs, Impact City Teams - have assured us that the content of the

survey is highly useful for a variety of planning needs; and the
first question we generally get from these potential users is
"When can we get the data?"

"Two additional points should serve to demonstrate the anticipated
relevance of the survey for users. The National Advisory Commission
on Criminal Justice Standards and Goals has adopted the use of
victimization surveys - a la the NCP - as a major recommendation
for utilization by local criminal justice practitioners in evaluating crime control efforts in their communities. Secondly, the
survey mechanisms (questionnaires, training guides for interviewers,
interviewing modes, etc.) have been validated, as you know, through
a comprehensive developmental process spanning 2 1/2 years. As a
result, these techniques can easily be applied in local communities
who need specific crime data for their areas - applied without the
costly and time-consuming developmental effort required for a
statistical survey of this type."

It should also be noted that plans for the survey were always subject
to cost considerations. Even after the survey's inception in July 1972,
some of our original plans had to be modified due to cost considerations.
We had anticipated obtaining data for the United States as a whole, for
regions, for cities by size as well as information on the central cities
in the 15 largest SMSAs in 1973. However, on the basis of detailed
cost projections, we had to postpone interviewing in the central cities
of two SMSAs scheduled for 1973 surveying (San Francisco-Oakland and
Miami). Other factors affecting survey plans involved methodological
limitations which we were constantly uncovering. For example, the
objective of obtaining a complete measure of the incidence of crime was
limited by problems associated with interviewing persons under age 12.

In July 1972, NCP was established and another attempt was made to document
the objectives and uses in a paper prepared for inclusion in the report
of the National Advisory Commission on Criminal Justice Standards and
Goals. This paper reflected the basic thinking at the time the
program was put into operation. This paper appears as Appendix A to the
National Advisory Commission's Report on the Criminal Justice System.
A reprint of the appendix is attached but excerpts pertaining to
objectives and uses are repeated here. The Commission identified data
necessary for the development of effective crime reduction programs,
much of which can be supplied by the NCP. These needs are as follows:

"...a city program whose objective is to reduce street crime
poses obvious but rarely answered questions such as the following:

How much street crime has there been in the past few
months? Is it increasing or decreasing?

What portion of the street crime is committed for an
apparent economic motive, such as hold-ups or
purse-snatchings?

Is economically-motivated street theft changing at
a faster or slower pace than street violence where
economic gain is not involved, such as in rape or
assault?

Is substantially all street violence and theft the
result of an essentially random encounter between
an assailant and an unknown victim, or does street
crime involve a significant number of victims and
offenders who know each other in some social capacity?

When fewer people walk the streets due to real or
imagined fear of crime, do street robberies rise
because of the lessened mutual protection or deterrent
effects that people provide from their sheer number
and presence; or conversely, do street robberies
decrease because fewer potential victims place themselves in the risk setting?

In what ways does fear modify citizens' behavior in
regard to the utilization of mass transit, restaurants,
downtown shopping, or other public services? How does
this relate, if at all, to the actual occurrence of
crime?

Where and when does street crime occur? Does it shift in
time and space; if so, under what circumstances?

How much assaultive violence in the city streets is
attributable to juvenile gangs? Is this pehnomenon
rising, cresting, or slackening?

Who are the victims of street attacks? Women? Men?
The young? The old? Blacks? Whites?

"These and a multitude of other questions are the kinds of issues
facing a planner who desires to make a serious attack on just one of
the many problems confronting the criminal justice community - in
this example, street crime. It is immediately apparent that the
answers to many of those questions are quantifiable in the sense
of explicit numerical measures. It is also true, though less
apparent, that few such measures have been available in the past;
and the ones that have been available have generally suffered
various deficiencies, thus rendering analysis and/or evaluation
highly suspect, if not totally futile." 1/

In addition to identifying data needs which can be addressed through the
victimization survey, the Commission went on to discuss specific uses
to which victimization data can be put:

"The victim survey, whether localized, regional, or national in
scope, is enormously useful as a statistical device. Since victim
surveys were first used in the mid-60's by the Presidential
Commission on Law Enforcement and Administration of Justice
(hereinafter referred to as the Crime Commission), a sizeable number
of valid and largely independent uses have been identified, and
the list is still growing.

1/ National Advisory Commission on Criminal Justice Standards and Goals,
Report on the Criminal Justice System, 1973, p. 200.

"Types of Crime Amenable to Study

Thus far in the development of victim survey methodology, a large
body of statistical research has been compiled which demonstrates
the utility of the method in estimating assaultive violence,
personal theft, burglary, and commercial robberies. This suggests,
of course, that the victim survey is not the statistical panacea
for measuring every conceivable type of predatory offense which can
victimize the public. For example, such offenses as shoplifting
and consumer fraud have proven to be particularly elusive from the
victim survey approach. (See section on Limitations of Victim
Surveys.)

"The demonstrated value of a well-designed victim survey lies in its
capability for measuring such phenomena as interpersonal violence,
especially of the stranger-to-stranger variety. For example, it
can give separate figures on the number of serious assaults where a
weapon was used, the number of assaults where no weapon was employed,
the number of attempted assaults with or without a weapon, the number
of forcible rapes and the number of attempted rapes.

"For personal theft, the victim survey is suitable for measuring the
number of armed robberies, the number of strong-arm robberies, the
number of forceful purse-snatchings, and the number of these same
events which also result in physical injury to the victim.
Similarly, measures of household theft can be ascertained: the amount
of burglary, attempted burglary, or larcenous theft. Auto thefts
can be estimated from a victim survey.

"Victim surveys are applicable to measuring the amount of commercial
robbery and commercial burglary when the appropriate questionnaires
are administered in business establishments and other institutions.

"Nationally, the Law Enforcement Assistance Administration has focused
its victim-survey program on the measurement of the types of common
theft and violence described above. Not only are these types of
crime feasible for measurement in a purely methodological sense, but
more importantly, they substantively represent most of the offenses
which large segments of society regard as serious. Moreover, LEAA
is placing considerable emphasis upon differentiating the person-to-
person offenses by whether the victim and the offender know each
other. Stranger-to-stranger violence is radically different from
domestic violence both in terms of criminal justice system response
and in terms of the degree of public fear and resultant behavior
alteration.

"Measures of Change for Evaluation

A victim survey administered periodically in the same locale will
provide measures of change. This is vital for the valid evaluation of crime control and prevention programs. Since agency
statistics only provide estimates of the crimes known to the police,
these measures cannot be suitably employed for "before" and "after"
assessments in a given crime control project. For example, a project
with a dual objective to reduce street assaults and to improve

police-community interaction may have the effect of increased citizen
reporting of victimizations to the police, thus invalidating before
and after comparisons derived exclusively from police statistics.

"A victim survey, on the other hand, is not as sensitive to citizen
vicissitudes in reporting crimes to the police - measures of change
from this source are thus more validly taken as true change rather
than paper change.

"Social and Economic Framework in the Study of Crime

To study the broader impact of crime, one of the most significant
uses of victimization surveys is the assessment of the socio-
economic and demographic framework surrounding violence and theft.

"What is the age and racial distribution of theft victims? Who
are their assailants? What kinds of businesses are most
susceptible to burglary or robbery? What is the cost of crime
in terms of physical injury, dollar loss, property damage,
insurance protection, medical expenses, altered living habits,
and other variables? These questions are the kinds of detailed
queries which can be determined from a well-executed victimization survey.

"Moreover, a victim survey is the only practical method for
ascertaining the degree of victim proneness. For example, how
frequently during a given interval of time does an armed robbery
hit the same victim? Do characteristics of persons suffering
multiple victimizations in a limited time frame differ from those
suffering a single victimization?

"A further, long-range use of victim survey data is in the
application of mathematical models in the prediction of crime
amount. Such projections could be plausibly constructed, if,
for example, it can be determined that the demographic
characteristics of victims over long periods of time remain
fairly stable or change in some empirically predictable fashion.
The use of such mathematical prediction devices, however, implies
the need for amassing continuous, or periodic, victim survey data
for model input.

"Crime Versus Fear of Crime

Public surveys are especially valuable in providing insight on
the relationship between crime victimization and citizen reaction
to crime. Citizen attitudes toward crime can be a particularly
useful barometer to policy makers in regard to whether crime is
or is not generally regarded as a major problem for the community.
Moreover, citizen reactions due to fear of crime may or may not
be manifested by lessened utilization of public services and
entertainment, by migration, by the acquisition of protective
devices, and by other behavioral alterations in life - style.

"An attitude survey, used in conjunction with a survey to measure
victimization experiences, can produce many important findings on

the degree and manner by which people change their lives due to
fear of crime. This type of information used in concert with
actual measures of victimization risk (as derived from the victim
survey) can go far toward helping students of the crime problem
learn whether fear of crime is increasing and if so, whether
justifiably so. These two types of measures alone, if available,
would have enormous implications for legislatures, policy-makers,
and the media.

"Comparative Data

Another important contribution of victim surveys is that valid
comparisons between two or more cities or other geographic areas
can be made in regard to the crime situation. This is easily
managed when a standardized victim survey using identical
questionnaires, survey collection procedures, interviewer training techniques, and uniform data reduction methods is administered
in more than one city or other small area. Differences in crime
amount or type thus observed would be reflective of real variations between cities.

"Users of these statistics would thereby be spared the nagging
uncertainties that arise from comparing crimes known to the police
city-by-city. Crimes known to the police are subject to citizen
differences in reporting victimization city-by-city and to variable
jurisdictional practices in defining and recording crimes, rendering inter-city comparisions of these data questionable. 2/

Now that the program has been in operation for some time and some of the
data results have been analyzed, it seems appropriate to reassess the
objectives and uses in terms of the future. It was never intended that
the objectives and uses should be set in concrete, but rather the
program is seen as viable, subject to change and growth to meet the
constantly changing demands of LEAA and the public. Since most of the
persons associated with the NCP program now have been working on it
since the initial developmental stages, it was deemed that an independent
or "fresh" look at the program would be useful. For this reason, a grant
was awarded to the National Academy of Sciences (NAS). It is anticipated
that the NAS final recommendations, due in January 1976, will result in
a number of changes in the NCP effort.

In conclusion, we would like to point out a few practical applications
of victimization survey results that have become apparent through our
analysis of the survey results, it was only possible to outline general
uses of the data. Now we are beginning to see how these general uses
can be tailored to the existing problems. For example, in mid-1972,
we received a request for information on the crime problem among the
elderly by the Honorable Harrison A. Williams, Jr., Chairman, Subcommittee on Housing for the Elderly. It had long been thought that the
elderly were particularly susceptible to the risk of victimization.
Apparently many new programs were being considered to protect the elderly
from the ravages of crime. At the time of the request, we could not
provide any insight into the problem of the elderly as victims of crime.
Now, however, we can say that generally, the rates of personal victimization are inversely related to the age of the victim. Thus, it appears

2/ Ibid, pp 201-202.

that the elderly are less subject to victimization than other groups of the population. In terms of program planning, this information signifies the need to focus on younger age groups if we want to develop programs which will affect the most victim prone groups.

The city of Portland, one of LEAA's impact cities, is attempting to use the results to support implementation of certain new programs. For example, in Portland, the NCP survey results indicated that over half of serious crimes were not reported to police. In recognition of this problem, the Chief of Police plans to make a concerted attempt to address the factors contributing to underreporting of criminal incidents by increasing citizen cooperation with officials in deterring and detecting crime, and in apprehending and prosecuting criminals. The survey results also showed that during the time period covered, robberies and burglaries constituted the most serious problem. Several steps have been taken to reduce these crimes, including: the creation of a Strike Force to deploy police officers on an overtime basis in high crime neighborhoods, the installation of silent alarms in some commercial establishments, and implementation of a street lighting program in three high crime areas. The survey showed that half of the crimes against persons occurred in a street, park, field or similar locations which will be affected by the street lighting program. These are only some of the exciting uses that can be made of victimization survey data. As persons in the criminal justice system become more familiar with the potential resources provided by victimization data, and these data become more easily available, we are positive many more practical applications of the results will be made and documented.

Glossary

AGGRAVATED ASSAULT Attack with a weapon resulting in any injury and attack without a weapon resulting either in serious injury (e.g., broken bones, loss of teeth, internal injuries, loss of consciousness) or in undetermined injury requiring 2 or more days of hospitalization. Also includes attempted assault with a weapon.

ASSAULT An unlawful physical attack or an attempted attack by one person upon another. Excludes rape and attempted rape, as well as attacks involving theft or attempted theft, which are classified as robbery.

BIAS As used in sampling, bias is the difference between the true value of a population parameter and the average value of a survey estimate of that parameter, for indefinitely many replications of a specified survey process and estimating procedure.

BOUNDING OR BOUNDED INTERVIEW The procedure of excluding from reported data any event known to have occurred outside the specified reference period. As employed in the NCS, the procedure excludes from a fixed reference period any event that was reported in an earlier interview as having occurred prior to that same fixed reference period.

BURGLARY Unlawful or forcible entry of home or business premises, usually, but not necessarily, attended by theft. Includes attempted forcible entry.

CLASSIFICATION Although a victimization can involve more than one NCS crime, each victimization is classified into a unique and primary NCS crime category according to the most serious crime that allegedly occurred. The descending order of seriousness for personal victimizations is: rape, robbery, assault, and larceny. After the primary classification has

229

been determined, the event is placed in the appropriate subcategory, for example, attempted rape with theft. (See Appendix D for a detailed description of the NCS classification system.)

CLUSTER A fixed group of elementary units of a population. In large samples, the elementary units of a population often are arranged exhaustively into a set of clusters, and the sampling operation secures a sample of clusters from the full sets. In the NCS, the household survey samples clusters of approximately four neighboring elementary units (housing units); the commercial survey samples clusters of approximately 15 business establishments.

COEFFICIENT OF VARIATION The square root of the ratio of variance of an estimate to the square of the expected value of the estimate.

COMMERCIAL ESTABLISHMENT (OR BUSINESS ESTABLISHMENT) An economic unit, generally at a single physical location where business is conducted or where services or industrial operations are performed, e.g., a factory, mill, store, hotel, movie theater, bank, or sales office. *Note:* A place of business that is not recognizable as such from the outside is included in the victimization surveys in the household survey rather than in the commercial survey.

COMMERCIAL INCIDENT See *Incident*. Crimes of burglary, attempted burglary, robbery, and attempted robbery at commercial establishments are considered commercial incidents.

CONTROL CARD The basic record for each sample unit. A control card is prepared and maintained for each sample household. It identifies the household, its membership, and all facts necessary to accounting for and classifying experience of that household in later tabulations. It is also an operational tool in the Census Bureau regional offices for maintaining control over interviewers and the sample itself.

CPS Current Population Survey. A continuing national household interview survey of the civilian noninstitutional population of the United States, conducted each month by the U.S. Census Bureau since 1943. It is the basis for estimates of employment, unemployment, income, and many other characteristics of the population.

FORCIBLE ENTRY A form of burglary in which force is used to gain entry (e.g., by breaking a window or slashing a screen).

HEAD OF HOUSEHOLD The person who is regarded as head by members of the household; most frequently, the principal breadwinner of the family is considered as head.

HOUSEHOLD A household consists of (a) all persons, whether present or temporarily absent, whose usual place of residence at the time of interview is the housing unit (see *Housing Unit*), and (b) all persons staying in the housing unit who have no usual place of residence elsewhere.

HOUSEHOLD INCIDENT See *Incident*. Crimes of burglary, attempted burglary, household larceny, attempted household larceny, and motor vehicle theft are considered household incidents.

HOUSEHOLD LARCENY Theft or attempted theft of property or cash from the home or its immediate vicinity. Involves neither forcible entry nor unlawful entry.

HOUSING UNIT A group of rooms or a single room occupied as separate living quarters; that is (a) when the occupants do not live and eat with any other persons in the structure and (b) when there is either direct access from the outside or through a common hall or complete kitchen facilities for the unit.

IMPACT CITIES A set of eight central cities in which LEAA funded various anticrime programs. Victimization surveys also were sponsored by LEAA in these cities in 1972 and in 1975. The term impact cities has been used as a convenient descriptor of this set of victimization surveys.

INCIDENT A specific criminal act involving one or more victims and offenders.

INTERVIEWER VARIANCE That part of the total variance of an estimate that is contributed by differential biases of individual interviewers.

MEAN SQUARE ERROR The sum of variance and the square of bias. The square root of mean square error is a more global measure of the total error of an estimate than is standard error.

MEASUREMENT ERROR Errors in estimates from sample surveys can be classified in different ways. A distinction is made between sampling error and measurement error. Sampling error arises because any particular sample of a universe does not include all the units in the universe and therefore may not be a precise reflection of that universe. Measurement error is all other or nonsampling errors in the sample estimates and includes such factors as incorrect individual responses, nonresponses, and editing and processing mistakes.

MOTOR VEHICLE THEFT Stealing or unauthorized taking of a motor vehicle belonging to household members, including attempts at such acts.

MULTIPLE VICTIMIZATION If a person has been victimized on more than one occasion in a specified time period, he is considered to have experience multiple victimization for that time frame. (Note that it is a broader concept than series victimization.)

NCJISS National Criminal Justice Information and Statistics Service, a component of the Law Enforcement Assistance Administration of the U.S. Department of Justice.

NCP National Crime Panel A term sometimes used to designate the national component of the National Crime Survey, as contrasted with the city-level component.

NCS National Crime Surveys The NCS includes the National Household Survey, the National Commercial Survey, the set of City Household Surveys, and the set of City Commercial Surveys—all concerned with criminal victimization. When the context is clear, NCS refers to the National Household Survey only.

NONINTERVIEW Failure to secure data for a unit that is a member of the designed sample. The noninterviewed unit might be a household, a business establishment, or a person. The context indicates which type of these units is meant.

NONSAMPLING ERROR See *Measurement Error.*

NSR Non-Self-Representing A term to denote that a sampling unit is selected with less than certainty, i.e., with probability less than 1.0.

OFFENDER Person who is alleged by an NCS respondent to have committed crimes in one of the seven major categories surveyed.

PERSONAL INCIDENT See *Incident.* Crimes of rape, robbery, assault, personal theft, and corresponding attempts are considered personal incidents.

PERSONAL LARCENY WITH CONTACT Theft or attempted theft of purse, wallet, or other property by stealth directly from the person of the victim, but without force or the threat of force.

PERSONAL LARCENY WITHOUT CONTACT Theft, without direct contact between victim and offender, of property or cash from any place other than the victim's home or its immediate vicinity. Also includes attempted theft.

PSU Primary Sampling Unit The term *elementary unit* is used to denote an individual member of a population under study, e.g., a household or a person. For efficient sampling of human populations, the operation is often carried out in stages. In the first stage, large clusters or groups of elementary units are chosen with known probability of selection for each large cluster. The large cluster is a primary sampling unit. In subsequent stages, subsamples of elementary units are selected from within the sample PSU's.

RAPE Carnal knowledge through the use of force or threat of force, including attempts. Statutory rape (without force) is excluded.

RECALL DECAY A name given to the phenomenon that the greater the distance between the date of interview and the date an event occurred the less likely is the event to be reported, other things being equal. (This is a widely prevailing phenomenon in retrospective interviewing.)

REINTERVIEW A control and evaluation procedure in which a previously interviewed sample household is again interviewed by a different interviewer (usually a supervisor) with respect to the same subject matter and reference period (see Chapter 2). Successive interviews of the same households for differing reference periods are not called reinterviews.

RESPONDENT The person responding for the sample unit, i.e., for a household, business establishment, or a person. If the data for a sample unit are supplied by the person most intimately related to the inquiry—the person himself or the person designated as household or establishment spokesman—the responding person is said to be self-respondent; if data are supplied by another person, the responding person is said to be a proxy-respondent.

REVERSE RECORD CHECK An evaluation of respondent reporting, secured by starting with a sample of records, querying the persons represented by the records, concerning topics that are the subject matter of the records—but not revealing to the respondent that the questioner is aware of the record—and then comparing respondent replies with the record information.

ROBBERY   Theft or attempted theft, directly from a person or a business, of property or cash by force or threat of force, with or without a weapon.

ROBBERY WITH INJURY   Theft or attempted theft from a person, accompanied by an attack, either with or without a weapon, resulting in injury. An injury is classified as resulting from a serious assault if a weapon was used in the commission of the crime or, if not, when the extent of the injury was either serious (e.g., broken bones, loss of teeth, internal injuries, loss of consciousness) or undetermined but requiring 2 or more days of hospitalization. An injury is classified as resulting from a minor assault when the extent of the injury was minor (e.g., bruises, black eye, cuts, scratches, swelling) or undetermined but requiring less than 2 days of hospitalization.

ROBBERY WITHOUT INJURY   Theft or attempted theft from a person, accompanied by force or the threat of force, either with or without a weapon, but not resulting in injury.

ROLLING REFERENCE PERIOD   Suppose "annual victimization rates" were published quarterly, in each case being based on experience in the preceeding 12 months. The reference periods for successive publications would overlap, and the majority would not coincide with calendar years. The "annual rates" would be said to rest on a rolling reference period.

ROTATION OR ROTATION GROUP   A set of addresses that is retained in the sample for 3½ years and that is contacted for successive interviewing at 6-month intervals. After retention for 3½ years, the set of addresses is rotated out of the sample and replaced gradually over a 6-month interval by a new rotation group (see Chapter 2).

SAMPLING ERROR OR SAMPLING VARIABILITY   See *Variance* and *Measurement Error*.

SCREEN QUESTIONS   In the NCS, the screen questions are an introductory set of queries intended to identify all victimization events (within scope of the survey) that have occurred in the reference period. Some screens are for detection of household crimes and others for personal crimes. Later questions elicit details about the events that are uncovered by the screen questions.

SEGMENT   Another term for clusters. When used as a verb, segment means the process of dividing a population or a part of a population into clusters.

SERIES VICTIMIZATION   Several incidents are combined into a single series victimization when the interviewer finds that (a) the incidents are very similar in detail, (b) there are at least three incidents in the series, and (c) the respondent is unable to recall dates and other details of the individual incidents well enough to report them separately. Details recorded for the series are those of the most recent incident (see Chapter 6).

SIMPLE ASSAULT   Attack without a weapon resulting either in minor injury (e.g., bruises, black eye, cuts, scratches, swelling) or in undetermined injury requiring less than 2 days of hospitalization. Also includes attempted assault without a weapon.

SMSA   Standard Metropolitan Statistical Area   The SMSA is a formal standardized delineation of an economically and socially integrated metropolitan area. An SMSA usually contains a central city of 50,000 or more population and is defined in terms of contiguous whole counties, except in New England, where the boundaries follow city and town lines. Official SMSA definitions are released by the Office of Management and Budget in the Executive Office of the President of the United States.

SR   Self-Representing   Term to denote that a sampling unit is selected with certainty, i.e., with probability 1.0.

STANDARD ERROR   The square root of the average squared difference between estimates secured from particular instances of a survey process, and the average of estimates obtained from all possible replications of that process. It is the square of variance. In probability surveys, estimates of standard error can be calculated from the sample data.

STRANGER/NONSTRANGER   The victim's classification of the alleged offender. The alleged offender is classified as a nonstranger if a relative of, or either a well-known or casual acquaintance of, the victim.

TELESCOPING   Incorrect placement of the time of occurrence of an event as reported by a respondent. Reporting the event as more recent than actual occurrence is forward telescoping, and reporting an event as earlier in time than actual occurrence is backward telescoping (see Chapter 2).

THEFT   The unlawful taking of property with intent to deprive the rightful owner of it. Also includes attempts.

UCR   Uniform Crime Reports   The term refers to a system of reporting by local law enforcement agencies to the Federal Bureau of Investigation (FBI). The reporting program seeks uniform classification and counting of known offenses, persons arrested, and persons charged with a selected list of criminal actions.

UNBOUNDED INTERVIEW   Reported data that are not adjusted by the bounding procedure.

UNDERCOUNT, UNDERREPORTING, OR UNDERCOVERAGE   Terms used to describe the situation in which a survey process (either a census or a sample) results in estimates that are lower than true counts would be. Undercoverage can have a variety of causes (see Chapter 2).

UNLAWFUL ENTRY   A form of burglary committed by someone having no legal right to be in the premises even though force is not used.

VARIANCE   A measure of the precision of a sampling and estimation process. Arithmetically, variance is the square of the standard error of a sample estimate. Knowledge of an estimate from a probability sample and the standard error of that estimate permits setting probable lower and upper bounds on the statistic that would be obtained in a complete enumeration of the universe.

VICTIM   A person, household, or business establishment that is the directly injured party to a criminal incident. (See *Incident* and *Victimization*, and note that for crimes against persons, the number of victimizations is often greater than the number of incidents becuase more than one victim is involved in some criminal incidents.)

VICTIMIZATION   A specific criminal act as it affects a single victim. In criminal acts against persons, the number of victimizations is determined by the number of victims of such acts. Because more than one individual may be victimized during certain crimes against persons, the number of victimizations is somewhat higher than the number of incidents. Each criminal act against a household or commercial establishment is assumed to involve a single victim, the affected household, or establishment.

VICTIMIZATION RATE   For crimes against persons, the victimization rate, a measure of occurrence among population groups at risk, is computed on the basis of the number of victimizations per 1,000 resident population age 12 and over. For crimes against households, victimization rates are calculated on the basis of the number of incidents per 1,000 households. For crimes against commercial establishments, victimization rates are derived from the number of incidents per 1,000 establishments. Note that the victimization rate is not a ratio of number of population units victimized to number exposed to risk, nor a probability of a given person being victimized (see Chapter 2 and Chapter 7).

VULNERABILITY   As used in victimization statistics, the likelihood or risk of being victimized. (See Chapter 6 for discussion of ecological, status, and role vulnerabilities.)

Bibliography

Abrams, Mark. "Social Indicators and Social Equity." *New Society,* November 23, 1972, p. 454.

Amir, Menachim. *Patterns in Forcible Rape.* Chicago: University of Chicago Press, 1971.

Argana, Marie G., Thompson, Marvin M., and Gerson, Earle J. "The Measurement of Crime through Victimization Surveys." Paper presented at the Annual Meeting of the American Statistical Association, December 27, 1973, New York.

Babbie, Earl R. *The Practice of Social Research.* Belmont, Calif.: Wadsworth Publishing Co., 1975.

Bauer, Raymond A., ed. *Social Indicators.* Cambridge, Mass.: MIT Press, 1966.

Becker, Gary S. "Crime and Punishment: An Economic Approach." *Journal of Political Economics* 76(1968):78.

Biderman, Albert D. "A Social Indicator of Interpersonal Harm—A Discretionary Grant Final Technical Report." Washington, D.C.: Bureau of Social Science Research, December 1975.

———. "How to Avoid Criminal Justice Indicators Wherein Worse Means Better." Unpublished.

———. "Information, Intelligence, and Enlightened Public Policy: Functions and Organization of Societal Feedback." *Policy Sciences* 1(1970):217–30.

———. "Notes on Immunizing Effects of Exposure and 'Risk' in Victimization Surveys." Washington, D.C.: Bureau of Social Science Research, November 1975.

———. "Notes on the Significance of Measurements of Events and of Conditions by Criminal Victimization Surveys." Washington, D.C.: Bureau of Social Science Research, July 1975.

———. "(A Pilot Study of) Public Survey Approaches to Crime Phenomena—Report on a Design for a National Study." Washington, D.C.: Bureau of Social Science Research, April 1966.

———. "Regarding a Proposed National Criminal Justice Statistics Center." *Hearings Before the Subcommittee on Census and Statistics of the Committee on Post Office*

237

and Civil Service, House of Representatives. 90th Congress, 2d session, May 1968, pp. 182-94.

Biderman, Albert D., and Reiss, Albert J., Jr. "On Exploring the 'Dark Figure' of Crime." *The Annals of the American Academy of Political and Social Science* 374(1967):1-15.

Biderman, Albert D. et al. *An Inventory of Surveys of the Public on Crime, Justice and Related Topics.* Washington, D.C.: U.S. Government Printing Office, 1973.

——. *Report on a Pilot Study in the District of Columbia on Victimization and Attitudes toward Law Enforcement.* Report of the President's Commission on Law Enforcement and Administration of Justice. Field Surveys I. Washington, D.C.: U.S. Government Printing Office, 1967.

——. "Survey Research on Crime, Criminal Law and Criminal Justice in the United States." *Secondary Analysis of Sample Surveys, Uses, and Needs: Proceedings of World Association for Public Opinion Research/ESOMAR Congress.* 9-13 September 1973, Budapest, Hungary. Amsterdam: ESOMAR, 1974, pp. 175-92.

——. "Surveys of Population Samples for Estimating Crime Incidence." *The Annals of the American Academy of Political and Social Science* 374(November 1967):16-33.

——. "The Impact on Criminology of Surveys of the General Public." *Proceedings of the 20th International Congress of Psychology.* August 1972, Tokyo, Japan.

——. "Time Distortions of Victimization Data and Mnemonic Effects." Washington, D.C.: Bureau of Social Science Research, July 1970.

——. "Uses of Surveys for Estimating Crime Incidence." *American Statistical Association: Proceedings of the Social Statistics Section, 1968.* Washington, D.C.: American Statistical Association, 1968, pp. 107-11.

——. "Victimology and Victimization Surveys." In *Victimology: A New Focus,* Vol. 3, ed. by Israel Drapkin and Emilio Viano. Lexington, Mass.: Lexington Books, 1975.

——. "When Does Interpersonal Violence Become Crime?–Theory and Methods for Statistical Surveys." Paper presented at a meeting on "Access to Law," Research Committee on the Sociology of Law, International Sociological Association, 25-28 September 1973, Girton College, Cambridge, England.

Bishop, Yvonne M. M., Feinberg, S. E., and Holland, P. W. *Discrete Multivariate Analysis, Theory and Practice.* Cambridge, Mass.: MIT Press, 1975.

Blanken, Gary E. "Current Estimates from the Health Interview Survey, United States–1969." *Vital and Health Statistics,* Series 10, No. 63. U.S. National Center for Health Statistics. Washington, D.C.: U.S. Government Printing Office, April 1973.

Boggs, Sarah L. "Urban Crime Patterns." *American Sociological Review* 30(1965):899-909.

Bradburn, Norman M. *The Structure of Psychological Well-Being.* NORC Monographs in Social Research, No. 15. Chicago: Aldine Publishing Co., 1969.

Bradburn, Norman M., and Caplovitz, David. *Reports on Happiness: A Pilot Study of Behavior Related to Mental Health.* Chicago: Aldine Publishing Co., 1965.

Campbell, Angus, and Converse, Philip E., eds. *The Human Meaning of Social Change.* New York: Russell Sage Foundation, 1972.

Cloward, Richard A., and Ohlin, Lloyd. *Delinquency and Opportunity.* New York: Free Press, 1960.

Cohen, Albert K. *Delinquent Boys: The Culture of the Gang.* New York: Free Press, 1971.

Cormack, R. M. "The Statistics of Capture–Recapture Methods." *Oceanographic Marine Biology Annual Review* 6(1968):455-501.

Cressey, Donald R. *Delinquency, Crime and Differential Association.* The Hague: Mattinus Nijhoff, 1960.

Dodge, Richard W., and Turner, Anthony G. "Methodological Foundations for Establishing a National Survey of Victimization." Paper presented at the Annual Meeting of the American Statistical Association, August 23–26, 1971, Fort Collins, Colorado.

Ehrlich, Issac. "Participation in Illegitimate Activities: An Economic Analysis." In *Essays in the Economics of Crime and Punishment,* by Gary S. Becker and William M. Landes. New York: National Bureau of Economic Research, 1974.

Engel, Arnold, and Burch, Thomas A. "Osteoarthritis in Adults by Selected Demographic Characteristics, United States, 1960–1962." *Vital and Health Statistics,* Series 11, No. 20. U.S. National Center for Health Statistics. Washington, D.C.: U.S. Government Printing Office, November 1966.

Ennis, Philip H. *Criminal Victimization in the United States: A Report of a National Survey.* Report of the President's Commission on Law Enforcement and Administration of Justice. Field Surveys II. Washington, D.C.: U.S. Government Printing Office, 1967.

Executive Office of the President, Office of Management and Budget. "Standards and Guidelines for Federal Statistics." Revised Circular A-46. Washington, D.C.: Office of Management and Budget, May 3, 1974.

Feinberg, S. E. "The Multiple Recapture Census for Closed Populations and Incomplete 2^k Contingency Tables." *Biometrika* 59(1972):591–603.

Folsom, R. E. *et al.* "The Two Alternate Questions Randomized Response Model for Human Surveys." Paper presented at the Biometric Society Meeting, Ames, Iowa, April 26, 1972.

Gibson, E., and Klein, K. *Murder, 1957-68.* A Home Office Research Report. London: Her Majesty's Stationery Office, 1970.

Glorig, Aram, and Roberts, Jean. "Hearing Levels of Adults by Age and Sex, United States, 1960–1962." *Vital and Health Statistics,* Series 11, No. 11. U.S. National Center for Health Statistics. Washington, D.C.: U.S. Government Printing Office, October 1965.

Gray, Percy G. "The Memory Factor in Social Surveys." *Journal of the American Statistical Association* 50(1955):344–63.

Greenberg, B. G., Abul-Ela, A. A., Simmons, W. R., and Horvitz, D. G. "The Unrelated Question Randomized Response Model: Theoretical Framework." *Journal of the American Statistical Association* 64 (1969):520–39.

Hall, George E. "The Program of the Statistics Division of the Law Enforcement Assistance Administration." Paper presented at the 1971 meeting of the American Statistical Association, August 23–26, Fort Collins, Colorado.

Hamill, Peter V. V., Johnston, Francis E., and Lemeshow, Stanley. "Body Weight, Stature, and Sitting Height: White and Negro Youths 12–17 Years, United States." *Vital and Health Statistics,* Series 11, No. 126. U.S. National Center for Health Statistics. Washington, D.C.: U.S. Government Printing Office, August 1973.

Hentig, Hans von. *The Criminal and His Victim.* New Haven: Yale University Press, 1948.

Joerg, Karen. "The Cleveland–Akron Commercial Victimization Feasibility Test." Draft of the Statistics Division Technical Series Report No. 2. U.S. Department of Justice, Law Enforcement Assistance Administration, no date.

Kalish, Carol B. *Crimes and Victims: A Report on the Dayton-San Jose Pilot Survey of Victimization.* Washington, D.C.: U.S. Department of Justice, Law Enforcement Assistance Administration, June 1974.

Logan, W. P. D., and Brooke, E. M. *The Survey of Sickness, 1943 to 1952.* General Register Office, Studies on Medical and Population Subjects. London: Her Majesty's Stationery Office, 1957.

McClintock, F. H. *Crimes of Violence.* London: Macmillan & Co., 1963.

McClintock, F. H., and Gibson, E. *Robbery in London.* London: Macmillan & Co., 1961.

McIntyre, Jennie. "Public Attitudes Toward Crime and Law Enforcement." *The Annals of the American Academy of Political and Social Science* 34(1967):34-46.

MacMahon, Brian, and Worcester, Jane. "Age at Menopause, United States, 1960-1962." *Vital and Health Statistics,* Series 11, No. 19. U.S. National Center for Health Statistics. Washington, D.C.: U.S. Government Printing Office, October 1966.

Merton, Robert K. "Social Structure and Anomie." *American Sociological Review* 3(1938):672-82. Reprinted in Merton, Robert K. *Social Theory and Social Structure.* Glencoe: Free Press, 1967.

Miller, Walter B. "Lower-class Culture as a Generating Milieu of Gang Delinquency." *Journal of Social Issues* 14(1958):5-19.

Moors, J. J. A. "Optimization of the Unrelated Question Randomized Response Model." *Journal of the American Statistical Association* 66(1971):627-29.

Moser, C. A., and Kalton, G., eds. *Survey Methods in Social Investigation.* 2d ed. New York: Basic Books, 1972.

Mulvihill, Donald J., and Tumin, Melvin M. *Crimes of Violence,* Vol. 11. Staff report submitted to the National Commission on the Causes and Prevention of Violence. Washington, D.C.: U.S. Government Printing Office, 1969.

Neter, John, and Waksberg, Joseph. "A Study of Response Errors in Expenditures Data from Household Interviews." *Journal of the American Statistical Association* 59(1964):17-55.

——. *Response Errors in Collection of Expenditures Data by Household Interviews: An Experimental Study.* Bureau of the Census Technical Paper No. 11. Washington, D.C.: U.S. Government Printing Office, 1965.

Pittman, D. J., and Handy, W. F. "Patterns in Criminal Aggravated Assault." *Journal of Criminal Law and Political Science* 55(1964):462-70.

President's Commission on Law Enforcement and Administration of Justice. *Task Force Report: Crime and Its Impact—An Assessment.* Washington, D.C.: U.S. Government Printing Office, 1967.

——. *The Challenge of Crime in a Free Society.* Washington, D.C.: U.S. Government Printing Office, 1967.

Reiss, Albert J., Jr. *Studies in Crime and Law Enforcement in Major Metropolitan Areas.* Vol. 1. Report of the President's Commission on Law Enforcement and Administration of Justice. Field Surveys III. Washington, D.C.: U.S. Government Printing Office, 1967.

Reppetto, Thomas A. *Residential Crime.* Cambridge, Mass.: Ballinger Publishing Co., 1974.

Reynolds, Paul Davidson *et al. Victimization in a Metropolitan Region.* Mimeographed. Minneapolis: University of Minnesota Center for Sociological Research, 1973.

Scott, Marvin B., and Lyman, Stanford M. "Accounts, Deviance and Social Order." In *Deviance and Respectability,* ed. by Jack D. Douglas. New York: Basic Books, 1970.

Sellin, Thorsten. *Culture Conflict and Crime.* New York: Social Science Research Council, 1938.

Shaw, Clifford R. *et al. Delinquency Areas.* Chicago: University of Chicago Press, 1942.

Skogan, Wesley G. "The Use of Victimization Surveys in Criminal Justice Planning." In *Quantitative Tools for Criminal Justice Planning,* ed. by Leonard Oberlander. Washington, D.C.: U.S. Government Printing Office, 1975.

——. "Crime and Crime Rates." In *Sample Surveys of the Victims of Crime,* ed. by Wesley G. Skogan. Cambridge, Mass.: Ballinger Publishing Co., 1976.

Sparks, R. F., Genn, H. G., and Dodd, D. J. *Surveying Victims.* London: John Wiley & Sons Ltd., 1976.

Stinchcombe, Arthur. "Institutions of Privacy in the Determination of Police Administrative Practice." *American Journal of Sociology* 69(1963):150–60.

Stoudt, Howard W., Damon, Albert, McFarland, Ross, and Roberts, Jean. "Skinfolds, Body Girths, Biacromial Diameter and Selected Anthropometric Indices of Adults, United States, 1960–1962." *Vital and Health Statistics,* Series 11, No. 35. U.S. National Center for Health Statistics. Washington, D.C.: U.S. Government Printing Office, August 1973.

Sudman, Seymour, and Bradburn, Norman M. *Response Effects in Surveys.* Chicago: Aldine Publishing Co., 1974.

Sutherland, Edwin H., and Cressey, Donald R. *Principles of Criminology.* 7th ed. Philadelphia: J. B. Lippincott Co., 1966.

Svalastoga, K. "Homicide and Social Contact in Denmark." *American Journal of Sociology* 62(1956):37–41.

Turner, Anthony G., and Dodge, Richard W. "Surveys of Personal and Organizational Victimization." Paper presented at the Symposium on Studies of Public Experience, Knowledge and Opinion of Crime and Justice, March 16–18, 1972, Washington, D.C.

U.S. Department of Commerce, Bureau of the Census. *Concepts and Methods Used in Manpower Statistics from the Current Population Survey.* Current Population Reports, Series P-23, No. 22. Washington, D.C.: U.S. Government Printing Office, June 1967.

——. *National Crime Survey, Central Cities Sample Survey Documentation.* Washington, D.C.: U.S. Government Printing Office, May 1974.

——. *National Crime Survey Documentation.* Washington, D.C.: U.S. Government Printing Office, 1976.

——. *National Crime Survey, Interviewer's Manual* (and current revision). Washington, D.C.: U.S. Government Printing Office, 1974.

——. *Public Use Samples of Basic Records from the 1970 Census: Description and Technical Documentation.* Washington, D.C.: U.S. Department of Commerce, 1972.

——. Supplement No. 1 to *Public Use Samples of Basic Records from the 1970 Census: Description and Technical Documentation.* Washington, D.C.: U.S. Department of Commerce.

——. *Standards for Discussion and Presentation of Error in Data.* Census Technical Paper No. 32. In *Journal of the American Statistical Association,* Vol. 70(Part II), No. 351, September 1975.

——. *Statistical Abstract of the United States: 1975.* Washington, D.C.: U.S. Government Printing Office, 1975.

——. *National Crime Survey, Central Cities Sample, Five Largest Cities Survey Documentation.* Washington, D.C.: U.S. Department of Commerce, May 1974.

——. *The Current Population Survey: A Report on Methodology.* Census Technical Paper No. 7. Washington, D.C.: U.S. Government Printing Office, 1963.

U.S. Department of Justice, Federal Bureau of Investigation. *Uniform Crime Reporting Handbook.* Washington, D.C.: U.S. Government Printing Office, 1966.

U.S. Department of Justice, Law Enforcement Assistance Administration. *Crime in Eight American Cities: Advance Report.* Washington, D.C.: U.S. Government Printing Office, July 1974.

——. *Crime in the Nation's Five Largest Cities: Advance Report.* Washington, D.C.: U.S. Government Printing Office, April 1974.

——. *Criminal Victimization Surveys in the Nation's Five Largest Cities.* Washington, D.C.: U.S. Government Printing Office, April 1975.

——. *Criminal Victimization Surveys in the Nation's Five Largest Cities* (Final Report). Washington, D.C.: U.S. Government Printing Office, April 1975.

——. *Criminal Victimization Surveys in 13 American Cities.* Washington, D.C.: U.S. Government Printing Office, June 1975.

——. *Criminal Victimization in the United States: Advance Report January–June 1973.* Vol. 1. Washington, D.C.: U.S. Government Printing Office, November 1974.

——. *Criminal Victimization in the United States: 1973 Advance Report.* Vol. 1. Washington, D.C.: U.S. Government Printing Office, May 1975.

——. *First Annual Report of the National Institute of Law Enforcement and Criminal Justice.* Washington, D.C.: U.S. Government Printing Office, 1975.

——. *LEAA Newsletter.* Vol. 4, No. 6. December 1974, p. 5.

——. *LEAA Newsletter.* Vol. 5, No. 1. June–July 1975, pp. 9–15.

——. Public Information Office. April 15, 1974. *News Release.*

——. *San Jose Methods Test of Known Crime Victims.* Statistics Technical Report No. 1. Washington, D.C.: U.S. Government Printing Office, June 1972.

——. *Uniform Crime Reports: Crime in the United States, 1973.* Washington, D.C.: U.S. Government Printing Office, 1974.

U.S. Department of Labor, Bureau of Labor Statistics. *Employment and Earnings,* Vol. 22, No. 9. Washington, D.C.: U.S. Government Printing Office, March 1976.

U.S. National Center for Health Statistics. "Health Survey Procedure: Concepts, Questionnaire Development, and Definitions in the Health Interview Survey." *Vital and Health Statistics,* Series 1, No. 2. Washington, D.C.: U.S. Government Printing Office, May 1964.

Warner, Stanley L. "Randomized Responses: A Survey Technique for Eliminating Evasive Answer Bias." *Journal of the American Statistical Association* 60(1965): 63–69.

Wilkins, Leslie T. *Social Deviance.* London: Tavistock, 1964.

Wilks, Judith A. "Ecological Correlates of Crime and Delinquency." Appendix A in *Crime and Its Impact—An Assessment.* Task Force Report of the President's Commission on Law Enforcement and Administration of Justice. Washington, D.C.: U.S. Government Printing Office, 1967.

Wolf, Preben, and Hauge, Ragnar. "Criminal Violence in Three Scandinavian Countries." *5 Scandinavian Studies in Criminology.* London: Tavistock, 1975.

Wolfgang, Marvin E. *Patterns in Criminal Homicide.* Philadelphia: University of Pennsylvania Press, 1958.

——. "Uniform Crime Reports: A Critical Appraisal." *University of Pennsylvania Law Review* 111(1963):708–38.

Yarrow, Marian Radke, Campbell, John D., and Burton, Roger V. "Recollection of Childhood: A Study of the Retrospective Method." Monograph 5. *Society for Research in Child Development* 35 (August 1970), Ser. No. 138, University of Chicago: LB1103-S64, Reading Room 4.

Biographical Sketches of
Panel Members and Staff

CONRAD F. TAEUBER is Director of the Center for Population Research, a unit of the Kennedy Institute for the Study of Human Reproduction and Bioethics at Georgetown University in Washington, D.C. He was formerly Associate Director of the Bureau of the Census with responsibility for Demographic and Social Surveys and Censuses. He received his B.A., M.A., and Ph.D. from the University of Minnesota, the latter in 1931. Prior to coming to Washington, he taught at Mount Holyoke College, where he served in the Works Progress Administration and the Department of Agriculture. He was also Chief Statistician of the Food and Agriculture Organization of the United Nations. His work in relation to statistical surveys and censuses has included assignments with the United Nations and the Inter-American Statistical Institute.

ALBERT D. BIDERMAN is Research Associate and Assistant Director at the Bureau of Social Science Research, Inc., Washington, D.C. He received a B.A. in economics from New York University in 1946 and an M.A. and Ph.D. in sociology from the University of Chicago in 1952 and 1964, respectively. His interest in surveys of citizen experiences with and attitudes toward crime developed from his review in 1963 of the state of social indicators and from pilot studies for developing the victimization survey method test he conducted for Presidential commissions on crime in the mid-1960's. He has been devoting extensive effort in recent years to work toward improving federal social statistical programs both as a consultant to government agencies and as a member of several professional association committees on government statistics and social indicators.

HERBERT JACOB is Professor of Political Science and Chairman of the Department at Northwestern University. He received his A.B. from Harvard University in 1954 and his Ph.D. from Yale University in 1960. He also has taught at Tulane University and at the University of Wisconsin–Madison and has been a Fellow of the Center for Advanced Study in the Behavioral Sciences. His principal research focuses on American trial courts, especially criminal courts, and he has made extensive use of survey methodology.

WILLIAM M. LANDES is Professor of Economics at the University of Chicago Law School, a member of the senior research staff of the National Bureau of Economic Research, and editor of *The Journal of Law and Economics.* He received an A.B. in 1960 and a Ph.D. in 1966 from Columbia University. His principal research has been in the application of economic theory and quantitative methods to the study of the legal system. He has published numerous papers in that area. He also has taught at Stanford University, Columbia University, and the Graduate Center of the City University of New York.

PHILIP J. McCARTHY has been Professor of Economic and Social Statistics in the New York State School of Industrial and Labor Relations at Cornell University since 1948. He received a B.A. degree from Cornell in 1939 and a Ph.D. degree in mathematical statistics from Princeton University in 1947. Among his special assignments have been the following: consultant to the Bureau of Labor Statistics and the National Center for Health Statistics, member of the 1960 Price Statistics Review Committee of the National Bureau of Economic Research, two separate terms as an Associate Editor of the *Journal of the American Statistical Association,* and member of the American Statistical Association Census Advisory Committee. His publications are primarily in the area of survey sampling methodology.

PATRICK V. MURPHY is President of the Police Foundation. He received a B.A. from St. John's University, a Master of Public Administration from the City College of New York, and has graduated from the Federal Bureau of Investigation's National Law Enforcement Academy. Since he began his career in the law enforcement field as a New York City patrol officer in 1945, he has held numerous posts. A partial list includes Chief of Police in Syracuse, Commanding Officer of the New York City Police Academy, Public Safety Director of the District of Columbia, first Administrator of the Law Enforcement Assistance Administration, Commissioner of the Detroit Police Department, Commissioner of the New York City Police Department, and Dean of Administration and Police Science of the College of Police Science at the City University of New York. The Police Foundation, of which he became President in 1973, is an independent institution dedicated to fostering improvement and innovation in policing.

MORRIS ROSENBERG is Professor of Sociology at the University of Maryland. He received a B.A. from Brooklyn College in 1946 and an M.A. in 1950 and a Ph.D. in 1953 from Columbia University. He has previously taught at several universities and for many years was a member of the Laboratory of Socio-Environmental Studies at the National Institute of Mental Health (NIMH). Most of his publications have dealt with social psychological research and social research methodology. He is currently a member of the Epidemiologic Studies Review Committee of the NIMH.

MARVIN E. WOLFGANG is Director of the Center for Studies in Criminology and Criminal Law at the University of Pennsylvania. He was formerly Chairman of the Department of Sociology at the University of Pennsylvania. He has served as consultant to the President's Commission on Law Enforcement and Administration of Justice and as Director of Research for the Commission on the Causes and Prevention of Violence and has been President of the American Society of Criminology and the American Academy of Political and Social Science. He received a B.A. from Dickerson College in 1948, and an M.A. and a Ph.D. from the University of Pennsylvania in 1950 and 1955, respectively. His extensive publications include works on violence, deliquency, crime, and justice.

BETTYE K. EIDSON PENICK is a Senior Staff Officer with the Committee on National Statistics of the National Academy of Sciences. She received a B.A. degree from the University of Tennessee, an M.A. from the University of Georgia, and a Ph.D. in social relations from the Johns Hopkins University in 1971. She was formerly Assistant Professor of Sociology at the University of Michigan and Director of the Detroit Area Study, the graduate training program in survey methodology at Michigan. Her publications are in the areas of race relations, formal organizations, and community conflict.

MAURICE E. B. OWENS is a Staff Officer with the Committee on National Statistics of the National Academy of Sciences. He received a B.S. from North Carolina State University in 1966, a M.S. from Virginia Polytechnic Institute in 1968, and a Ph.D. from George Washington University in 1974. He was a mathematical statistician at the Naval Research Laboratory from 1967 to 1974. His publications include theoretical and empirical investigations in the engineering sciences, analytical examinations of system formulation and design problems, computer applications, and goodness-of-fit tests.

WALT R. SIMMONS is a statistical consultant. Formerly, he was Assistant Director of the National Center for Health Statistics and statistical and economic advisor at the U.S. Bureau of Labor Statistics, the War Manpower Commission, and the Social Security Board. He received an A.B. degree in 1934 and an M.A. in mathematics in 1936 at the University of Kansas and did graduate work in statistics at the American University 1946–50. His teaching includes mathematics and economics at the University of Kansas and appointments as Adjunct Professor in Statistics at the University of Stockholm (1970) and at American University (1950–65). Mr. Simmons has wide experience in theory and practice in sampling and large-scale surveys, in which fields he has many published papers.

RICHARD F. SPARKS is Professor at the School of Criminal Justice, Rutgers University, Newark, New Jersey. He received his B.Sc. from Northwestern University in 1954 and his Ph.D. from the University of Cambridge, England, in 1966. During 1964–67 he was Lecturer in Criminal Law and Criminology, Faculty of Law, University of Birmingham, England; from 1967 to 1974 he was Assistant Director of Research at the Institute of Criminology, University of Cambridge, England. His recent research interests include the methodological problems of victimization surveys and the legal control of multinational corporations.

Index

247

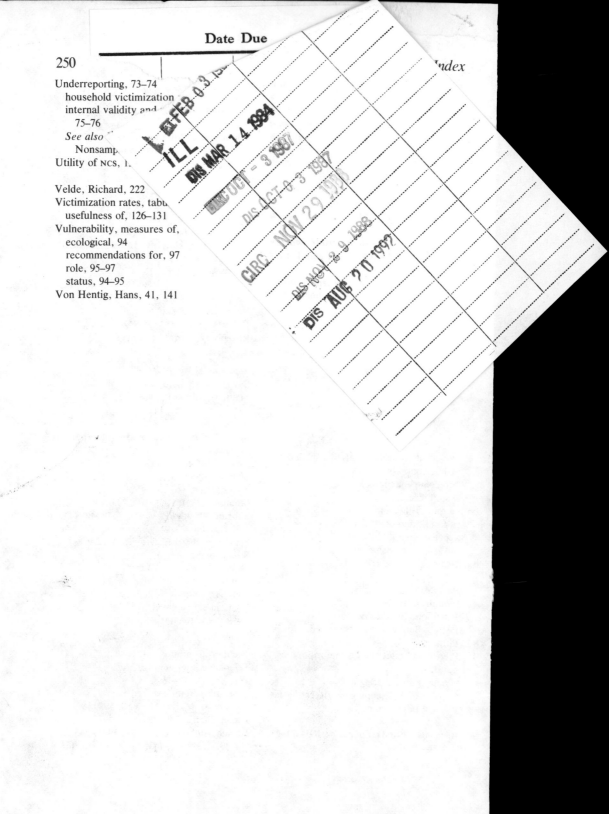